The Call of the Farm

To Tracy
For everything—
With love.

The Call of the Farm

AN UNEXPECTED YEAR OF
GETTING DIRTY,
HOME COOKING,
AND FINDING MYSELF

ROCHELLE BILOW

THE EXPERIMENT
NEW YORK

The Experiment, LLC
220 East 23rd Street, Suite 301
New York, NY 10010-4674
www.theexperimentpublishing.com

The Experiment's books are available at special discounts when purchased in bulk for premiums and sales promotions as well as for fund-raising or educational use. For details, contact us at info@theexperimentpublishing.com.

Library of Congress Cataloging-in-Publication Data

Bilow, Rochelle.
    The Call of the farm : an unexpected year of getting dirty, home cooking, and finding myself / Rochelle Bilow.
        pages cm
    ISBN 978-1-61519-214-4 (pbk.) -- ISBN 978-1-61519-215-1 (ebook)
    1. Billow, Rochelle--Homes and haunts. 2. Food writers--United States--Biography. 3. Seasonal cooking. 4. Farm life--New York--Finger Lakes Region. I. Title.

    TX649.B534A3 2014
    641.5092--dc23
    [B]

                                    2014016967

                    ISBN 978-1-61519-214-4
                    Ebook ISBN 978-1-61519-215-1

Cover design by Jaya Miceli
Cover illustrations © csaimages.com
Author photograph by Anthony Aquino
Text design by Pauline Neuwirth, Neuwirth & Associates, Inc.

Manufactured in the United States of America
Distributed by Workman Publishing Company, Inc.
Distributed simultaneously in Canada by Thomas Allen & Son Ltd.

First printing August 2014
10 9 8 7 6 5 4 3 2 1

CONTENTS

A NOTE

This, like all good memoirs, was written as my reaction to and remembrance of the story that follows. In the event that something went fuzzy, I have attempted to clarify details with the relevant parties. Most names have been changed. Any lapses or leaps in chronology or detail are merely representative of time's funny way of letting memories fade, and are in no way an attempt to fabricate or misrepresent the events or people portrayed. My aim is to share my story exactly as it happened to me.

INTRODUCTION

REALLY LIKE GRANOLA. IT'S ONE OF THOSE FOODS THAT I FIND impossible to stop eating once I've started. It's delicious whether sweetened with maple syrup or spiked with cardamom, and I especially enjoy it if there's a hint of salt. But when I was younger, I didn't just like granola, I *adored* the stuff.

When I was about six or so, I flew into a temper tantrum one morning upon discovering that the box containing that oat-filled goodness was empty. As I bounded downstairs to the kitchen, I joyfully announced to my mother, "I want granola for breakfast." I was so proud, so pleased with myself—what a wonderful thing, to know exactly what one wants! But then I noticed a nervous look on my mother's face and I frowned inwardly. *Let's see where this goes,* I thought, clenching my fingers into my palms and waiting.

"We are all out of granola," my mother said firmly. She seemed very matter-of-fact, and perhaps slightly empathetic.

Oh no. "But. I. Want. It," I said, squeezing my fists at my sides, my neck growing taut.

"Well, I'm sorry," my mother said, her patience wearing thin (to her credit, I was often upset about trivial things like breakfast cereals). "But you can have toast with jam, or scrambled eggs, or graham crackers." She paused, then repeated for emphasis: "We are all out of granola."

I completely lost my shit. If I'm being honest, there's the possibility I took off a shoe and hurled it across the room as I shouted, "I WANT GRANOLA." My sister, quietly eating toast—not granola; I checked—covered her ears.

Everything turned out okay in the end; I probably ate some apple with peanut butter or another equally tasty thing after calming down, and then went about my day. When my parents relayed the whole affair to a family friend a little while later, I rolled my eyes at how it was being re-told. *This hardly seems fair*, I thought, and protested vocally. "I didn't do it like that!" I whined, but I knew the claim was futile. I *had*, actually, yelled as loudly as my parents claimed, and what was more, I didn't feel sorry for it. I had been looking forward to eating that granola all night. I fell asleep dreaming about it, picturing the way the flakes would become soft with milk, the way my teeth would crunch the almonds and the bigger clusters of oats. I was fucking excited about it, in a way that was bigger and more real than anything else in my life, and the joy I felt upon waking—the joy connected to realizing that *today was the day* I got to eat that brilliant cereal—was full and whole in a way that made me feel content and excited and completely overwhelmed all at once. So, yeah. I was upset about it being gone.

Even though I've learned to tone down the theatrics, I am still completely, unapologetically obsessed with food, and I have spent the years since that tantrum cultivating a lifestyle that gives it the proper recognition and devotion I feel it deserves. To this day, I am frequently overcome with a crippling feeling of distress when my life refuses to play out the way I'd like it to, both in terms of edibles and aesthetics.

"I don't know, Rochelle," an old boyfriend said to me once, "You are just very exhausting." My sister concurred recently, while we were sipping tea and coffee together and discussing our family dynamics. As she brought her mug up to her lips, she considered our respective roles. "I mean, I do think you're the most intense one of all of us," she said.

As I matured, some of that intensity grew focused on an ever-increasing interest in food, cooking, and eating. Just as easily as I had decided I wanted a bowl of granola, I decided that immediately after college I would attend culinary school and work as a line cook before becoming a food writer. "Don't you think it's perfect, combining my ability to write with this passion that I have?" I said to my mother and father, serving them lamb loin chops that I'd attempted to roast with a basil pesto crust. Something had gone terribly wrong, though, and the meat was almost raw, the crust a soggy mess. They nodded grimly and I bent back down over the cookbook I had been studying.

Culinary school turned out to be an excellent choice. There I learned not only how to properly cook lamb, but how to butcher a chicken. I was taught how to make a béchamel sauce, and beurre blanc and béarnaise, too. I discovered the correct way to roll out puff pastry from scratch, and to compose the perfect tarte tatin. I know now how to filet a fish, baste sea scallops in butter, and cook a steak to a perfect medium-rare.

While I was in culinary school, I began interning at Aldea, a Portuguese restaurant in Manhattan with an ambitious menu and a kitchen that opened into the dining area. My internship eventually turned into a "real job," and soon I was cooking in the *garde manger*, or salad and appetizer station, every day before I went off to culinary classes, which were held from 5:45 to 10:45 in the evening. On nights that I didn't have school, I was at Aldea from midmorning until past midnight. It was thrilling and exhilarating and altogether exhausting.

Line cooking was a formative experience as well, though much less enjoyable. The stress and heat and yelling of the kitchen were much too much for me, and I found the late nights and constant pressure to *never fuck up, ever* really rattled my nerves. I was living in Manhattan, and that stressed me, too. I eventually realized that I had gotten very far off-course from my original goal of writing about food. I was exhausted and unhappy, and so I moved back to Syracuse, where I grew up, in hopes of crafting a freelance food-writing career in a more slow-paced environment.

I love Syracuse in the way one loves a slightly challenging adopted dog. No matter how many times it piddles on the carpet, you still care for it because it's yours and no one else's, and it loves you back and feels like home. I love Syracuse, but it is not a particularly ideal place to cultivate a life out of food writing. So I struggled for three years, cobbling together local and national jobs and bouncing from receptionist gig to receptionist gig in an attempt to pay my bills. I wrote a monthly column for the local newspaper, and loved the opportunity to create and test recipes, to cook all morning and spend the afternoon writing about flavors and textures and techniques.

I was trying pretty hard to make food writing "happen," but the bitter truth of not actually earning enough to fill my car with gas had me pretty down and out. Seeking a sense of placidity and calm, I turned to alternative healing, and, drugged under the influence of lemongrass essential oils and Native American flute music, began to explore the concept of "intention"—the idea that what we think, we create. Influenced by the glut of New Age-y, self-improvement books I was reading at the time, I started to believe that if I just put all of my thought energy toward what I wanted to happen, it would.

So I began to daydream, all day long, and kept myself open to all and any opportunities, no matter how unlikely they seemed. When my editor at *Edible Finger Lakes*, a local magazine with a food beat, assigned a short profile on what the movers and shakers around Syracuse liked to eat, I had a feeling that something big would come of it, that it would be an important story. I immediately contacted my friend, a restaurant reviewer for the daily paper. "The eggs and raw milk at Stonehill Farm are my favorites," she said confidently. "Or the hot tomato sauce at Pastabilities." I figured the restaurant had gotten enough press as of late and off I drove to the farm.

This book is about what happened after that. It is about my big, intense emotions, and how they sometimes terrify other people, and about my penchant for obsession, and the incredible, enveloping love I have for food and everything that surrounds it. It is about desire, and sex, and heartbreak. It is about, above everything else, consuming delicious things.

SPRING

LATE FEBRUARY

The first time I visited Stonehill Farm, I felt overwhelmed, my senses assaulted. The air was thick with a cacophony of smells—not offensive, necessarily, just different to my sterile, suburban apartment complex–oriented nose—and the landscape looked wild, free, the slightest bit dangerous. The workers were men, their cheeks wind-burnt and their hands rough—a result, I assumed, of time spent weeding vegetables and doing other outside work in the cold weather. I knew nothing about farming, other than it was necessary for the type of food I wanted to consume. Otherwise, I considered it irrelevant to my interests as a cook and writer.

I was at the farm because I had been given an assignment from *Edible Finger Lakes* magazine to write about the best and most-loved foods in Syracuse, and a tip from a friend had brought me to this operation on one of the lakes. The story seemed like an easy one to write: All I had to do was come up with a few dozen words about the eggs and raw milk that the farmers produced. But when Cliff, Stonehill's manager, offered me a full tour, even though it wasn't necessary, I found it hard to say no. As exotic as the farm felt when I first arrived, by the time I left an hour later, brown paper–wrapped lamb chops in hand, I felt a deep urge to be smack-dab in the middle of it all, surrounded by chickens and cows and pigs and knee-deep in manure, and I had no idea why.

It frightened me a little, but having just successively quit my job as a receptionist at an advertising agency and ended a year-and-a-half relationship—two seemingly unrelated events borne out of a frantic realization that I felt restless and "unfulfilled"—I was actively seeking enlightenment, self-awareness, and a deeper satisfaction with life.

As Cliff walked me around the barnyard, the end-of-February wind whipped around us and I turned up the collar of my coat. I observed the beef cows huddling together for warmth—Cliff told me the name of each one—and smiled at the pile of pigs rooting around their troughs for forgotten food scraps. The dairy cows were lucky enough to be cozied up in the barn, and Cliff took me to see them, too. "We're a full-diet farm," he said, explaining that not only did he and his crew raise livestock for food, they produced raw milk, had a flock of two-hundred laying hens, and grew over four acres of vegetables. "Everything you need for a balanced diet, we try to provide to our members." I looked at him curiously. "We're a CSA, so if you buy a share of the farm, or really, a yearly membership, you get to pick up food every week."

"Even in the winter?" I asked.

"Even in the winter. There's a handful of us who work here full-time—Toby, Ian, Jack, and myself—and Dylan and Logan are here part-time."

Across the field, I saw a tall man with a full beard walk out of an Airstream trailer and slip on a pair of boots as he zipped up his jacket. "And you all live here, too?" Cliff nodded. "Here and there; we're all spread out in different houses. But we're all on the farm. That's Jack. He and Hazel—his girlfriend—live in the 'Stream.'"

It all felt so foreign to me that I couldn't help but imagine what it might be like to live and work there. I looked down at my pleated black peacoat, considering what I'd look like in a sturdy, stiff canvas jacket like Cliff's, and I pictured myself chucking hay bales to the outdoor cows, as the bearded man had begun doing. Although the scent of manure had flooded my nostrils upon my arrival, by now all I smelled was fresh air. As I watched Cliff lean down and tousle a pig's floppy ears, I realized that this was a place that could, despite its unfamiliarity, excite and nurture me. I felt a throbbing sensation in my heart that slid down to my stomach. At that moment, I knew, quite certainly, that I would find a reason to return. February hadn't yet hinted at spring, but I had a feeling that a change was coming soon—and I wanted to be a part of it.

The next week, hoping to extend my time at Stonehill, I pitched the idea of a profile piece to my editor at the Syracuse paper where I had been writing a monthly food column for the last year. "It's a new farm, and they're doing everything the right way," I said, unaware of what, exactly, I even meant by the word "right."

"They do their field work with horses"—I paused, realizing I didn't actually know what field work was—"and they're all young, bright, and creative. I think it'd make a great story." I held my breath as I waited for him to respond. Until this point, I had written strictly cooking how-to and recipe stories. They were fine enough, and seemed to resonate well with the paper's readership, but they didn't feel authentically "me"—whatever that meant. My father had grown up on a dairy farm in northern New York, and I wondered if that thread of connection could be a clue to finding my voice.

To my surprise, my editor gave me the green light, and I eagerly jotted off an email to Cliff to schedule a day to volunteer and interview him in greater depth. *If nothing else*, I thought, *it'll make for a good tongue-in-cheek story.* I saw opportunities for self-deprecation in detailing my attempt at farm work and physical labor, and showed up to Stonehill at nine that morning wearing tight blue jeans, hiking sneakers, a black polyester long-sleeved shirt, and a big sweater. I had dabbed a bit of blush on my cheeks and swiped my lashes with mascara—just in case, though what the "case" might be, I wasn't quite sure.

IN ADDITION TO RAISING BEEF, PIGS, AND CHICKENS FOR MEAT, keeping hens for eggs, and growing vegetables, the farm was a licensed raw-milk dairy. On my previous visit, Cliff had given me a half-gallon jar of the stuff, and after drinking and cooking with what was the thickest, sweetest milk I'd ever had, I washed the jar and filled it with homemade biscuits dotted with cheddar cheese and black pepper. I tied a blue ribbon around the neck, untied it, paused, and then tied it back on again. It might be a little kitschy but, I reasoned, maybe the farmers would find that endearing. I really wanted them to like me, because I was pretty sure I already loved them.

A friend once told me that my impulsiveness—my eagerness to dive into new things, fearlessly and fully, without exploring or considering them first—is both my best and worst quality. In the back of my mind, I knew that I should continue to search for meaningful work as a food writer, but on that drive back to Stonehill, in the very bottom-most corner of my heart, I could feel that this was the first step to some predestined plan in which I would move to the farm and work toward creating a new life there. The details of how, and why, were vague at best, but I had time to figure them out.

And so with that determination, I listened as Cliff outlined a list of chores for me to complete that day. First on the list was tossing hay bales down a trapdoor and re-stacking them in the dairy barn. He showed me how to lift the bale by the twine and chuck it away from my body in one fluid motion. I nodded as he explained, but didn't try it myself until he had disappeared from sight. I guessed the act would feel awkward for me, and I was embarrassed to make a mistake in front of him. I was right—it was uncomfortable, but I thrilled at the weight of the bale, the feeling of hay pricking through my borrowed work gloves, made for a man and two sizes too big. *This is hard work*, I thought as I considered how I had always relied on my hands to work—be it writing or chopping vegetables. Tossing hay around seemed only natural, if a little cumbersome at first.

I stood on a wagon parked in the middle of the barn and began hauling bales from one side of it to the other, down the trapdoor, with as much speed as I could muster. At one point, I lost my footing and fell, my shin catching the side of the wagon and taking off a layer of skin. Raw and pink, my leg pulsed and I chided myself for being clumsy. My cheeks grew blush, too. I cared what these people thought of my farming ability, but I wasn't sure why. I was just there to write a story, after all—not carry the weight of Stonehill Farm on my back.

Once the hay was stacked, however precariously, I walked to the horse barn where Cliff had shown me how to groom the Percherons. There were two short black mares, Pat and Pearl, that Cliff owned, and two taller grey geldings, Bear and JD, that belonged to Ian, a farmer I had met briefly the week before. All four horses were covered in caked dirt, and the task in front of me looked enormous. The outdoor air was chilly, though, and I welcomed the relative warmth of the barn. I got to work, each stroke releasing a cloud of dirt into the air. After ten minutes, my sinuses were under attack and I was blowing dust out of my nose. My arms were sore and tired, which surprised me. I was just brushing a few horses; surely I was stronger than that. After half an hour, I set down the comb, exhausted. (I would later learn that, even in the muddiest seasons, no one on the farm ever spent more than a few minutes grooming—not because they didn't care; they cared deeply—but really, it just seemed wise to give up on aesthetics when there was so much work to be done.)

I was running my hand down Bear's neck, scratching with my fingers as I reached his withers, when I heard footsteps in the doorway. I quickly picked the comb back up and began to brush him again.

"Hey there," said the voice attached to the footsteps, and I peeked out from behind Bear.

"Hi," I said to Ian. His shaggy blond-brown hair poked out from beneath a knit cap. The cold morning air had produced a shock of red across his high cheekbones, making them look even sharper. My eyes traveled from his slender pink lips—which were almost curled up to a smile—up to the bridge of his nose, which boasted a generous splash of freckles. A small ring looped out of his left nostril.

I continued to groom Bear as Ian worked in the barn, using a pocketknife to slice open a hay bale and divide it into four piles on the ground. "Getting ready for tomorrow," he said, before using a big push broom to collect all of the spare pieces of hay and straw into a pile behind the horses. I stole a quick glance and tried to take in as much of him as I could—even under the layers of thick wool, I could tell he had a strong back and chest that whittled down into a trim and narrow waist.

Within the first five minutes of sharing the space, I was filled with a sense of intoxication and excitement. Maybe I was completely crazy, but I very much wanted this man's presence around me. I knew nothing about him, save his first name and his two horses, yet his energy traveled through the coldness and seemed to linger at the tip of my nose. Why was I so taken by him? I thought back to our initial meeting the week prior and immediately remembered his stride. He walked like he had somewhere to go, with his chest out and his shoulders back. He seemed so confident, so sure of himself, that he must be, I had figured, someone worth getting to know.

We talked and worked together for the rest of the morning as I forged on with what is surely, to date, the longest groom the horses have seen. We talked about how old he was (thirty-two) and about his favorite music (pretty much all of it, plus he played the guitar). I was very into a jazz band called Sister Sparrow and the Dirty Birds and wanted to know if he had heard of them; it seemed like just the right bit of trivia to inject into conversation—if he wasn't familiar, I'd have something to share. If he was, all the better. He hadn't, and I told him I'd have to give him a copy of their album. We also discussed dance—he had dabbled with a few modern classes in college and I had taken tap, jazz, and ballet in high school. It was a funny thing to have in common, but there it was. Then we chatted about farming, and why he did it. "I like it. I like it better than anything I've done," he explained with a shrug. We talked until it wasn't morning anymore, since I didn't have any additional chores to complete and, besides, I didn't want to end the conversation. So I stayed put.

Months later, when we spoke about that first encounter, I would insist that I felt nothing until I read his written word in the form of a poetic and charming email. "I wasn't flirting, that day in the horse barn," I insisted, both to him and to myself, "but I did like speaking with you."

When Ian looked at his watch and announced that it was noon, I felt shocked at how easily the morning had passed. He asked if I'd like to feed the pigs with him and, unsurprisingly, my mouth immediately formed the word "yes."

He showed me how to dip a five-gallon bucket into a trough of water and pour it into another bucket on the ground. "Using this keeps the water cleaner," he said, handing me the scooping vessel. I filled a bucket completely and struggled to walk with it, the rim banging against my shins and calves, spilling water over the sides. "And," he paused. "I don't know if this would work for you, but I find it more helpful to fill two buckets. That way you're balanced."

I blushed. I should have known that. Should I have known that?

After filling the pigs' tubs with water and their troughs with grain, we walked to the farmhouse to wash our hands for lunch.

THE AIR IN THE KITCHEN WAS THICK WITH THE SCENT OF BACON, AND pots and pans of varying sizes and states of cleanliness were scattered across the table and countertop. "So, it's self-serve," Cliff said, sticking a large fork into a stockpot full of spaghetti noodles and waving his hand at the stacks of plates and the mason jars stuffed with mismatched silverware that lined the open shelves on the wall. A sauce made with tomatoes, garlic, and hunks of various meats filled a cast-iron skillet. A quart of homemade pickled green beans stood open on the table next to the biscuits I had made. The ribbon lay crumpled next to the lid, and I was glad I had left it on after all. It might not have been a detail a group of men would appreciate, but it was *me*, and I was pleased to have introduced myself in that way.

I crowded around the table with the crew—Ian, Cliff, Toby, Jack, and Logan—and tucked in. The sauce was good, with a brightly acidic flavor and small bites of chewy fat. "What's in this?" I asked, unfamiliar with the texture of pork fat that hadn't been rendered.

"Bacon ends," Cliff said, referencing the scraps of bacon that go to the farmers once the cured belly gets too short to slice into strips.

There was homemade butter, too, and everyone applied it liberally—nestled into pockets of the biscuits, onto the pasta, directly over the red sauce. Cliff admitted that they didn't always make butter—there was never enough time—but that when they did, they savored it with everything. "We just don't cook with it," he explained. "It seems kind of like a waste to use it like that."

The discussion at the table was easy and loud, at times crude, but never offensive. I felt self-consciously feminine and threw in a few dirty jokes of my own. After lunch, Cliff got to work cleaning up (at the farm, the cook washes the dishes, a rule I would come to learn and loathe) and, full but not overly so, we all went back to work.

It appeared there wasn't much for me to do in the way of chores— most of the afternoon's tasks required a more refined skill set than I had to offer.

"You can clean out the dairy gutter," Cliff said, referencing the manure-filled track behind the cows' stanchions.

"Cool," I said, eager to show my pluck and pleased to have such a juicy task to write about. I made plans to meet Toby in the milking parlor after I washed the half-gallon glass jars for that afternoon's milking. But when I arrived there, he was already knee-deep in the job.

"I think I got this," he said, resting on the shovel and shooing me along. I would learn later that, much to everyone's amusement, he felt guilty about giving me such a dirty job, especially considering that I was wearing what he referred to as "nice clothes, for god's sake!"

I poked around the barnyard until I found Ian who, upon consideration, decided that the chicken coop could do with some fresh bedding. He showed me how to use a pitchfork to pile a cart high and wheel that over to the henhouse. It took a few loads to cover the existing layer of chicken shit with clean hay, and when I finished my throat was scratchy and raw. My respiratory system had certainly taken a beating, but my body felt stronger than ever and pleasantly spent. After that, I accompanied Logan as he made sap-collecting rounds from the maples across the barnyard, and I welcomed the chance to lean up against the old trees and give my arms a rest.

We hauled the sap to a makeshift burner outside and watched it boil away. A few brown leaves and pine needles drifted their way into the pot, and he stirred them in. "I'll strain it later. This adds something; it's like a tea, sort of," he explained.

Ian rounded the corner as I contemplated the surprisingly light, bright scent of sap in contrast to the heady sweetness of syrup. "I'm making dinner tonight. Would you like to help?" He had planned on a local black bean soup with roasted potatoes and winter squash. Eager to show off my sous chef skills, I followed his orders and got to work chopping potatoes. Once I had them in a dice, I followed culinary school rules and filled a big bowl with cold water, then dropped the cubes in.

"Um," Ian looked at me curiously. "Why are you doing that?"

"Well, if you don't cook them right away, they'll oxidize and brown," I answered, feeling smart.

"Oh. I was planning on just coating them with oil and herbs right now," he said. "But that's cool. I didn't know that." I turned the color of a radish and made an "oh well" face as I drained them in a colander.

The acorn squash was mottled with spots of mold and becoming soft around the edges, so we worked around it, keeping only the good parts for the roasting pan and throwing the too-far-gone pieces in the compost. I picked pieces of rosemary from a dried stem and chopped them finely with a heavy knife. After a liberal sprinkling of salt and pepper, into the ancient, grease-streaked oven they went.

It was nearing five o'clock, and I felt compelled to call it a day. My body ached and I longed for a warm shower, but mostly I didn't want to overstay my welcome. "Thanks for everything," I said to the crew, who had trickled in from the fields and barns as we cooked. I pulled on my jacket. "I'd really like to come back. For the story."

I had left my cell phone in the car all day and was sitting in the parking lot of the barn, checking the glut of emails that had piled up, when a *tap-tap* on the window startled me into the present. Ian's big grin on the other side of the glass motioned for me to roll down the window.

"Taking notes?" he asked playfully.

"Maybe. Maybe, I'll share them with you." I grinned back like the Cheshire cat. "Hey, here's my card if you ever . . . want to get in touch." I drew out the sentence in attempt to sound casual as I handed over my contact information.

"Great. I will be."

I waved, pulled out of the lot and then remembered the CD in my disc drive. I turned my car around and drove up beside him. "Hey. Remember Sister Sparrow?" He nodded. "Here. I have an extra copy. My favorite track is number three." He looked slightly amused, and set the disc down next to a rusty piece of equipment he was fixing.

I waved once more and drove away for good. Even as I approached the city, I could perfectly picture every patch of still-bare trees; every flop-eared, spotted pig; every big, uncontained scent. I breathed in deeply, sure I could smell hay through the windows. Then I thought about Ian. I wondered if he had noticed the glances I stole at the lunch table, and whether he had anything else to teach me. Stonehill Farm was vivid and bright in my mind, but just to be sure I had all the details correct, I figured I should visit one more time.

EARLY MARCH

I woke the morning after I volunteered with a tightness in the back of my legs and a pulled muscle across my shoulders. The feeling was not unlike the one you get after a vigorous run or a hike in the woods. I stretched and peered out the window. It was sunny, finally, and March already felt so different from the last day of February—it held more promise. I slid out of bed, scratched at my ribs, arched my back, and yawned. Somehow, I had gone a quarter of a century without appreciating just how satisfying a good stretch really was.

The next few days I spent as per my norm: reaching out to food publications in hopes that a desperate editor would bite at my pitch, testing and writing recipes, and working on the stories already lined up in my docket. I had been freelance writing for a few years and, while I was pleased with the gains I had made, I still couldn't seem to cobble together enough work to support myself financially. A high-profile or high-paying gig sent thrills through me, but they were sporadic and rare. I had fallen into a predictable pattern of taking a day job in an administrative or receptionist role, assuming the minimal workload wouldn't distract me from my real goal of being published. But like clockwork, after a few months of slacks and blouses, of answering phones and opening mail, the work began to feel unsatisfying and I'd carve out a promising-enough opportunity in writing to justify leaving. I had just done it again, this time leaving a creative advertising agency with a young staff and beer on tap in the back of the office. My co-workers thought I was crazy for giving up such a great job, but I felt crazy for giving it a shot in the first place.

With Stonehill on my mind, I devoted the majority of my time to writing the farm profile for the newspaper. A series of email exchanges with Cliff helped me to better understand the established roles and inner workings of the farm. I learned that while he managed the enterprise, the land was leased from a woman named Beth, whose family had owned the plot for more than a hundred years. Cliff had fallen in love with farming at North Farm in upstate New York, where he learned how to operate a full-diet, draft horse–powered, Community Supported Agriculture operation. CSAs had been gaining popularity in the last few years, becoming more than a fringe movement in rural America. Instead of grocery shopping at big box stores, or even trekking out to a regional farmers' market, CSA customers purchased a share of the farm—sometimes promising manual labor, too—and received a week's worth of just-harvested food. Most CSAs were vegetable-focused, and that's what made Cliff's special: he wanted his farm to give people everything they needed to be self-sustaining, at least in terms of the foods they ate. So after leaving North and working on another full-diet farm in Vermont, he decided to strike out on his own with a similar model. He purchased a pregnant cow and gave himself a deadline: before she gave birth, he had to find a place to establish his operation.

His childhood friend Logan heard about Beth's land in central New York, and suggested Cliff check it out. It had been a functioning dairy farm, and then a working sheep farm before sitting idly for a few years. Cliff entered a lease-to-own agreement with Beth, packed up his bags and his cow, and made the leap. With Logan's help, he cobbled together a small staff; another friend, Ash, worked with livestock and butchery, and together they formed a tight crew.

Ash moved on after a year to pursue a degree in teaching, and Cliff hired a former colleague from North Farm to take over his role. Jack was an artful butcher with a youthful face often disguised by a full beard. Bringing a fanatical passion for perfection in caring for and raising livestock, he made the transition to Stonehill in the winter of 2011. Ian had also worked at North and, after an offer from Cliff, he joined the team in January of 2012 as the vegetable manager. Toby, a young, aw-shucks kind of guy from a small town in Colorado had been working on a vegetable farm out west when he heard an interview with Cliff on a Greenhorns radio broadcast and sent a letter of interest. He wasn't sure Cliff would respond, or if that's how one even went about getting hired, but Cliff took the chance and offered him a job. Toby had been at Stonehill since October of 2011, working with Ian in the vegetable department and with Cliff in the raw milk dairy. Dylan rounded out the crew, spending two days a week organizing and operating the weekly CSA pickup.

The farm was an intricate operation, with each employee working in a specialized field that seemed equally foreign and complicated to me. I grasped the idea that Jack managed livestock, but had no clue what that entailed. I knew nothing about the miles and miles of electric fencing set up, taken down, and rearranged every spring, summer, and fall, nor did I understand the importance of grazing and pasture plans. If the cows ate from only one patch of grass, it'd never regrow properly—and they'd never get proper nutrition. So Jack worked out the best and most efficient means of shuttling cows all over the fields, to spread the grazing (and the manure) around. Although I was aware that cows ate grass, I had never considered that there was someone behind the scenes orchestrating the whole buffet. Similarly, I knew vegetables were planted in and harvested from the ground, but I had not once thought about how they got there and what was necessary for them to grow. My father had grown up on a dairy farm, and I liked milk just fine—I was even attuned to the raw, or unpasteurized, movement—but I had never spent any real time in a milking parlor (before watching Toby shovel out the gutter, that is.)

My grandfather milked almost one hundred head of cattle when my dad was growing up. I had spoken with my father about his childhood over the years, but never at length, and mostly about things that mattered more to me as a rambunctious young girl, like "Did you get to play in the hay barn?" and "How cute, really, are dairy cows?" I resolved to revisit the conversation with him. It might help flesh out my story, I figured, but it would also probably answer a few questions I had about myself and the path I had just leapt onto. I wondered if he missed farming, and if he thought I should pursue it.

As I worked toward an intimate and engaging narrative for the article, I was still trying to untangle how a full-diet farm actually operated. Having very little farming experience, I wasn't aware that "full-diet" was a rather unique concept in modern agriculture, with most operations specializing to the point of growing a single crop. If I was going to write a good story, I had a lot to learn.

One afternoon later that week, as I chewed on the end of a pen and considered synonyms for "manure," I felt my telephone vibrate: a new email. The subject line read "As promised," and it was from Ian. My heart beating faster than normal, I opened the letter and read. It was simple and borderline benign, the type of email that probably meant nothing, but could be easily reinterpreted by an eager young woman. He outlined what he'd done that day (worked on the cultivator, watched snow falling over the fields and paddocks), what he'd listened to (a mix of NPR and pop/hip-hop), and his thoughts on the Sister Sparrow CD (a decidedly New Orleans vibe that would be good in a dark bar). He thanked me for my work on the farm and said I was very helpful. He asked if he'd see me again sometime soon and wished me happy writing.

I rested my chin in my palm and re-read the entire thing. I couldn't tell if he was flirting, but I liked the way he wrote. His note had flow and elegance, a firm grasp on syntax and style. I was definitely falling, and hard.

Later that night I met my friend Katie at a wine tasting she was working in Syracuse. She did marketing for a vineyard on Seneca Lake, and I had written some promotional pieces for the Finger Lakes Wine Country Tourism Association, so when work brought her out my way, I eagerly volunteered to help. We struck up a friendship and enjoyed collaborating on events—working next to her felt like spending the evening with a girlfriend and good wine.

In between pouring glasses of various vintages, I read her the email, trying not to give away my own feelings about what it might mean. "What do you think? Is this flirtatious? Should I be excited? Am I getting too excited?"

She wrinkled her nose and thought for a minute before responding. "I don't know. It's hard to tell."

"He's very handsome," I said, thinking of his strong jaw line. My cheeks grew warm at the thought of him.

"Well, write him back and find out!" she said, meting out an ounce of Riesling for a curious taster.

I thought about him for the remainder of the night, wondering what it might be like to kiss him and whether he might be wondering the same thing. "Would you like to try some Gewürztraminer?" I repeated again and again, the "r" and "v" sounds in the middle of the word knocking together like two runaway trains.

That night I sat cross-legged on my bed, surrounded by a Wendell Berry book and my story notes, and wrote back to Ian. I asked what a cultivator was (I really did want to know), told him about the wine event (leaving out the amounts that I had sampled), and, in general, used irresponsibly flirtatious language.

I pressed send, lay back with a satisfied smirk, and closed my eyes.

The next week, I returned to the farm for another day of volunteering. It was grey and windy, with a persistent drizzle that eventually turned into a downpour. I arrived midmorning, and saw Dylan, Jack, and Cliff behind the barn, chopping slabs of pork fat into small pieces.

"We're rendering lard today," Cliff explained as Jack slowly heated the chunks in an enormous metal stockpot over a propane burner. "Grab a knife and jump in." I held the plastic blue handle of a large butcher's knife and got to work, every so often stopping to breathe in the scent of hot fat that was permeating the air and, surely, my clothes and hair. A pan of hot water sat in the middle of the table, and I quickly realized its value as my knife gummed up with fat and grease. Every so often, we'd dip our knives in the hot water and continue "cutting. There was a great deal of fat to work with, and by the time we had tackled it all, the crook of my index finger had begun to blister, just the way it had when I worked as a line cook.

Dylan and I were put in charge of watching the lard as it melted, making sure the pan didn't scorch before the fat reached 265 degrees. We occasionally scraped the bottom with a large metal spatula, peering in with worried looks. It was Thursday and the CSA members would be arriving in just a few hours, their reusable canvas bags ready to be filled, so Dylan also needed to begin readying the barn for that afternoon's pickup. He showed me how to sweep out the space with a big push broom, reaching into the corners where feathers, bits of stone, and so very much dust had gathered, then pile it into a rusty old shovel and fling the contents outside. We sorted through big plastic bags of carrots and beets taken from storage, composting any that looked substandard—there were a great many, at this point—and we piled the good ones in wooden crates.

Meanwhile, the lard situation was beginning to look perilous. The big red tent we were under wasn't faring well in the wind, threatening upset at every gust. The rain came down at such a slant that it pelted straight into the stockpot. I didn't know much about making lard, but we both surmised that adding water to a pot that was actively working to evaporate it was probably not the best recipe for success, so we set a lid slightly askew over the top of it all and tried to fix the tent situation. When Dylan left to make the noon meal, Cliff took over the project and I was put to work stacking more hay bales.

Gathered in the kitchen, everyone seemed cold and miserable until they heard what was for lunch: pork hock stew with black beans and red chiles, plus a potato casserole made with fat Kennebec potatoes sliced thinly on a mandoline, the delicate rounds layered on their sides in a baking dish, then doused in melted butter and roasted until their edges were a toasty golden-brown. My breath caught in my throat when I saw Ian open the door and swap his boots for slippers. I gave him a small wave and ducked into the kitchen, suddenly feeling less brave than I had over email. The kitchen was an inviting place to escape to; Dylan was an excellent cook, the kind who researched and dutifully followed recipes. He also wasn't shy about the amount of lard he tossed into the cast-iron pans.

I still felt timid around the crew, not sure if and when it was appropriate to jump into a conversation or start my own. So I focused on the meal, relishing the way the potato ridges shattered under my teeth, the way their middles melted softly on my tongue. Generously salted and coated in fat, they served as a fine foil to the spicy beans. Everyone drank milk out of pint and quart jars, so thick it left an opaque lining on the glass.

The crew took a full hour for lunch, and they all spent it together. There was a penchant for lingering at mealtime, revisiting the kitchen for "just a scoopful more," and savoring the last few bites. The concept seemed odd to me, having eaten lunch alone at my desk or downing a quick sandwich in the car while I ran errands for so long.

"Ugh, food-baby," said Logan, rubbing his distended stomach. Everyone nodded in agreement and slouched in their chairs, chatting idly, until Ian popped up and clapped his hands, eager to get back to work. The conversation between us had sparked and crackled, building on the silent acknowledgment that we had spoken earlier, *in private*. I was reluctant to let him go, and teased him. "Leaving so soon?" I asked, arching my back and running my fingers through my hair in an attempt to seem casual. "Horses won't feed themselves, Ro," he said, using my nickname, which I had signed my email with. I squeezed my fingernails into my palms under the table: *He noticed.* One by one, the farmers stood, because the pigs wouldn't feed themselves, either, and the milk didn't just flow freely. I sat, looking to Cliff for direction.

"Hey, she can wash eggs," Dylan said, rubbing a newly cleaned lunch plate with a bleach-stained kitchen towel.

I shrugged and smiled. "Sounds good to me."

I was shown the walk-in cooler where dirty eggs were kept after collection from the henhouse, and told how to fill a five-gallon bucket with warm, soapy water. "Just so you know," Dylan warned, "There's a steer in there. Like, hanging from the ceiling."

"Cool," I said, trying to sound nonchalant, but inside, trying to fight off nerves. I had been a vegetarian from ages fourteen to nineteen, and even though I had been eating meat regularly for years, I had really only ever considered animals as living things or as food, never as that vague in-between stage.

"I figure I should warn people. You never know." He pushed the door open to reveal four quarters of a cow that didn't yet look like steak, but was definitely not an animal anymore, either.

I was then shown how to gently scrub away any mud, feathers, or shit from the eggs, how to dip them in a clean-water rinse before laying them to air out on a wire-mesh table. I was taught to wait patiently until they dried completely before packing them, small-side down, in egg cartons, and then I was left alone to do it all.

As I washed each egg, I turned it over in my hand, admiring the variance in colors, from pale beige to dusty sand to deep caramel. Some eggs were too large to fit into cartons—double yolks, for sure, I was told—and some had hairline cracks along their sides. Those, called house eggs, I placed in a separate carton to be used by the farmers. As I washed, Jack worked to finish wrapping the bacon and sweet Italian sausage he had made that week, and Cliff furiously ladled still-warm lard into jars through a funnel (we'd learn later, as it cooled, that the attempt had been a roaring disaster, the lard mottled with chunks of half-congealed fat and drizzly, rather than creamy, in texture).

I was just finishing up the last batch of eggs when four o'clock rolled around. The weekly pickup, or distribution, was about to start, and CSA members were starting to stroll in. The guys had changed into button-down shirts that, while threadbare and greyish in hue, were made handsome with the addition of a tie and worked well in contrast with their ripped work pants and barn boots.

I hung around, watching the farmers interact with the customers for a few minutes. A family with three young children spoke with Cliff, the eldest girl tap-dancing on the concrete floor in her sneakers. This was a community, but not yet mine. "Thanks for everything—I think I'm going to head out," I whispered to Cliff.

"Wait," he said with a smile. "Here."

He handed me two of the firmest acorn squash, plus some of the large red beets I had helped to sort and a handful of white onions with hints of green sprouts poking through their tops.

"Hey, thanks. Thanks so much," I said, hugging the package to my chest. Already, thoughts of a squash, halved and doctored with butter, sage, and brown sugar were brewing in my mind. I could hardly wait to get home and make dinner.

As I walked through the milk house—the room adjacent to the parlor where milk was filtered and jarred, then distributed to customers—and into the parking lot, I ran into Ian and was surprised at his appearance. I had been thinking about him so much that I almost forgot what he actually looked like; in my daydreams, his hair was blonder, his gait smaller. In reality his hair was just shy of brown, and he walked quickly. I looked him up and down, taking in the beard that, while patchy in places, gave him a wild, animalistic look. I gave an approving nod; this version was better.

"I'll see you tomorrow," Ian said. Cliff had mentioned earlier, when we were chopping lard, that all of the farmers, plus a handful of volunteers and friends, were going to watch *Wet Hot American Summer* on a projector in the living room.

I swallowed a big gulp of air. "Really?" A trickle of excitement ran down my spine. Between the emailing and the lunchtime flirting, I wondered if Ian was feeling the same sort of anticipation about me.

"Sure, why don't you come for dinner beforehand?"

I hesitated. I wanted to, but was worried about being fair. "I don't know. I won't be volunteering, and I don't feel right eating without putting in the work."

"It'll be fine," he said casually. "You can come as my guest."

My coy smile hinted nothing of the toothy grin I was hiding inside, or maybe it did. "Okay. Then I will."

I turned on my heel and floated all the way home. And I didn't come back down until the first bite of acorn squash, the last of a winter treat and sweet with the promise of spring.

LATE MARCH

Friday night came quickly. I spent the early part of the evening at my parents' home, talking with my father as he built a fire in the living room. They lived a short distance from the farm, just a thirty-minute drive away in a small town called Onondaga Hill.

"You're getting serious about farming, then?" he asked after I described the lard-making process from the day before.

"Really," I said. "It just seems like—I don't know—something I want to learn more about. Like something that's in me already. Does that make sense?"

"Of course," he said. "It's been years since I lived on the farm, but I miss it now and then. I do." He smiled. "I really miss certain parts of it, like waking up early and working outside. There were these work overalls we all wore, too . . . " His voice faded off, and I was quiet, letting him reminisce. He lit a match and tossed it into the fireplace. The newspapers ignited and the flames quickly spread to the kindling. "It's the sort of thing that just feels good, that never leaves you."

"I'm beginning to understand that," I said. "Ian told me it felt better than any other job he's done."

My father raised an eyebrow. "Ian, hmm?" I had spoken about him once or twice already that evening, and although I thought I did so casually, I realized my tone may have betrayed me. "Will he be there tonight, too?"

"Well, yeah." I muttered my answer. "Everyone will."

"Just don't do anything too quickly," he said, closing the fireplace door.

"God, Dad!" I said. "It's just a movie!" But, inwardly, I admitted that my father certainly knew me well.

I ARRIVED AT THE FARM IN JEANS AND A WHITE KNIT SWEATER WITH a cowl neck, a bottle of my favorite Finger Lakes Meritage in either hand. I wore boots with faux fur around their ankles, and Toby jokingly asked how many gerbils had died for the fashion.

The atmosphere was casual, not quite a party yet. The living room still looked pretty sparse, and I figured that the pace would pick up when the rest of the guests arrived. Toby and Ian were playing guitar—"When Doves Cry" by Prince—and a few people were in the kitchen, finishing dinner preparations. I waved at Ian, who nodded in response, and I sat on the floor between the two of them, listening without looking at them as they worked through the chord progressions. Toby had just mastered the chorus when I was put to work making a salad with mesclun bartered from a friend with either better luck or a heated greenhouse. I was used to having raw greens year-round, but the care with which Cliff handed the bunch to me told me that these were something special. I rummaged through the haphazardly arranged pantry until I found some walnut pieces and plump raisins. I threw them in with the greens and whisked together a vinaigrette made from balsamic vinegar, raw sugar, Dijon mustard, salt, and pepper. The olive oil was housed in a large metal can, and it gushed quickly into the bowl with a *glug-glug-glug*.

Cooking in the kitchen at Stonehill didn't feel natural, not in the way that churning out tarts and scones at home, or plating foie gras at Aldea, the restaurant where I had worked in Manhattan, did. I felt like I was in someone else's space, with foreign ingredients. I didn't know where to find anything and, with Dylan commandeering the kitchen, I felt more in the way than helpful.

I poured a few ounces of wine into a half-pint jar and set it down on the table. The glass didn't leave much room to aerate the Meritage, but I swirled it anyway, slowly and carefully, the way I had learned in the tasting rooms on Keuka and Seneca Lakes. When I held the wine to my face, I was rewarded with a waft of heady baking spices, stewed plums, and wet soil. I felt calmer, more comfortable, and went to sit in the living room as Toby picked out a Carrie Underwood song on his guitar.

By the time we had eaten our fill, figured out the projector, and put it in place, it had grown dark. We all piled in front of the screen, on couches and chairs, on blankets on the floor. I sat next to Ian and leaned back against the couch cushion, patting Logan's knees with my palm before the film began. It was a funny movie and everyone laughed a lot, goaded on by one another. I began to feel a little flushed from the wine, so when Ian filled his glass with water from the tap, I motioned for it and asked if I could have a sip. He looked at me curiously, as if I had crossed some boundary that wasn't necessarily bad, and I emptied half the glass's contents. "Thanks," I whispered, setting it back in his hand and turning my attention to the movie.

After the credits, as cushions were put back in their place, I got to know the other guests a little better. I spoke with a volunteer who had grown up on a farm and, feeling nostalgic, offered to do weekend chores. I got to know a woman with a horse rehabilitation farm who had brought dehydrated kale chips to share. She was there to pick up JD, one of Ian's Percherons, who had sustained an injury.

"Are you sad?" I asked Ian later that evening as we sat on the ripped leather couch. "Will you miss him a lot?"

Ian shrugged. "I'll miss him, but I don't know if I'm sad, exactly. He'll have a good life there and if he ever recovers I'll get him back." He seemed so rational, but I detected a bit of quiet nostalgia in his voice. "It's not like they're pets," he said, which made Toby laugh so hard he coughed.

"Yeah, okay, Ian," he said, rolling his eyes. "You're in love with those horses."

I watched Ian's expression soften and hugged my knees. "I really love animals, too. Especially baby ones."

"Don't love them too much!" Jack hollered from the kitchen. "You can't run a farm with lots of pet pigs and cows running around."

After most people had left, I washed dishes in the kitchen with Cliff, placing wet plates in the draining rack before he retrieved them and wiped them dry with a towel. I tried to take notice of where he put each one, committing it to memory. "So culinary school, huh?" Cliff said.

"She cooks potatoes all fancy-like," Ian said, sauntering in to steal a kale chip. I said "*Hey!*" and flicked soapy water his way with my fingers.

"Yeah, culinary school. The French Culinary Institute," I said, rubbing at a bowl with the sponge. "Learned a lot, paid a lot of money . . . " I paused. "Learned a lot."

Cliff considered this while depositing a handful of forks, tine-sides up, into a pint jar on the counter. "Would you want to maybe cook a few meals a week here?" I smiled hugely, showing all my teeth. "You could maybe do lunch and dinner three times a week—say Monday, Tuesday, and Wednesday?" I had agreed before he even offered a few bags of vegetables each week in return.

The next week felt more structured. I wrote, stacked more hay bales, and began creating meals for the farmers. My first experience cooking at Stonehill was a disaster, although everyone ate seconds and smiled encouragingly throughout lunch, even if the crew agreed that they'd had better. I had asked Cliff what protein was available to cook with, and he admitted that besides ground beef, not much. That was fine by me; I didn't eat much meat and didn't much care. I asked him to thaw a few pounds the night before and got to work planning a shepherd's pie topped with puréed carrots and parsnips spiked with nutmeg and a hint of cinnamon. When I arrived that morning, though, I found two brown paper–wrapped packages submerged in a stockpot of hot water. I squeezed one between my thumb and first two fingers and found it still hard. "Sorry . . . I forgot," Cliff said, throwing on a Carhartt jacket and running out the door to tend to a crisis.

I shrugged and started a new pot of water to boil the root vegetables. Logan came in to measure out ingredients for pizza dough. We chatted idly as I mashed the carrots and parsnips with spoonfuls of butter and cream, letting showers of fine salt and pepper fly through my fingers. The mixture was awfully chunky; I had attempted to purée the whole thing with an immersion blender to a limited degree of success when an old-fashioned potato masher would have done the trick. I just threw up my hands and called it good enough. Then I added what was supposed to be a scant amount of maple syrup for a hint of sweetness, but lost control of the jar and a good third-cup sloshed in.

"Shit," I said, throwing in a bit of ground cayenne in an attempt to reconcile, or at least balance everything.

With lunchtime rapidly approaching and the meat still only partially thawed, I mixed it as best I could with a beaten egg, more salt and pepper, and ground sage. I was hoping for breadcrumbs, but couldn't find either those or fresh bread, so I just plopped the whole mass in a glass casserole dish, spread the lumpy maple carrots over the top and placed it in the oven. I crossed my fingers. It would be good. It would be fine. It would be calories.

LATER THAT WEEK I WENT BACK TO NEW YORK CITY TO VISIT SOME old friends. Having lived in the city for a year while attending culinary school, I still felt ties to the place and was eager to be back in what, despite not having been able to hack it, I still considered to be the center of the universe. But something was different this time: the city felt too large, too aggressive. What I used to process as a pulsing energy now felt oppressive. I was eager to get back to the farm; I didn't yet belong there, but at least it felt quiet, and peaceful.

And, of course, there was Ian. Our email exchange had picked up quickly after the movie night, becoming increasingly playful, and we danced around the idea of spending another evening together. A local high school was presenting a stage version of *Sweeney Todd*, a concept I found hilarious. He countered that we simply stage our own production, with a bucolic pasture backdrop and apple trees. His easy and casual humor thrilled me, and I finally suggested we attend a documentary film produced by an old college professor of mine. He agreed and we made plans to go on Friday, when I returned from the city.

On the bus ride back from New York, I sat with my forehead against the windowpane. I couldn't get him off my mind, and I knew I was entering dangerous territory. Daydreaming, where I let expectations and elaborate fabricated story lines quash the beauty and simplicity of real human interaction, had never done me much good, at least in the way of men. So I tried to calm down and spent the rest of the time working on a travel guide to the city of Syracuse that I was writing for *USA Today*.

Neither Ian nor I had been clear about whether or not the documentary viewing was a date, or if anyone else was invited. I hoped it was, and that they weren't, but when I arrived at the farm that evening, it was abuzz with activity and I began to question my excitement. Ash, the farm's original butcher, a solid man with enormous arms, was visiting and the kitchen table was laid out with edibles from both his travels and the farm's larder: soft pretzels, Andouille sausage, and a large bulb of winter kohlrabi, still covered in a thick layer of mold. The kohlrabi was presumably to become part of that evening's dinner, provided someone mustered up the energy to cut through its callous exterior.

"Hey! Hi!" I said to the crew, pulling up my socks and tiptoeing across the floor, which was streaked with melted snow and bits of hay. Apparently, I noted, the farmers at Stonehill didn't always take off their boots when they passed through the house. "I'm Rochelle," I said, extending my hand to Ash.

"Want a piece of sausage?"

"Well, I won't say no." I popped it in my mouth and chewed. It tasted pleasantly spicy, and was seasoned well. In the other room, the familiar strains of guitar sounded. "*It's all about the money, money, money,*" Toby crooned a pop radio song as Ian backed him up with harmony.

"Ready to go?" I called out to Ian from the kitchen, peering around the corner to check the wall clock. The crew in the room averted their eyes and I heard what sounded like a faint snort. It became clear to me that not only was no one else invited, Ian had been mercilessly teased about his plans. "Bye, everyone." I smiled as I yanked my boots back on. A few moments later, Ian joined me outside. "I can drive," I offered, and we both got into my old eggplant-colored Honda Accord.

Certain I knew the way in theory but unsure of it in practice, I took a wrong turn and we arrived at the theatre late. There weren't many seats left and, reluctant to disturb the viewing, we tiptoed a few rows down until we found an empty one. "You sit." Ian motioned to the chair and settled onto the stairs beside it.

I sat close to him, our legs almost touching. There seemed to be a current of electricity running between us—just being near him made me feel energized. He leaned in to whisper something about the film, and I caught the scent of chewing gum, some combination of tangerines and tropical fruits.

I brought my lips close to his ear and paused, taking a breath. "You smell like the beach," I said quietly.

He whispered back matter-of-factly. "Before we left I had a piece of sausage, then a pretzel with peanut butter. Ash was like 'Oh, that's a bad move before a date,' and gave me a piece of gum."

I smiled in the dark, then sat back and folded my hands. So it *was* a date.

After the movie we had a few beers at a hole-in-the-wall dive bar in town. We talked about wine, how I had gotten into it and what I looked for in a good glass. I let my eyes grow far away with the description of a perfect dry Riesling, rife with wet stone and juicy lime. We spoke about his family, his bachelor's and master's degrees, and what type of writing I really wanted to do.

"Narrative nonfiction, I guess," I said, running my right hand through my hair. "I like to tell stories, and I feel like I have some pretty good ones."

He pressed a little further, hinting at a preference for written work with more practicality. I blushed for what seemed like the hundredth time that week. "Well, substance is important to me, too." He told me about a book he'd just read, a memoir about farming and food, and said that I'd be welcome to borrow it if I'd like. "I think you'd connect with it," he said.

"Why?"

"Well, she seems to experience things kind of emotions-first, and, if I'm not mistaken, that's your deal, too."

"You can read me like," I said, taking a pause for dramatic emphasis, "a book."

He leaned in closer. "Well, some things are obvious."

While we were in the dim bar, the air had grown thick with a hazy fog. I drove us back slowly and nervously, unsure of where the street for the farm was and if I could get us there safely. Ian guided me gently. "There's a small dip in the road here," he said. "Now a curve to the right. Here. Here's our turn."

I took the turn a little too widely and he laughed. We traveled a quarter-mile up the road and the farm opened itself up to us. I turned into the driveway next to the farmhouse and parked my car behind Jack's pickup truck. Ian and I opened our car doors at the same time and he came around to meet me. We both stood by the passenger-side door, facing one another. I was breathing more quickly than usual.

"Well. Thanks for coming," I said sheepishly. "And thanks for the beer."

"You're welcome. Thanks for inviting me."

We stood in front of each other, our hips close, my eyes at his shoulders. My body swayed tentatively, closer to and then farther from his. He grabbed my waist and steadied me, then placed his mouth on mine. We kissed there in the driveway, the dim moonlight bathing our hair. I moved my hand up to his neck and held it tightly. We stayed like that for a few minutes, our movements slight but deliberate, until we both finally pulled away.

"I should go," I said. He nodded and began to walk away, toward the house.

A few steps, and he paused. "You know, you don't *have* to. You don't have to go."

My heart lurched. I didn't want to go. "But I do."

He nodded, smiled, and disappeared into the dark.

I inhaled deeply, filling my lungs with clean air that smelled like a combination of coldness and sap. "Oh . . ." I murmured. I tried to make out his body in the night, grasping at the memory of his breath. I took one step forward and walked directly into the front bumper of my car.

EARLY APRIL

Weeks passed as grey slush turned into new growth and I drew deeper into the farm.

Officially, I was cooking lunch Mondays, Tuesdays, and Wednesdays in exchange for fresh vegetables and the occasional carton of eggs or half-gallon of milk. Unofficially, I was spending just about every waking and sleeping hour at Stonehill.

I arrived around 8:30 each morning, after the crew had finished breakfast, and was put to work. Some days, I was given odds-and-ends tasks: cleaning a storage space in one of the barns, taking out the compost, sorting through half-squishy onions in search of a few good ones for distribution. But most often, when I wasn't cooking, I worked in the greenhouse with Ian. With no prior farm experience, I was surprised to learn how much work had to be done in that small, warm structure before moving out to the field.

It was hot already, with some days climbing up to eighty degrees. The men worked without shirts, and after an initial bout of shyness, I did too. An afternoon spent weeding in the greenhouse was unbearably hot, so with sweat trickling down the curve in my back, I'd pull my tank top over my head, working in just thin cargo pants and a jogging bra. One day as I filled flats with celery seeds, Cliff and Ian, back from a walk around the vegetable fields, came over to check on me.

"And the employees are now working shirtless. This is despicable," Cliff said in mock frustration, throwing his hands in the air.

"Hey. Hey!" Ian rebutted, equally in jest. "This is my greenhouse and I will run it how I see fit."

My resolve to take things slowly after our first date hadn't lasted long: I visited the farm the next day. Ian and I took a walk in the woods, weaving between the trees until we came to a clearing that overlooked a valley. I could see fields for miles, but it was Ian who noticed an ancient tree stand, no doubt originally built for hunting deer. "Wanna climb up?" he asked, and held the rickety ladder as I ascended, more certain the wood would weaken and crumble under my feet the higher I got. We sat talking in the tree stand for an hour, until both our stomachs began to grumble. "Dinner?" he asked. "We could make something."

"I brought some whole wheat pappardelle," I said. "From a local guy."

"Do you always travel with pasta?" he asked, jumping off the ladder a few feet above the ground.

"Only when I think it'll come in handy," I said, extending my hand and hopping from the ladder into his arms. We made our way from the forest into the kitchen, where I put him in charge of chopping onions and carrots. We sautéed those with ground beef, then simmered it all with canned tomatoes before ladling it over the pasta, which was thick and chewy—as al dente as pasta came. Once we'd cleaned up, we made our way to his room in Beth's farmhouse and began watching a movie on his laptop. It all felt very comfortable. Ian fell in and out of sleep throughout the film, and once it was over I snuggled in closer to him and told him that I should leave. He was already in pajamas.

"You shouldn't," he said, and this time, it was enough to convince me. So I stayed, and we began kissing feverishly, and then he took off my clothes and I took off his. My entire body shuddered with pleasure when he touched me, his hands deliberate and confident.

So now, back in the greenhouse, Ian's comment felt like sharing a secret. I caught his eye and winked. We all laughed, and Cliff grabbed a few of the flats I had finished seeding.

"Impressive," I said, noting the four-deep stack.

"You're gonna be strong enough for this soon," Cliff said, walking toward the house.

"Wait, I'm *going* to be strong?" I called after him indignantly.

"Yeah! Going to." He disappeared into the mudroom. The interaction heartened me; I had turned down the opportunity to attend a wine-tasting event and write about it for a couple of hundred dollars, and had been feeling guilty. But between the warmth of the sun and the friendly banter with Cliff and Ian, I found resolve in my decision. I was happy here, and that seemed reason enough to justify it.

To begin the seeding process, soil was mixed with water until it reached optimal texture and consistency, then a tool was used to form and deposit blocks of soil into shallow, homemade wooden flats. Ian usually performed this task, mixing the soil with a shovel as I lined each flat with old newspapers. On more than one occasion, I came across my cooking and recipe column in the local paper, and would quickly turn it upside-down, smoothing out the paper and adding the flat to a stack of finished ones. I was proud of my writing, but slightly embarrassed by the cutesy photos that accompanied the articles.

One evening around that time, a couple stopped Ian and me as we were walking to dinner in Syracuse. "Are you Rochelle?" the man asked. I nodded and extended my hand, excited to meet someone who read my columns and articles.

"Oh my god. Yes," the woman said, and they both began to giggle.

He took a dramatic pause. "We have this picture of you taped to our fridge." Both Ian and I raised our eyebrows. "You're like, wielding this enormous knife with this even bigger smile on your face and it. Is. Totally creepy." My grin grew slack and he barreled on. I knew what picture he was describing, and it mortified me. ". . . But creepy in an amazing way!"

I groaned and excused myself from the conversation as quickly as possible, calling to mind all of those upside-down sheets of newspaper, discarded and composting in the field. "Well, that was awesome," Ian chuckled to himself as we walked away, but for a good few minutes I was inconsolable. Something about the exchange embarrassed me deeply, and while I couldn't quite put my finger on what it was, I had a feeling that it had to do with the fact that my career wasn't quite where I felt it should be. Five years ago, when friends asked what I meant by "food writing," I casually said, "You know, like *Bon Appétit*." While I was thankful for the platform I had, I couldn't help but feel a little like I was falling short.

Back in the greenhouse, once the flats were lined and filled, we deposited seeds into the small indentations of each soil block.

Depending on their germination needs, some blocks received just one small seed; others were given five or six, or even nine. The pads of my fingers felt clumsy in those early weeks, unable to drop the right number of seeds in the correct space. Once, I lost control of a cluster of head lettuce seeds in my palm and it showered out over the entire flat. I began to apologize profusely. Ian waved the mistake aside in a generous show of forgiveness. "It's not *good* that it happened, of course. But it happens." A few weeks later, when the lettuce began to grow, the flat looked like the night sky, each smattering of Jericho seedlings a tiny constellation in the rich, dark soil.

The full flats were carried outside and set on a makeshift table. A thin layer of soil was spread over the top, then the entire thing was watered and brought to the germination chamber, a dark and warm closet off the kitchen that I had also found to be ideal for proofing bread dough made with coarse whole wheat flour.

Despite the monotony, I preferred placing seeds in the blocks, letting Ian cover the flats with soil and water. It took time to get the amount of soil correct; Ian would point out when there was too little in a corner, too thick a blanket in the middle. I gave up temporarily and cozied myself inside the greenhouse, surrounded by seed packages that promised peppers, eggplant, celery, and cabbages, sweet herbs and bitter greens. Ian didn't let me snuggle into complacency for long, though, and insisted I practice covering the flats with soil and watering them thoroughly. Once I got the hang of it, I grew to love carrying the saturated flats from the sawhorse tables to the garden cart and into the germ chamber. At the end of the day, a damp, dark stain streaked my T-shirt, a telltale sign of the wet wood I held against my body as I hauled the heavy containers full of young seedlings. I was getting stronger.

Ian was all business in the greenhouse, unafraid to gently reprimand anyone who deviated from his system or underperformed. I noticed a similar attitude toward Bear and Duke, as he refused to accept poor attitude or anxiety as excuses for anything less than exemplary work. Duke had come to Ian by way of a draft horse rescue organization, and while he was no JD, he had a certain amount of spunk and promise. *Ian demands so much of the horses, and of me,* I wrote in my journal. It was true, though not upsetting. I felt, for once in my life, accountable for my actions. In the past, my insufficiencies or mistakes had often been waved away or forgiven easily; not here. There was a kindness in the teaching, but an urgency, too. I could almost feel myself growing and improving. The darker the pasture grew, the more of a farmer I became.

AFTER THE WORKDAY, AWAY FROM THE VEGETABLES, THINGS WERE different. Ian kissed bigger, better than anyone I had ever met, coaxing my lips open with his, exploring my mouth eagerly. We took walks in the twilight, with fizzy glasses of Campari, sparkling water, and gin in hand. We watched the sun set in the never-ending fields, dipping low behind the bushy green trees. We explored the woods that bordered the farm and touched each other urgently in the dim candlelight of his bedroom.

After dinner and a short shower, he would light a stick of incense, stretch his legs and limbs, and settle into bed. He spent his evenings composing letters to faraway friends and reading thick nonfiction books before I coaxed the binding from his hands. Some nights he sat at the wooden writing desk next to one of the windows and pulled out his guitar. Wearing only blue hospital scrubs as pants, his hair still damp and sticking to the back of his neck, he played to no one in particular. He knew "Skinny Love" by Bon Iver and sang it as often as I requested. I would lie underneath the patchwork quilt and hum along with the melody. "*Come on skinny love; just last the year,*" his body would start to sway, and I felt connected and satisfied in a way I never had before. I felt lucky to be in his bed.

One night as we lay with the blankets kicked down toward the foot of the bed, kissing lazily with his body draped over mine, my arms pinned over my head, his hands on my wrists, he buried his face in my underarm. "Are you wearing perfume? Do you wear perfume?" He asked.

"Not perfume, no," I said. "But I do put on essential oils. Lavender, mostly. Sometimes lemongrass, or bergamot." I paused. "I used to wear vanilla extract," I admitted.

He thought about this, then spoke again. "Would you consider not wearing anything? I want to smell *you*."

My chest turned crimson. "Of course," I said, and the next day tucked my oils deep into the back of my sock drawer at home.

Later that week, he tried again, breathing in deeply as I giggled and told him that his facial hair was tickling my skin. "You're still wearing something," he said, disappointed.

"No, no," I insisted. "I promise I'm not."

"Deodorant? Are you wearing deodorant?"

Ah. "Yeah, that."

"Well . . . would you consider not doing that either?" he asked, and I said, "Okay," and from then on would coax him over and proudly lift my arm, my fingers reaching for the sky, whenever I felt particularly strong with the scent of the day's work.

I kept a few sets of clothes in Ian's room—tank tops and sweaters with pills and holes all along the sleeves—and when they got very dirty, I took them home to wash them. I took Ian's clothes, too, because they were there and soaked in sweat and grass stains, and needed washing, and because I was falling for him and wanted to. "God damn," Toby would say as I carried a hamper full of Ian's torn T-shirts to my car. "You are one lucky son of a bitch," he'd say, and shake his head at Ian.

The first few weeks I stayed over, I feigned a half-hearted desire to leave after an hour in bed, to drive back home. But with my cheek on his chest, his arm resting lazily over my bare back, I had to convince myself just to walk to the bathroom and brush my teeth. "Nnno," he'd mumble through a half-dream, pulling my arm toward him until I collapsed back onto the mattress. It was comfortable and exciting all at once, and I felt alive.

Sharing his bed seemed right and simple, but sleep didn't come as easily. Each noise from the barnyard and creak from the old house kept me awake, perhaps as much as my whirring mind did. As soon as I was able to ignore the rooster's untimely crows and the shrieks and squeals from the pigs, Ian would shift in his sleep and I would remember that I was there with *him*. That I wanted him. I feared

I might be moving far too quickly, but every night that I felt his breath on the nape of my neck, hot and soft, every morning I woke to a vermilion sun illuminating the room, I could think only one thing: *I cannot ever lose this.*

APRIL WAS MUCH HOTTER THAN ANY OF US WERE EXPECTING. ONE day in the middle of the month proved extra muggy, and we were all panting by early afternoon. I had been working on dinner—short ribs braised in orange juice and soy sauce, with roasted black radishes—when Cliff tore into the farmhouse, letting the screen bang against the door frame. "We're going swimming!" he said, grabbing a threadbare pale blue towel from the bathroom that I realized with some guilt I had been drying my hands on for two months.

"We are?" I instinctively turned off the oven and began covering the various bowls and pots I had in the works with spare towels. I didn't have a bathing suit with me at the farm—I didn't even have a pair of pajamas—but it didn't feel like that mattered. "Okay! Ready," I said, running outside after him. The rest of the crew had left for the water already, except for Lara, a spunky farmer from Pennsylvania and a new addition to the crew, and Ian. We slid into Cliff's Subaru, Lara and Ian tucked into the back.

Cliff and Lara had begun a flirtation, and I smiled as I listened to them chatter during the drive to the lake. She was short, like me, with sun-lightened brown hair and big, round eyes. The two of them made a great pair, I thought; they were both quiet, private people, with big plans and peaceful, patient self-control. They brought the farm's "couple" tally up significantly—if you cared about that sort of thing. If you counted Ian and I, six out of eight of the crew were part of a "we." Our friend, the cheesemaker at Alfalfa, a sheep dairy down the road, had begun referring to Stonehill as "sex camp," a term that made me giggle, Ian frown, Lara roll her eyes, and Cliff shrug.

It was still too early to swim legally at the beach—the lifeguard stand sat empty, and warning signs dotted the lawn above the waterline. No one seemed to pay that detail any mind, so I ignored it as well. Someone had brought along a bar of soap, and everyone chattered excitedly about not needing to shower that night. Jack and Cliff were the first ones in the water, diving in and surfacing seconds later, shaking water out of their hair and beards with giddy laughs. Ian was next, and I was impressed. He'd spent time after college living and working as an acrobatic cliff diver, performing tricks from heights as tall as sixty feet, so I was expecting a show. I think everyone was, both in this instance specifically, and in his life in general. His body arced gracefully and hit the water like a sharp knife. He left only the faintest hint of a ripple, and stayed underwater for a very long time before coming up yards from where he'd landed. I hadn't dove since my fourth-grade swimming class, and I found the idea of plunging in headfirst terrifying. The irony of this was not lost on me, though, and as I tucked my knees into my chest and hit the water rear end–first, I thought about how funny it was to be so brave in some ways, yet such a coward in others.

I had stripped off my tank top and pants, shimmying down to a pair of red gingham-print brief underwear and a pink sports bra, and after hoisting my body up out of the water, I stood watching Logan and Cliff practice back flips into the lake, Logan first removing his glasses and setting them on the grass. I shivered beside them, crossing my arms over my stomach. I was suddenly very aware of how closely the thin cotton of my undergarments hung to my skin. My hair was split into two low pigtails, secured with elastic bands just below my ears, and my curls rested, stringy and soaked, on my shoulders.

"Hey," Ian said quietly, fresh out of the lake, his mouth at my ear. I perked to attention, listening for what I assumed would be a flirtation. I leaned in closer, so his lips were almost touching my skin. "Pull your underwear up a little bit. I can see the line of your pubic hair."

"Hey!" I said, embarrassed and surprised. I smacked his shoulder, but adjusted the fabric.

"I just thought you'd want to know." He shrugged then rolled his shoulders back before executing a second perfect dive.

We all drove back to the farmhouse, where Jack and Toby made white Russians for everyone using that afternoon's milk and a bottle of vodka that had been sitting on top of the freezer. I finished warming the short ribs, then begged for a few extra minutes from the farm crew. "Let me just pull the meat from the bone," I said.

When dinner was ready, we flung open the windows and let the cool night air waft in. For ten minutes, the only sound was the clink of silverware. I relaxed into the quiet and savored the bright note of citrus in each bite.

THE WEATHER STAYED HOT, AND FOR THE NEXT WEEK WE LUXURIATED in sunshine as we worked. I was beginning to understand the undercurrent of routine as I found my place in it. One Thursday after lunch, we lingered over cups of tea made with holy basil and discussed the very important matter of a farm Easter dinner. The holiday had already passed, but, Jack suggested, it might be nice to celebrate it together. There was a whole ham left over from distribution, and he offered to smoke it. Dylan and I agreed to glaze it with honey, and to make a big pot of mashed potatoes. Underneath the table, I found Ian's knee with my hand and squeezed tightly. He placed his palm over my knuckles and squeezed back.

Later that afternoon in the greenhouse, as Ian and I thinned seedlings, pulling extra chard plants from the soil blocks and discarding them on the ground, he asked me a question.

"How are you able to be here so much?" He rolled a seedling between his thumb and forefinger before tossing it.

I paused, reluctant to tell the truth. The truth, of course, was that I didn't have a real job, that freelancing wasn't taking up all of my time or earning enough money, that I was grasping onto farming as an opportunity for a fresh start and new beginning. I could have said that, but it seemed embarrassing. I yanked out a few more young chard plants before choosing my words carefully. "I guess as a freelancer I'm able to kind of create my own schedule. If I have an assignment due in two weeks, I can work on it a little bit each day, or I can knock it all out at once." He nodded, waiting for me to continue. "And I think I write faster than most people. I'm able to come up with a concept and just go for it. In fact"—I began to gain a little more confidence—"I rarely even use outlines. I just write."

"That's interesting," he said, and I could tell he meant it.

"And, although writing doesn't pay well, I do make some money from public appearances." I told him about a culinary event I was hosting at a hotel in the Finger Lakes, how two hours of speaking about local food and wine would send me home with enough to pay rent.

He seemed genuinely intrigued by this. "When you break down our hourly rate in farming, it looks pretty bleak."

"Well, how much do you make?" I lingered on the question, wondering if it was out of line.

He told me. It was not a lot of money; a lot less than my most recent secretary's salary.

"Oh, wow," I said. "That works out to . . ." I cut myself off, realizing that if I considered how infrequently I actually booked events and secured stories, my hourly freelancing rate couldn't be much better.

"Our housing is covered, too," Ian said, and I thought about his bedroom with its big windows, dusty but cozy, old and full of character. There was no kitchen, save the communal one everyone shared, but then I considered how much I paid for rent when I lived in Manhattan. My oven hadn't even worked and I shared the space with a mouse. He shrugged. "It's not ideal, but I kind of like it. It can be fun to live in the middle of all that energy, with people coming and going all the time."

"All that energy," I repeated, thinking about the way I felt when surrounded by people; claustrophobic and exposed, anxious and desperate for solitude. I did well with strangers—I liked anonymous conversation that had a clear expiration date—and I loved being with close friends, but I had few of those. It was the in-between that made me uncomfortable, and it was the in-between that seemed to be so present at Stonehill. I loved quiet evenings with the core farm crew, when we all sat around the table eating ice cream out of the same container, attacking it with spoons. I disliked the constant flow of visitors and volunteers, but it had never, until that moment, occurred to me that I might actually be one.

LATE APRIL

Even as my confidence regarding my role on the farm was faltering, in the kitchen I was fearless.

Suddenly given a field's worth of fresh, quality ingredients and nothing before me but time and hungry farmers, I relished the opportunity to create elaborate meals layered with flavors and seasoned generously with fat. I steamed beets in the oven with water and black pepper, the way I learned at Aldea, covering the roasting pan with a large cookie sheet to trap in moisture. When they were cooled and sliced, I marinated them for hours in olive oil and more pepper, before finally tossing them with yogurt and showers of dill or chives plucked from the herb garden. I closed my eyes as I peeled off the membrane from pork tongue, still slightly uncomfortable with the texture. After finely chopping the organ, I tossed it in a hot pan simmering with dried chiles, scallions, and canned tomatoes, and I served the whole thing with tortillas and shredded raw cheese, plus the fixings for gin and tonics.

The kitchen was chaotic, in the way farmhouse kitchens always seem to be, the countertops covered with glass jars full of fermenting vegetables, sprouting grains, and milk that someone had forgotten to place back in the refrigerator. Upon opening the fridge, you were just as likely to discover beef testicles as soil-caked carrots. The small stainless steel sink was set into the back corner, underneath the only two windows in the room. Despite a "no boots in the house, ever" rule, the linoleum floor always seemed to be littered with bits of hay and trails of dirt. "Food that comes out of this kitchen," a friend had said once, "is very alive. It isn't dirty—not in that bad way—but it is definitely alive."

The meals marched on. Brioche buns studded with poppy seeds cradled beef burgers that had been stuffed with pungent blue cheese from a nearby Jersey herd. I constructed cakes bursting with walnuts and sage, or beets and dark chocolate. Although I was never really one to follow recipes, in those early days I pored over grease-stained cookbooks, trying to find ideas that would impress the crew without being too fussy. I spent all afternoon one Wednesday chopping yellow onions, leeks, and scallions for a three-onion soup spiked with cumin and flavored with bacon. I cut a big slab of cured pork into large hunks and rendered out some of the fat, using that to cook down the onions. As the farmers wandered in after evening chores, they each lifted the lid and stuck their nose deep into the pot. "This is great," Lara said, dipping her spoon into a deep bowl she had dished up. "I just ate a piece of bacon that was, like, seventy percent fat." Noticing my worried look, she added, "And I mean that in a really excited way."

Working outside all day fosters large appetites and a true appreciation for food. There's something so satisfying about lifting heavy things, about walking far and fast, about using every muscle in your body, and then coming inside to the intoxicating combination of scents that only the slow cooking of raw ingredients can create. Sharp onions turn sweet; smoky bacon grease and earthy root vegetables meld together and perfume the air. I was volunteering almost daily on the farm, and when I wasn't there, it was all I spoke about to my friends—friends who spent their days cooking in restaurants. "Must be nice," they scoffed as I recounted peeling beets in my socks. I'd smile knowingly: You couldn't pay me enough to lure me back into the frenzied heat of a professional kitchen. "The farmers must feel so lucky with a culinary school graduate cooking for them," one friend noted.

I cringed at the compliment. "Oh, I have a pretty captive audience. And really, with all of the produce, meat, milk, eggs . . ." My voice trailed off as I thought about the farm eggs I was working with daily, their yolks vibrant orange and pert. "I'm the lucky one," I said, and I meant it.

Spending most nights with Ian but not actually being employed by the farm, I didn't start my mornings with chores, as was required of the crew. Ian set his alarm for 4:45 a.m. in preparation for the upcoming summer's earlier hours, and most mornings he was up and out of bed with little effort. He'd roll over, kiss my neck, then slide my sleep-limp arms from around his waist. By the time he brushed his teeth, I had stirred slightly and rolled over on my side. I watched him stretch, circling his arms quickly around his head, and counted as he completed a quick series of push-ups on the wooden floor, usually stopping at thirty-two, but looking like he could do a lot more. He worked through this routine with efficiency and precision, each muscle in his back shifting and moving, and I hated to see him finish as he stood up and shook the tightness from his body, ready to start the day.

After he dressed and left the room, I'd curl up in bed for a few more minutes before feeling restless. Inspired by the increasingly bright sun, I'd do a few stretches of my own and then lace up my sneakers and bound outside for a run. I'd always been a runner, so I was pleased to learn there was a four-mile loop around the farm that started with a treacherous hill, peaked at a well-manicured golf course, and ended right back where it started. I ran that most days, though once I went exploring along a path I thought might add up to about five miles. I got lost, ended up running eight, and didn't make it in for breakfast until the crew was halfway through their hash browns.

THINGS ON THE FARM CHANGED STEADILY AND QUICKLY: LARA JOINED the team and, although she had a passion and talent for growing vegetables, she was to spend her first season working with Jack and the livestock. She came fresh off a farm in Pennsylvania, where she had learned about Stonehill and written Cliff a letter, inquiring if he had a place for one more farmer. He hadn't, but she kept in touch and, eventually, her expertise in both livestock and produce made her too attractive to pass up. I liked watching her work, her strong arms and shoulders making the most difficult tasks look simple. She used power tools to build mobile chicken coops for the meat birds (in addition to the laying hens, every spring through fall, Stonehill raised Cornish cross chickens to be slaughtered and given out with the CSA share). Lara's farm know-how left me duly impressed and a little intimidated. Meanwhile, a steady flow of volunteers moved through the fields and the barns, washing eggs and glass jars, stacking hay.

I was beginning to understand that Stonehill Farm's "normal" was actually a lack thereof.

One morning, Cliff asked me if we could schedule a meeting within the next few days.

"Is everything okay?" I asked, picking at my cuticle, which had acquired a sort of patina, with dirt and sweat lodged in crevices of my skin.

"Sure is. I just want to check in."

That afternoon we sat at the dining-room table, which was covered in a cluster of odd items: dog-eared copies of seed catalogues, a water glass left over from lunch, a screwdriver, a few broken pencils. Cliff opened a big white three-ring binder that appeared only during meetings and was kept meticulously organized, its tidy sheets a stark contrast to the disarray of the barnyard. The page he turned to was empty, save for my name written at the top in his looping, graceful handwriting.

"So, hi," I said, pulling my knees to my chest, my toes hanging over the edge of the chair.

"Hi." He clicked his pen a couple of times. "I was hoping to talk to you about how this is all going—and to get a feel for what your goals are at Stonehill."

"Oh. Sure." I wasn't entirely prepared for such a thorough question, but I welcomed the communication. "Well, I'm really excited to be here, to be cooking and to be a part of the crew." This seemed somehow insufficient, and his thoughtful gaze made me feel I should add more. "I love it here," I said, speaking from a part of me I hadn't yet acknowledged—even to myself. "It feels so, so right in a surprising but completely encompassing way." I paused, wondering if he understood what I meant. I felt different from everyone else at Stonehill—more like Ian's new girlfriend than a real farmer—but I had to admit that a sense of peace filled my mind when performing the repetitive tasks. The physical work soothed me, and I was sure that, with time, I'd become much better at it. I wondered if Cliff felt that way when he began farming, but suddenly grew too shy to ask.

"I'm glad," he replied. "I worry a little bit, though, that you might someday resent all of the work you're doing here, because it's, well, for free."

"Hm." I considered this, and knew he was right. "I don't resent anything now," I said. "But someday, I guess if I'm being honest, I would like to work here. And, you know, get paid for it. I mean, maybe even have a room over at the farmhouse."

Cliff laughed and wrote that down underneath my name. *Would like to live and work here.*

"I can tell you that I'm not currently in a position to hire anyone. But I understand that you do a lot here, and you work hard. It's been really nice having you cook." I smiled at the compliment, which seemed very real coming from a farmer. "I want to make sure it's fair for you. Are the vegetables working out? Is it enough for now?"

"Well, I'm not really taking much home. But that's because I'm pretty much always here. Do you think that someday, there might be an opportunity for me to be a part of the crew?"

"Yes," he said. "We might be able to hire you part-time next month," he said. "If you're interested in that. Dylan's finding it hard to balance his other job with this, and he'll be leaving at the end of the month."

My heart jumped into my throat, and I hid a laugh. With both of us perched on mismatched chairs around a dirty kitchen table, wearing socks and smelling of manure, this was by far the most casual business meeting I had ever had.

"I am!" I sang, setting my feet on the floor and leaning into the table. "And part-time's actually perfect, because it leaves me room to write."

"Cool," he said. "As long as you're okay with the volunteer thing for now?"

I nodded vigorously. "I really am. I mean, I'm learning so much—that alone is incredibly valuable." I thought about my realization the week prior that I might actually be an interloper in a tight-knit crew. "Thanks for teaching me, and for letting me hang out here."

"Thanks for being here."

I couldn't wait to set off for the greenhouse to tell Ian the good news. As I pulled on my barn boots, stuck all over with spent dandelion seeds, I thought about how lucky I was to have found the farm.

THAT WEEKEND, AS IAN AND I LAY LAZILY IN HIS ROOM, DEBATING whether or not we should move, dress, or leave the bed, he suggested a horse ride. "I haven't been out on Bear in a while," he said. "Interested?" I sat up like a shot.

"Yes! Yes, yes, yes!" Bear was my favorite of the farm's four Percheron workhorses; he was the tallest and largest, but also the most calm and cool—almost loving, in a subdued sort of way. When we got to the barn, Ian demonstrated how to bridle a horse and lead him out of the stall. I stood back so I wouldn't get stepped on by Bear, and watched as Ian coaxed the metal bar of the bit in between the horse's lips. "I used to be kind of scared to do this," he said, sticking his index finger into the side of Bear's mouth and working it until he relented and accepted the bit. "But you just kind of have to do it to get comfortable." He slipped the horse's ears through the top of the bridle and slung the reins over his neck. Ian walked Bear, ever cool and calm, outside to an overturned feeder that was about two feet tall. I stood on it and, aided by Ian's grip, pulled myself onto Bear's back. Ian jumped up easily after me, and I nestled against him, my thighs and abdomen cupping his backside, my arms tight around his body.

"Come up," he said, his voice drawing out the first word in command. Bear stepped forward and off we went. We walked across the road (I held on a little tighter), and into the hayfield. "Hey, do you want to try something?" Ian asked. "Do you want to maybe not talk for the ride? Just . . . listen?"

"Yes," I whispered, and turned my ear to the sky, to the birds and the breeze.

I had never seen the farm look more beautiful. The tall grass waved gently in the wind, beneath a sky dappled with grey and trees lush with new life. As we neared the forest on the edge of the field, I ducked, narrowly missing a scrape of maple branches against my forehead. Acutely aware of Ian's body against mine and the smell of his skin, I was overcome with an intense sense of gratitude, disbelief, and a slight loss, for all of the years I went without this feeling. I tried to hold it back but I began to cry. Ian turned his head slightly toward me. "Are you all right?" he asked, confusion in his voice. Bear carried on.

I nodded and used the back of my hand to wipe tears away from my lower lashes. "I am. I'm crying because I'm happy, and I'm sorry I do it all the time—I know I do—but everything really is fine. It's *great*." I inhaled deeply, filling my chest with springtime air, and counted to five, then released the breath in a slow stream. Everything really was fine.

"Okay," he said, his tone still a bit unconvinced. Suddenly I feared I had made some kind of intangible mistake, that I had shown too much of myself too quickly. Ian stayed quiet, and I followed his lead, trying not to worry.

THE NEXT FRIDAY MORNING I SAT AT THE FARMSTAND WITH DYLAN, watching him exchange conversations with customers alongside wooden crates full of potatoes, beets, and stinging nettles. The root vegetables were snapped up eagerly, but it took a little more convincing to move the nettles. Although they have sharp prickles all over their stems and the tops of their leaves, they soften their sting the moment they meet boiling water, and I liked the strong flavor of their greens with scrambled eggs. Ian had told me that he was planning on leaving the farm for the weekend to visit Saratoga. He had spent the later part of his childhood and teenage years there, and many of his friends still lived in the area. "I try to make it once a month," he had told me.

At four o'clock, he poked his head into the barn. It was quiet during a rare lull in the afternoon, and he asked if I wanted to come to his room while he packed his bag. I nodded, grabbed my mason jar of water, and followed him across the road. While he took a quick shower, I ran my finger along the spines of his book collection, a mix of used textbooks, guide books for weeds and plants and trees and horses, some fiction titles I recognized, and big, thick volumes with short, geographical names like *HAWAII* and *AFRICA*.

He came back to the room wearing dark blue pants and a forest-green polo shirt, his wet hair deepening the color around the collar. I sat on the bed and watched him roll up a few T-shirts and a pair of shorts and place them in his backpack. "I wanted to talk to you about something," he said. "And it's not that big of a deal, so I don't want to make it one. And—I don't know how to start things like this, so . . . " He expelled air from his lungs with a push. "I'll just go for it."

I curled up into myself, anxious and expectant.

"When you came to the farm, I was really planning on being alone for a while," he said. "I just didn't plan on being in a relationship right now. That's my bottom line. I got out of one this winter, and I think you did, too? Really recently?" I nodded. Ian continued. "So I want to . . . keep having fun. I like seeing you and I like you, but I'm wondering if you feel more . . . serious about this than I do."

Each pause seemed painfully large, and I answered swiftly to loosen the knot that was tightening itself around my chest. "Sure. I understand. I don't want a relationship, either." (*Why are you lying?* my voice hissed in my head.) "I mean, hell, I just got out of one. I want to take it slow—get to know you." My words bumped into themselves as I worked to get them out of my mouth and into his ears as quickly as possible.

"Okay, cool." He opened a tin of loose organic tobacco mixed with herbs—sage, mint, and mullein—and hand-rolled a cigarette for later that evening. "I don't want you to think I don't like you. You're smart, and a good writer, and I . . . " His voice trailed off. "I think you're a good person." He licked the paper to seal it shut.

I offered a casual shrug and a close-lipped smile in return. "I think you're cool, too. It's cool. Now get out of here. You've got friends to meet."

"Are you sure?" He seemed nervous, as if sharing this thought had been just as uncomfortable as turning it around in his mind.

"Yes," I said. But when he kissed me good-bye, it was warm and hard and he put his hands on my face and I forgot everything that I had just said.

EARLY MAY

With May came spinach, my birthday, an official spot on the farm crew, and Shae. The spinach went into salad after salad, frittata after quiche, my birthday came and went, and Shae arrived and stayed. She was Ian's friend; the two had met on a plane to Kenya eleven years earlier, forming a bond when Ian convinced her to try her first Bloody Mary on the flight. ("It won't be very good, since it's on a plane," he had said, "but it's worth doing anyway.")

The two had grown closer as the years progressed, and Shae became a fixture in the innermost circle of Ian's life. They shared the same friends, laughed together until tears pricked at their lashes, and fought like brother and sister. Ian spoke fondly of her as he described their relationship one weekend before her arrival. I had taken him to a walking path along Onondaga Lake, an iconic Syracuse landmark, pretty enough but sadly too polluted to be fit for swimming or fishing. He had rolled a cigarette and was lazily taking drags from it as we walked through the grey afternoon air. "She just finished her yoga teacher training. She's a very passionate person," he said.

"Ha. Then we'll get along." I grinned sideways. "What's next for her?"

"Not sure," Ian said, snuffing the cigarette and tossing it in a trash can. "She spent the last month applying for jobs. But she wants to work here—on the farm—for a while and take some time to figure it all out."

"Sounds good to me," I said, thinking of my own circumstances and hoping that she'd like me. I had met a few of Ian's friends on a trip to Saratoga a few weeks before (he had decided to invite me after the last month's snub) and I adored the way I felt around them— funny and charismatic, like one of the crew. I was beginning to see just how many friends he had, and how important they were to him.

Everyone seemed to like Ian, and it wasn't hard to see why: His eyes lit up whenever he spoke—with friends, acquaintances, strangers. You could even hear it in his voice if you happened to be speaking on the phone. It made me feel impossibly introverted, and it made me want to be more like him.

He caught me looking his way and wrapped me up in his thick flannel jacket, the panels of plaid reaching around my back as our chests touched. He kissed me in the middle of the path and his mouth tasted like sage and mint, with the faintest hint of tobacco. "I like the way your mouth tastes."

"Really?" He looked surprised.

"Yep," I said, reaching for his hand and immediately regretting it when I felt his body tense.

The next Wednesday, I spent the night away from the farm since I had a doctor's appointment early the next morning. Shae had arrived that night, and was staying in the guest room across the hall from Ian's. It was a nice room, bright and big, with a good view of the barns and, despite an unfortunate shabby blue carpet, looked very clean and open. It felt different and softer than Ian's room, which had wooden floors that collected tufts of dust in the corners and was decorated with pinned photos of friends. I had written Shae a note in permanent marker, welcoming her to the farm and expressing my regret that I couldn't be there to say hello in person. I signed it how I signed all of my letters to friends, "xo, Ro," with a cartoon drawing of a rabbit.

Upon arriving at Stonehill the next day, I parked my car in the gravel lot outside the barn and ran into Ian as I passed the silos. "Hi!" I said brightly, dropping my keys on the ground and leaping into his embrace. "Hi!" I repeated again, kissing his nose. "I missed you."

He nuzzled his nose into my neck before depositing me back down on the earth. "Missed you too."

He set off for the horse stalls and I walked around to the back of the barn, where Dylan was orchestrating distribution preparation. By that point, I knew the routine well: Thursdays were spent in a mad rush to ready the barn for the CSA pickup. Bushels of frilled mustard greens had been harvested earlier, along with tender leaves of mixed lettuce and bulbs of spring kohlrabi that were smaller, tighter, and brighter than the monstrous winter variety I had seen in the kitchen a couple of months earlier. All of this was covered with an old bed sheet, torn in various places, and sprayed damp with a cold hose. This would keep the vegetables pert enough until they could be stored properly in the cooler.

An unfamiliar figure was standing at one of the washtubs, swirling lettuce around in the cool water before picking it up with her hands and shaking excess water from it.

"Shae?" I said, walking to her. "Hi!" She was short—shorter than my five feet and three inches—with full hips and a head of tight, springy curls that seemed to bounce away from her head in every direction. Her eyes were piercing, with a persistent glimmer that made her look as though she were always on the edge of a wink.

She smiled a casual, easy grin. "Hey. Rochelle?"

I nodded and pulled up the legs of my pants as I sat on an overturned wooden crate and then reached for a burlap sack of onions. I wanted to get to know her, but there would be plenty of time for that later. Right now, the priority was readying vegetables for distribution in six hours.

The onions were in poor shape, mostly mushy and sprouting, with a pungent smell that distressed me so much I had to turn my head away from the task as I tossed too-far-gone ones into a pile for the compost.

We worked in alternating states of chatter and quiet, and I could sense that Shae was not a person inclined to fill silence out of obligation. She was comfortable with herself, with her place in the world. I felt an immediate respect, if not kinship, toward her.

Midway through the morning, Lara swung by our workstation. She had a leather tool belt slung casually over her left shoulder and a beige bird-watching hat hanging from her neck on a string.

"I am so tired," she said, plopping the belt down and reaching for a handful of spinach. She crumpled it into her mouth, chewing and making a face of approval as she tasted the leaves. "Not bitter; good," she said, swallowing.

"I have a breathing exercise that's good for that," Shae said. "For feeling tired. It's yogic. Here, follow me." She spread her feet wider than her hips and bent her legs until her thighs were parallel to the ground—a dramatic sort of squat. Lara set down the tool belt and crouched down. I abandoned my onions and followed suit. "Okay, now take air in and out as quickly as possible." She demonstrated, her breathing becoming heavy and aggressive, but not forced. Her face carried a look of great intensity, and the whole thing reminded me a little of a small animal readying itself to charge forward.

I tried in earnest to mimic Shae's body and breathing patterns, wondering if I was doing it correctly but feeling that if I had to ask, I probably wasn't. "*Hoo-hoo-hoo-hoo,*" little bursts of forced air escaped my nasal passages. I moved my hands into prayer position in front of my heart.

Lara tried for a few moments and then let her body dissolve into laughter, doubling over before standing up straight. "This isn't working for me," she said, shaking out her arms and legs.

Shae wrapped up her round of breathing and straightened, too. "Well, it works when you do it right," she said in a tone that was both matter-of-fact and unaggressive, a genuine smile on her face.

Shae and I worked together regularly after that. She was technically a volunteer, and besides cooking, I didn't have much direction in the way of farm tasks. Extra hands like ours always seemed to be put to work in the vegetable field where there was endless work to be done. We weeded tiny carrots with our hands, pricking our fingers on horse nettle and thistle until she wised up and started wearing gloves. She even bought me a pair with a blue flower pattern. When it rained too hard to yank weeds, we were sent to the field with a garden cart to pick rocks. The field was full of them, and our job was to remove any larger than a big dinner roll. The farm equipment could break or malfunction if it got caught on a rock, so it was imperative that the fields were combed thoroughly. We walked through the rows with the cart in between us, bending to pick up rocks and then dropping them in, taking turns pulling the cart to meet up with us every few yards. We talked all the while. Shae had a strong personality, and I found myself growing shy around her. Then one day she offered to cook dinner for me so I could go for a quick run after we finished our afternoon of rock picking.

"Are you sure?" I asked, pausing to stretch my arms downward until my fingers dangled down at my toes. I let them hang there. Shae cracked her back. "Okay, there's one thing that really bothers me, and it's that." I looked concerned. "It's not a big deal," she explained. "But if I offer to do something, you can pretty much assume that, yeah, it's okay." I blushed. "Be confident in yourself and know that if it wasn't cool with me, I wouldn't have offered."

"You're right. I'm sorry," I said. "And thank you."

She laughed, exasperated. "You don't have to say sorry for that, either."

"Are you shh . . . " I let the last word fizzle out through my teeth and we both chuckled, as we began piling rocks into our arms.

I didn't mind the physical labor of rock picking; I loved moving my body and building strength. But the job was dreadful in the cold May rain, which mucked up the field into a sludge of soggy mud within minutes. The wheels of our little cart were perpetually and literally stuck in the mud, and my cargo pants became immediately soaked. I hadn't yet acquired the bright orange waterproof bib overalls that everyone else seemed to own.

Had I known how dry the coming months would be, how arid-hot and parched, I would have relished every moment in that wet early May, letting the drops of rain bead on my nose and drip down the back of my neck, the curve of my spine. But of course we didn't know, and so we complained as we dumped load after load of rocks in a pile against a large tree in the woods bordering the field.

MY BIRTHDAY FELL ON A FRIDAY THAT YEAR, AND THE DAY BEFORE Cliff sat me down for another talk.

"Are you still interested in working here part-time?" he asked. "Because our CSA is only going to grow, hopefully speaking, and, now that Dylan's leaving, we'd really like someone to take on the role of CSA Manager."

My heart stopped. My mouth opened wide in a toothy smile. "Yes."

"Great," he said. "We can have you start officially next week. Maybe we should each outline some of our goals for this position, and meet back later to go over them."

"Absolutely," I said, already thinking of spreadsheets, databases, and pristine records chock-full of information about radishes grown and harvested and sold.

"Well, now, as a small token to make it official," he began. "Wait here." He bounded up the stairs to the bedroom he shared with Toby, which also functioned as his office. I heard him rummaging through drawers before he ran back downstairs and handed me a small black composition book, thin and the size of my palm. All of the farmers had notebooks like these; I often saw them scribbling copious notes on the pages. I knew Ian used his to remind himself of the chores and tasks to be done while Cliff scribbled down big ideas, dreams, and drawings.

Sure that my cheeks were a brilliant shade of pink that matched the sunburn on my shoulders, I gave him a quick hug before running out to join Shae, who was weeding garlic. I chatted excitedly with her about the new position, about the official title, about how I felt to be part of the crew finally. She replied with warmth, but also brought up a point I hadn't given much thought to over the last month—my writing career.

"So you'll still have time to write?" she asked, smoothing over a patch of disturbed soil dangerously near a garlic bulb.

"Definitely," I said, and without thinking about it, launched into a story I had told countless times. "As a freelancer . . ."

As I talked about my flexible schedule, Jack rode by on his bicycle, back from setting up electric fencing in the beef pasture. "Hey," he said, slowing down as he approached us. "Sounds like you're joining the ranks. Congratulations."

"Thanks!" I beamed, and Shae smiled kindly in my direction as Jack pedaled off toward the barn.

As we worked, talk turned to Ian.

"I knew he was dating someone—I knew it—when he stopped being as communicative," she said.

I took a swig of water from my jar and screwed the cap back on. "Really?"

"Yes. It's always like this." I felt an odd pit in my stomach at the thought of Ian being involved with other women. "When he starts dating someone, we don't hear from him as much, and we just *know*, because he's usually so close with his friends."

I felt guilty, but a thrill ran through me. Was it possible he was moving toward the level of excitement and involvement that I had been feeling for weeks?

"Anyway," she said with a conspiratorial grin. "It's a good thing I like you."

I AWOKE THE NEXT DAY TO A BOUQUET OF PINK AND WHITE wildflowers from Ian, the blossoms in a mason jar on his writing desk. "It was nice falling asleep with you when you were twenty-four and waking up with you at twenty-five," he said before sliding his mouth down my neck, chest, stomach. I closed my eyes and smiled, tangling my fingers in his hair.

That morning at breakfast Logan made pancakes with spelt flour, forming mine into the shape of a capital "R." I drizzled his homemade maple syrup over the top and ate it all with coffee piled high with freshly frothed milk. "Last year for my birthday," I said, my mouth full of food, "I ate dinner at Le Bernardin." I allowed myself to recall the thirteen courses of seafood, the complimentary champagne, and the thirteen subsequent tastes of wine.

We spent the morning weeding, the afternoon planting strawberries, and although I was excited to be working in an official capacity, heartened by Shae's words and Ian's tender kisses that morning, I couldn't help but feel a sense of unsettlement. Ian seemed to have grown agitated as the afternoon drew on, and I couldn't quite figure out why.

He told me later, that night in bed, that he had planned a day of surprises for me, a tour around Syracuse full of things and places I'd like, but that the workload was too great to leave. "That's fine with me," I told him. "Honestly, what I wanted on my birthday was to be here, working." I meant it, but he was still irritated at the idea that farming had to take precedence over his personal life.

Halfway through the berry planting, he set down the dibbler, a tool used to poke perfectly equidistant holes in the soil, and walked over to where I was crouched. I wiggled my toes into the ground and smiled—we had all taken off our boots to enjoy the feel of the cool dirt—then relaxed my lips as he sank down beside me. I was expecting a kiss, but instead he had come to inspect my work. He pinched a few plants between his thumb and forefinger and explained I hadn't been burying the roots quite deep enough, leaving them partially exposed and susceptible to weakness or death. He held a plant at its uppermost roots and showed me my mistake. "If these aren't buried properly," he murmured, "their roots will shrivel and they will die."

I nodded, biting at my lip, and assured him quickly that I would fix all of the plants I had put in the ground. I looked down at the row, dozens of strawberry plants already in the soil, and moved away from him as quickly as possible. My face was hot, stinging with embarrassment. *Why are you so upset?* I scolded myself. *It's your birthday.* But no matter how much I rationalized, I couldn't pull up the corners of my mouth, and that just made me sadder. Even though I had just gotten something I wanted desperately—a real job—and I was slowly assimilating into the farm's fabric, I felt unsettled, like it wasn't yet official. Like it wasn't real.

I held it together through the rest of the planting, and when Ian suggested I take the remaining afternoon to myself as he cleaned up the tools and put everything away, I listened to him. I pulled on my boots, filled a jar with water, and set off for a walk around the farm, consciously taking in as much of the springtime air as my lungs would allow. As I made my way down the path that cut the dairy pasture in two, I ran into Toby, who had just brought the cows out after milking. I saluted him and he waved back, and I continued walking until I reached the edge of the property, then turned around and looked at the barns and silo in the distance.

Was Stonehill my forever place? Could Ian be the lifetime love I was looking for? I thought back to the previous May and remembered what it felt like to be desk-bound. I couldn't say if I'd bury my own roots deep in the soil here, but trying to be present in that very moment, surrounded by the natural beauty, it felt good. I acknowledged a breeze picking up and started to make my way back to the kitchen. I didn't want to be late for my birthday dinner.

My mood improved at the meal, as Shae brought out bottles of sparkling wine and Campari and served organic pasta with a simple homemade tomato sauce. The food tasted so comforting yet light, in a way that the hearty food of the past few months had not. There wasn't a root vegetable in sight, and I happily ate and remembered what home cooking was like before Stonehill. A farm volunteer had dropped off homemade Italian bread, the kind with a crust that shatters into pieces when torn. We spread gobs of butter on it and used the heels to sop up sauce.

There was a cake, too, moist and bursting with shredded carrots and slathered with a sweet cream cheese frosting. Ian held his hand on my back as I blew out the candles, and he squeezed my shoulder tightly with the pads of his fingers. After we ate, Logan, Ian, Shae, and I took a walk into the fields and took turns tossing Styrofoam model airplanes in the air, trying to make them fly.

Once we grew tired of aviation, we all crept out to the coop where a batch of brand-new baby chicks was being kept warm under heat lamps. I picked one up and gently stroked my index finger down its back and wings. It chirped cheerily, joining in the chorus of high-pitched chatter from the rest of the birds. I smiled. Hundreds of baby chicks were a far better pet than any old housecat or dog.

It was late when we finally crawled into bed, and Ian had to wake early for the weekend's chores. We both lay on our sides, my palms tucked together and nestled under my cheek. "Did you have a nice birthday?" Ian said, his voice quiet but not quite at a whisper.

"I did," I said with a sleepy close-lipped smile. "You know what was the best part?"

"What?"

I blinked slowly and looked at him, counted a few freckles on his cheekbones before speaking. "All of it," I said, and rolled over so I was on top of him. "Every last bit."

"You can't choose a whole day as your favorite," he said, pretending to be serious.

"Well then," I lifted myself up like a Sphinx, my forearms on his chest. "You. You were the best part." He rolled over then, pinning me to the mattress with his lips. I stole a quick glance at the clock on his nightstand; it was well past a decent hour.

I had promised to help him feed the animals and water the greenhouse come sunrise, and as we faded into sleep, I knew we'd both be tired.

But, I thought to myself, drinking in the last streaks of color in the night sky, deep purples and rusty oranges, *this was worth staying up for.*

MID-MAY

"A trampoline?" I asked, swirling a particularly fatty hunk of bacon around a puddle of maple syrup on my plate. "How did that work, exactly?" It was a morning in early May, and a group of us had been discussing the deep, urgent need for fresh butter. At North Farm the workers used to make it, they explained, by bouncing a well-sealed milk can on a trampoline. I pictured them holding onto the steel handles tightly as they flipped and soared, and the idea seemed a little silly to me.

"An exercise trampoline," Ian clarified, and I laughed so hard I snorted.

"Oh! Well, I guess that makes more sense. You bounce the can on the trampoline—not yourself." I chewed thoughtfully on the bacon. "I've read butter-making instructions online that involve a food processor. Could you do it like that?"

"You could, probably, but it would make so little I don't think it'd be worthwhile. At North, eventually they started churning it in the milk can with a paint mixer attached to an electric drill."

"Huh." I had never seen a paint mixer, nor used an electric drill. This whole butter-making thing was beginning to look a little daunting. "Well, maybe I'll do it in the food processor this first time," I said, shoving aside my plate and opening my laptop. "I'm sure I can find the recipe." I read through a photo-guided tutorial for making it in a processor as the rest of the crew discussed the allure of springtime and fresh butter. Having never tasted the homemade stuff before my time at the farm, I couldn't tell you the difference between a batch made in May or in December—and probably, if I really considered it, I had never even tasted butter from grass-fed cows. I had grown to understand and love the subtle flavor differences in our milk from week to week, and had definitely noticed a richer quality and creamier, thicker consistency once the cows left the barn to graze the month prior. The way it clung to the glasses made me think of the way a good wine has legs, and that made me smile. But my attitude toward butter was one molded under cooking school influence: it was delicious, but the important thing was to use it liberally, and in tandem with wine, veal stock, plenty of shallots; not, necessarily, that it was of superior quality.

"Well, this'll be my project for the morning," I said, stacking the empty bowls and plates scattered across the table and carting them to the kitchen sink. "And for lunch, we can have fresh bread with fresh butter." Cliff explained that because the milk production had soared that week, there were plenty of half-gallons in the walk-in cooler, too old to sell to the public but still perfectly usable. All I had to do, he said, was make sure the bottles weren't disturbed and that the cream had settled on top, then use a ladle to skim it off. If I wanted to use the remaining milk to make yogurt, I could; or else just pour it into five-gallon buckets and cart it out to the pigs. We had enough milk to drink, he said, and besides, no one here had any real interest in the fat-free stuff.

After I washed the dishes, I collected the full jars, arranged them in a wooden bushel, and carried it into the barn. I opened a metal folding chair and set a second bushel on its side as a makeshift table, placing the first jar on it and unscrewing its top. I grabbed the small metal ladle from the milk house, along with a small milk can, and flipped the radio to the local NPR station. Settling into the chair and dipping the bowl of the ladle into the jar, I let the yellow-beige cream flood it, then poured it into the can. It hit the bottom in a luxurious stream. I repeated the process, until I noticed that the liquid filling the ladle had grown thinner and bluer, that it was milk rather than cream. After six bottles, I hung the ladle over the side of the can and rummaged in the temporary shop, a small room in the heart of the barn, for a plastic five-gallon bucket, unearthing one that looked dirty and felt greasy, but would be more than sufficient for transporting the milk to the pigs.

I poured the skim into the bucket, taking note to be more careful next time as it sloshed over the sides and splattered my boots. I repeated the process with the remaining jars, then covered the can of cream and set it in the utility sink in the milk house with a sticky note that read DO NOT TOUCH ME. After slapping the buckets on a garden cart, I walked to the pigs' paddock and surprised them with a mid-morning snack, feeling very authentically farmy and virtuous about everything.

The rest of the experiment was a tepid success. I filled the small bowl of the food processor with perhaps a bit more cream than was prudent, secured the top, and pressed the ON button. The cream, agitated and whirring, seeped out the sides of the machine and dribbled down its base, immediately soaking the countertop and dripping onto the floor.

"Ugh," I said, opening the top and scooping out a bit of dairy. I resumed the machine and then used old towels to mop up the mess. Twelve minutes later, the buttermilk had separated from the milk solids, and I eagerly strained and separated them, being careful to reserve the buttermilk for biscuits or, as Cliff had said that morning as he licked his lips, for drinking. I set the sieve over a metal mixing bowl to drain, then got to work scrubbing the grease out of the food processor.

As the kitchen returned to its normal level of chaos, I inspected my butter. It was yellow all right, with the consistency of good mayonnaise. I used a small spatula to stir in coarse flakes of sea salt and then scraped it into a ceramic bowl. Ta-da: butter. I tasted the excess from the spatula and considered the flavor. It had a definite barnyard funk, but I had always liked that sort of thing and considered it to be a job well done.

Toby was the first one in the house for lunch, and before he picked up his guitar, I brought out the finished product for him to taste. He stuck his finger in it. "Damn, girl," he said. "You made this?" I nodded, grinning widely. "It's so cool that we can do this here, so cool that we can make our own freaking butter."

"I know," I said. "I've always wanted food to be like this. I mean, I don't think I've always known it, but I've always wanted it."

The rest of the crew trickled in after that and spread the butter on slices of bread that a volunteer had made and dropped off that morning. I watched everyone's faces as they ate, expecting or perhaps hoping for groans of ecstasy, but instead observed quiet nods. The reception seemed lukewarm, and I wondered if I had done something incorrectly.

Afterward I grabbed Ian's arm as he was on his way back out to the greenhouse. "Hey," I said. "How was the butter?"

He hesitated, arranging his features into an I'd-rather-not-go-here look. "Well," he said, "Did you rinse it?"

"What?" I was perplexed.

"Did you rinse the butter? You need to get rid of the residual buttermilk or else it has a real . . . strong flavor. It gets funky and goes bad, fast, too."

"Huh," I said, intrigued and perhaps slightly humbled by what a scientific process this was turning out to be. "How do you do that?" Ian explained the process of spraying the finished butter with water and kneading it with clean hands to rid it of excess liquid. "Warm water for more spreadable butter, cold for harder."

"Well," I said with what I hoped was a nonchalant shrug. "Now I know for next time. And I think," I said, meeting his gaze with a you-were-right look of my own, "next time I will try the paint mixer thing. This was just more trouble than it was worth."

"Good idea, Ro," he said, and I gathered the collar of his shirt in my hand, pulled him toward me, and planted a hard kiss on his mouth before spinning him around and patting his backside with my hand.

THE NEXT WEEK I WAS BETTER PREPARED. I HAD GRILLED IAN IN BED about how—exactly how—he had made butter at North, and which of my neglected steps were necessary for a better product. I purchased a paint-mixing attachment at the local hardware store, and received a patient lesson in electric drill usage and safety from Ian.

Among the laundry list of important things I had not done on my first attempt was to heat the cream to sixty-five degrees before mixing it, so I plugged the utility sink and filled it with warm water, then set the can full of cream in it. I used a small thermometer, the kind I once carried around in the arm pocket of my chef's coat, to check the temperature and once the cream finally reached sixty-five degrees, I removed the can from the sink and set it on one of the coolers we used for rapidly chilling the jars after milking.

I made sure the mixing attachment was secure inside the drill, and immersed it in the cream. Clicking the drill to life, the metal apparatus began whizzing around the cream, sending ribbons of white from its center outward. Ian had told me the entire process could take up to fifteen minutes, so I settled my body into a comfortable position, sitting back on my left hip and holding the drill with both hands.

As I mixed, I periodically let my mind wander from the task at hand, and the attachment would creep up toward the top of the liquid, spraying cream all over my tank top and forearms. I wiped my arms onto my cargo pants, figuring that, with four days' worth of dirt, grass stains, and hay already clinging to them, they'd be no worse for the wear. Days later and still unwashed, my pants were rancid, and I tucked a very important lesson about dairy into the back of my mind.

Customers occasionally came through the door, looking surprised when the screen snapped shut aggressively behind them. "Hi!" I'd say over the drone of the drill. "If you're looking for milk and eggs, they're in the fridge right there. We just filled it this morning." I didn't know the majority of the customers, but they were all incredibly friendly and stopped to talk, tucking a jar or two of milk under their arms as I whirred away.

"That's three-fifty for a half gallon," I recited dutifully and cheerfully when asked, "and three dollars for a dozen eggs. Cash box is on the table." I'd incline my head toward the burlap sack–covered folding table that contained a lidded metal box, a stack of Cliff's business cards, and a bouquet of wildflowers in a pretty glass bottle.

At about minute twenty-five, I began to consider that something might be going wrong. Cliff had begun cleaning and sanitizing the equipment for that evening's milking, and I asked what he thought. "Mm," he considered it, but not too much. "Sometimes these things just take longer."

I exhaled with a *pffft*, blowing away a strand of hair that had escaped my braid. "Well, I think it's crap!" I said, annoyance creeping into my voice. I just wanted to make good butter before dinner. I just wanted to prove that I could do this well.

Sensing my frustration, Cliff moved quickly to lift my spirits. A grin spread across his face as he hosed down the inside of a milk can with extra-hot water. "Weighing in at a hundred and ten pounds in the right-hand corner of the milk house, it's Rochelle BUTTER-MAKING BIIIILOW!" His voice rose in volume like a sportscaster announcing a big fight. He let the can drop into the sink with a clank and raised his arms above his head in mock victory, then began dancing in a style that could only be described as a cross between a twerk and a krump. I giggled and blushed.

Ian passed by soon thereafter, having just returned some shovels to the front toolshed. "Something's wrong," I said. "I'm doing something wrong."

"Well, I did mention that it could take a while," he said, not worried in the least.

"It's been half an hour!" I wailed. He furrowed his brow, acknowledging the frustration. "Here, you try." Ian took the drill from my hand and stood over the milk can for a few minutes, watching the cream billow but show no signs of thickening or separation.

"Well, shit," he said. "I don't know, Ro." He rubbed the back of my neck with his fingers, resting the drill on the side of the can.

I relaxed into his touch for a moment before checking my digital wristwatch: 5:20. It was definitely time to get started on dinner. "I'll chalk this one up to a miserable failure," I said, detaching the mixer and running it under hot water, lathering it with dish soap. Cliff had begun milking the cows in the parlor, and I had to speak loudly to be heard over the din of the machine.

"It's not a failure," Ian said patiently as he slipped out the door to finish his chores for the day. "You're trying something new. You'll figure it out."

I carried the milk can back into the walk-in and secured the top, setting it underneath half a pig that hung from the ceiling, then grabbed two packages of eggs, tucking them under my arm. On my way out, I flipped off the light switch with my elbow and pressed the door closed with my hip, then set off for the cooler in the temporary shop, where I rummaged through bushels until I found what I was looking for: early mizuna and purple giant mustard greens, harvested perhaps a week too late, their leaves reaching big and wide, like fans. I crammed handfuls into a plastic shopping bag and tossed in a few onions, too.

Eggs for dinner always struck me as a luxurious sort of treat, rich and satisfying, and I loved how well they married with a glass of earthy Pinot Noir or buttery Alsatian-style Pinot Gris and a salad of bitter greens. *Well*, I thought, wiping down the prep table and rinsing the mustards under a stream of cold water, *we'll have the bitter greens, at least.*

I made a soufflé laced with sautéed onions, the mustard greens, which I quickly wilted in a hot pan with a splash of stock, and a shower of sharp Cabot cheddar cheese from a brick that had mysteriously found its way into the communal fridge. I rubbed a couple of ceramic two-quart ramekins with lard, feeling mildly annoyed that I couldn't use butter, then got to work whipping the egg whites into soft peaks that folded gracefully over themselves. I baked the soufflés in the oven and, thanks to merciful timing, pulled them out just moments before the crew came in for dinner, tired, hot, and dirty. The ramekins were met with words of praise and I had to admit they looked rather pretty, their tops gently domed and golden-brown. The first soufflé was cooked through perfectly, velvety and smooth in the middle, but the second one verged on still-raw, and I threw it back in the oven with the temperature cranked to 450. *Ah, well*, my shrug said. *These things happen.*

After dinner, I sat on the bed in my underwear and one of Ian's old T-shirts, rubbing raw shea butter into my calves and thighs as I whined about the day's frustrations. I was adamant, I told him as he moved through a series of yoga poses, that I was going to nail this butter thing.

"Why not call Patrick and Carla?" he suggested, referencing his friends who farmed upstate. We had paid a visit to their farm a few weeks prior, and they had both worked with Ian previously. "I know

Patrick made butter when we were at North. He'll probably have some insights."

"Do you think that's a good idea? I mean, will they mind?" The idea of reaching out to Ian's friends, independent of him, made me anxious.

He gave me an odd look and adjusted his body into warrior two pose, twisting his waist to face the door frame, rolling and relaxing his shoulders. "Yeah, why would they?"

"I don't know, because I'm socially awkward?" I said, flinging myself back on the bed and letting my feet dangle off the side.

"That's true," he said, moving into downward dog and laughing as I poked him with my big toe.

The next morning, I woke ready to try again. After breakfast, I sat on the steps outside the farmhouse and nervously dialed Patrick and Carla's phone number. Mercifully, it sent me to voicemail.

"Uh, hi. Hi, you guys. This is Rochelle . . . Ian's . . . Ian's . . . lady friend." I inwardly groaned at the word choice but barreled on. "I've been trying to make some butter here at Stonehill, but have been running into some problems. Ian thought you might be able to help me troubleshoot it a bit. So"—I took a breath. "Give me a call back and maybe I can make better butter. Okay, bye!" I ended the call and shook my head, walked to the barn to begin ladling cream off the top of a ten-gallon milk can Toby had saved just for me.

They called back shortly after and gave me some food for thought. What temperature was I bringing the cream to before mixing? (Sixty-five degrees, but perhaps I should consider doing it cooler, as if making whipped cream.) How long have the cows been on pasture? (About a month; because sometimes cream from hay-fed cows is fussy.) How long is it taking for the solids to separate? (Forever, and apparently they'd been running into that time frame themselves.) We said good-bye and I decided to try their advice of starting the cream a shade cooler. Armed with a good podcast and an extra fully charged battery for the drill, I started again. *I'm going to make some damn butter*, I told myself. *No matter how long I have to stand here.*

At the forty-minute mark, my arms felt sore and my legs ached from a bad habit of locking my knees as I stood over the milk can. Shae passed through and, sensing my frustration, asked if she could take over while I ran to get a sip of water, take a walk, get the hell out of there for a minute. Reluctant to rescind on my promise but sorely in need of a bathroom break, I handed over the drill and twisted my body at the waist, cracking my back. I wandered through the distribution space and out behind the trailer that was parked near the dairy cows' winter paddock. No one was immediately nearby, so I undid my pants and pulled them down around my ankles, then squatted in the grass, the tall blades tickling my thighs. In the paddock next to me, Bear lifted his head and chewed a mouthful of sweet springtime pasture, acknowledging me with a lazy sort of curiosity. I rested my elbows close to my knees and sat still for an extra moment after the stream stopped, then yanked my pants back up and headed into the milk house.

"Ro, you're gonna flip out," Shae said, holding the drill as though it was a murder weapon. "It made; it took."

I smacked my forehead. "Are you kidding me? Are you fucking kidding me? I walk away for *one minute!*" I took a deep breath. "I mean, I *am* happy. You made butter!"

"No, you did," she said generously. "I just happened to be here for the end of it."

"That's sweet of you," I said, taking the drill from her and poking at the daffodil-yellow clouds that bobbed in the buttermilk.

"Rochelle made butter!" she said as Cliff walked in, his baseball cap on backward.

"No, Shae did," I corrected, pouring out the buttermilk and catching it in a jar. The milk solids fell into the sieve with a *plop-plop-plop*, and I ran the faucet until it felt just barely warm on the inside of my wrist. The water that streamed out began murky, but once it ran clear, I shook the sieve and dropped the butter into the stainless steel sink; kneaded it for a few minutes, enjoying the sensation of fat sliding up in between my fingers. I transferred it into a big blue bowl and carried it to the kitchen, where I salted it and packed it into quart jars.

This time the butter was considered a smashing success, although, when asked, Ian did mention that perhaps next go-around, I might salt with a lighter hand. I tossed him a pained glance but had to concede that yes, I had inquired. "I just want to be honest," he said, and I halfheartedly agreed that I had indeed willingly opened myself up to the criticism, constructive as it was. My palate had always run, I explained somewhat defensively, toward salty, and to me, the butter couldn't have tasted more perfect.

As I scrubbed dishes in the kitchen, the crew played guitar and sang in the living room. The sun was low in the sky, and if I peered hard enough out through the screen and greasy window, I could see streaks of pink and rusty orange along the horizon. I pulled the heel from the night's loaf of bread out from under a kitchen towel, where I had hidden it before dinner. I dipped a clean knife into the quart jar and brought out a generous tablespoon of butter, slathering it on both the crumb and the crust, adding a sprinkle of salt on top. My elbows on the table, my chin in my hand, I dug my teeth in and tore at the bread, chewing happily, letting the butter coat my lips with a slick yellow sheen.

RECIPES FOR

SPRING

MAPLE POTS DE CRÈME

Pots de crème are a special-occasion dessert: sweet, sinfully smooth and pudding-like, flecked with the seeds of a vanilla bean. This was the first dessert I cooked for the crew at Stonehill, though I did it before I moved there full-time, letting the individual ramekins cool completely on my kitchen counter before tucking them into a pan lined with towels and driving very slowly to the farm. After drinking the farm's raw, non-homogenized milk, I couldn't help but feel it would be a perfect fit for this recipe—farm-fresh whole milk has a distinctly grassy note that can stand up to the sweetness of sugar and maple syrup. If you don't have access to raw milk, which can be hard to find due to state dairy laws, by all means use any good-quality whole milk, homogenized or not. You'll be cooking it, after all.

· SERVES SIX ·

2 cups raw or organic whole milk

1 vanilla bean or 1 teaspoon vanilla extract

6 egg yolks

⅓ cup raw sugar

⅓ cup pure maple syrup

Pinch of salt

Preheat the oven to 325°F.

Pour the milk into a small saucepan. Halve the vanilla bean lengthwise and scrape out the seeds.* Toss them, along with the pod, into the pan. Heat the milk gently until just barely simmering, then turn off

[CONTINUED]

the flame and let the milk sit for 5 minutes. Remove the pod and discard, or rinse and let dry before storing it in a bowl of sugar for flavored vanilla sugar, which tastes excellent in coffee and will keep for weeks.

In a large mixing bowl, vigorously whisk the egg yolks, sugar, maple syrup, and salt until light and fluffy. Slowly whisk in the warm milk, taking your time so as not to cook and scramble the eggs, and beat until smooth and fully combined.

Pour the mixture into six 4-ounce ramekins, then place them in a deep baking or casserole dish. Fill the dish with enough hot water to reach halfway up the sides of the ramekins. Cover the dish tightly with foil and bake for 35 to 40 minutes. The puddings are done when the edges of the custard are set but the interior is still loose and wiggly.

Let cool in the refrigerator before eating with whipped cream or shortbread cookies.

*If using vanilla extract instead of beans, add it to the egg, sugar, and maple syrup mixture along with the milk.

CRISPED POTATO CASSEROLE WITH SHAVED CHIVES

Potatoes aren't particularly "spring-y"—they're more of a summer food, really, in that you harvest them during summer—though if your crop is doing well, you may pull some new potatoes from the ground early. That said, properly stored potatoes carry us through the winter and put food in our bellies when the green stuff isn't quite ready for eating. To brighten and lighten things up, I add a flurry of fresh chives, of which there are plenty come April or sometimes even March.

· SERVES SIX TO EIGHT AS A SIDE DISH ·

4 medium potatoes, preferably of the waxy or all-purpose variety
(Peter Wilcox, Kennebec, Keuka Gold, etc.)

4 tablespoons (½ stick) butter, melted

Salt and pepper

½ teaspoon ground mustard seed

1 teaspoon ground celery seed

2 tablespoons finely cut fresh chives

Preheat the oven to 375°F.

Rinse and scrub the potatoes, then slice them as thinly as possible (a sharp knife or mandoline tool is very helpful here). I see no need to peel most root vegetables, as long as they're grown without chemicals or pesticides.

Place a large (9- to 10½-inch) cast-iron or heavy ovenproof skillet over medium heat. Add 1 tablespoon melted butter and let melt again. Once hot, layer the potato slices in concentric circles, slightly overlapping, until the bottom of the pan is no longer visible.

Use a pastry brush to rub melted butter all over the newest layer as you build the casserole, being liberal with your usage. Season with salt and pepper to taste and one third of the mustard and celery

[CONTINUED]

seed. Repeat the layering, buttering, and seasoning process two more times, until all of the potatoes have been used.

Remove the pan from the stove top and place it in the preheated oven. Roast for 30 minutes, until the potatoes are mostly tender and beginning to frill at the edges. Increase the heat to 425°F and roast for 10 to 12 more minutes, until the top is a deep golden brown. Remove from the heat and let cool slightly.

To serve, gently coax the potato cake out onto a cutting board, top with chives, and cut into wedges.

YOGURT-MARINATED CHICKEN
WITH MINT

Spring chickens are prized for a reason! There's nothing quite like the first in-season chicken of the year, and if it has been raised on pasture, all the better. I prefer to cook with whole chickens so I can use the carcass for stock. This dish pairs perfectly with a green salad and lemony vinaigrette.

· SERVES FOUR TO SIX ·

1 whole chicken, about 4 pounds and preferably organic

Salt and pepper

1 cup full-fat plain yogurt

⅓ cup fresh buttermilk

¼ cup plus 1 tablespoon roughly chopped fresh mint

2 tablespoons roughly chopped fresh tarragon

Zest of 1 lemon

2 tablespoons lard or butter

Pat the chicken dry, then place it breast-side down on a cutting board, with its cavity open toward you. Using sharp kitchen scissors, cut all the way down the left side of the spine. Repeat on the right side, all the way up to the neck. Remove the spine and save for making stock.

Use your hands to coax the carcass open completely and locate the long, opaque bone in the center of the chicken's chest. It's about the width of two fingers. Use a sharp knife to cut down either side of that, like you did with the spine. Be careful not to slice all the way through the meat. Wiggle your knife between the bone and skin, loosening it further, then set the knife down and use your hand to pull on the bone and remove it completely. Clean up any stray bits of cartilage, then season the carcass generously all over with pepper, inside and out. Hold off on the salt for now; adding it too early will dry out the bird.

[CONTINUED]

In a medium mixing bowl, whisk together the yogurt, buttermilk, mint, tarragon, and zest. Season with salt and pepper. Place the chicken in a casserole dish and rub all over with the yogurt mixture, covering completely. Cover and refrigerate overnight, or for a full day.

Preheat the oven to 425°F. Rinse the marinade off the chicken and pat completely dry. Season with salt and pepper.

Melt the lard or butter over high heat in a cast-iron or heavy ovenproof pan large enough to contain the whole bird. Once hot, place the bird breast-side down in the pan and sear until the skin is golden brown, 3 to 4 minutes. Flip the bird over and place in the preheated oven. Roast for 35 to 40 minutes, until the meat registers 165°F. Remove from the oven and let rest a few minutes before carving. Sprinkle an extra tablespoon of mint over the chicken just before serving.

HONEY BUTTER

Springtime butter is the best type. After the cows' first taste of fresh pasture, their milk is richer, creamier, and, sweeter—and the butter it creates is bright yellow and absolutely luscious. I like to add a little local honey sometimes; the combination is great on a slice of hearty bread. Although I had a hell of a time (to put it mildly) making butter on the farm, a small batch is much easier to handle at home. A food processor will work fine; there's no need to buy a paint-mixing attachment and huge milk can, unless you plan on churning it out for a big crew. And it's not necessary, really, to make sure the cream is at a specific temperature. Having a little patience will make the process more enjoyable (or so I've been told).

· MAKES ABOUT 1 CUP ·

1 quart fresh heavy cream (I prefer raw, although it's not a necessity; it's best to ultra-pasteurized in this recipe.)

½ teaspoon kosher salt

2 tablespoons clover honey

Pour the cream into the bowl of a large food processor or stand mixer, making sure it's no more than half full; if you overfill the bowl, the liquid will leak out or splatter.

Attach the lid and run the mixer for a few minutes, until the cream agitates and becomes whipped, stopping to scrape down the sides once or twice. Continue to run the mixer past the point of whipping; after 2 to 3 minutes the cream will break, separating into yellow clouds of milk solids (butter) and buttermilk. Strain out the solids, reserving the buttermilk for another use (such as the Maple and Bacon Cornbread on page 143).

Place the butter in a mesh sieve under a stream of cool running water and knead it gently with your hands until the water runs clear; you're

[CONTINUED]

rinsing off the residual buttermilk, which will keep your butter from spoiling before you use it up.

Turn off the water and knead the butter in a clean sink until all of the liquid has been squeezed from it, then place it in a medium mixing bowl. Add the salt and honey and use a wooden spoon to mix everything well. Pack in a jar and store in the refrigerator for up to one week.

SUMMER

LATE MAY

The anticipation of spring transformed seamlessly into frenzied action as summer rounded the corner. Rock picking turned into planting and marathon seeding sessions that began with Ian soil blocking before breakfast and wrapping up only when it was time for dinner. There was always more to be done. I had been helping out in the greenhouse for a few weeks, filling flats with celery, parsley, and lettuce seeds, but hadn't yet experienced what happened to them once they germinated and grew hardy enough to withstand the less-kind environment of an expansive field.

Everyone talked about the first transplant in hurried excitement over breakfast one Monday. "Hoo, boy," Jack said, clapping his hands once and rubbing them together vigorously. "First transplant of the season." A smile crept onto Cliff's face. I'd learned to read his expressions carefully, as he didn't often let his face betray his emotions. He was excited.

"We've got a crew," Ian said, ticking off names of available workers. "Arianne might come by and help, too."

"Ar-i-anne!" Ian responded with a laugh, drawing out her name and enunciating both the *i* and the *n* sounds with fervor. I felt a hot rush to my neck. I'd read her book, a memoir of farming, twice already. Arianne and her husband, TJ, owned North Farm upstate, where Cliff, Jack, and Ian had all worked and where they had met. Stonehill couldn't be talked about without a mention of North. Honestly, it was impossible to work there without feeling a slight, constant pressure to perform to North standards. "Well, at North, we used to . . ." became a familiar refrain that often set Lara's and Toby's jaws on edge.

I didn't mind the comparisons, convinced that I had a sort of sisterhood with Arianne, both being writer-types fresh from the city who'd fallen for genuine rough-and-tumble, at-times-difficult, farm men. "Besides," I explained to Toby one day as we weeded flats in the greenhouse, "I know shit about farming so I can learn from the way

North worked." Toby, on the other hand, had agricultural experience and did not, at the end of it all, appreciate the pearls of wisdom.

The celery seedlings were tall—a bit *too* leggy, Ian had said, but otherwise looking healthy—and colored a brilliant shade of green. In fact, I noted as my gaze wandered over the flats, the entire greenhouse looked verdant. Weeding, or "thinning" as I had learned more accurately, the seedlings was a daily task, one that I loved. It amazed me that within twenty-four short hours an entirely new plant could poke its leaves up from the soil. Plus it was pleasantly warm in the greenhouse.

"What's she doing in our neck of the woods?" I asked, running my finger around the inside rim of my coffee mug, collecting the frothed milk and licking it off.

"She was speaking at a conference," Cliff explained. That made sense; North Farm had, in many ways, led the way in the move toward sustainable, small, full-scale agriculture. Ian had fond memories of working with them, and told me that the combination of TJ's colorful personality and Arianne's eloquence placed them in high demand for events, inspirational and practical alike. I wanted to learn more about what life was like at North, and constantly asked Ian to describe the barns, the fields, and what life looked like there. I felt almost as if I had come from North myself, and yet I wanted to learn more about how Arianne and TJ made it work. If Arianne, a food writer with city grit on her shoes, could find bliss on a farm, maybe I could, too.

"I'm so excited I might throw up on her," I said.

"That'd be awesome," Ian said, as Cliff mimed simultaneously shaking someone's hand and vomiting.

THE FARM BUZZED AND HUMMED WITH ENERGY THE MORNING OF THE transplant. Ian coordinated it all, giving a task to each of us. Logan and Cliff were to start readying the rows, while Lara and I loaded up the wagon with flats from outside the greenhouse where they had been hardening off. Jack and Hazel were finishing the livestock chores, but agreed to lend a hand for at least a portion of the morning. As Ian hitched up Duke and Bear, Lara and I lifted flat after flat onto the rough wood planks of the wagon, careful to leave a space large enough for us to perch on.

"Come up," Ian said, pausing a moment and then using the reins to smack Duke's rear end. "Duke, come up," he repeated, annoyance bookending the phrase. The wagon lurched forward and I steadied myself with a hand on one of the flats. The vegetable field was already bustling with activity when we turned off the road.

Some of the crew had brought a small garden cart of flats so they could go ahead and start the planting before the full load arrived. I watched as Toby worked a stirrup hoe to unearth weeds, and Dylan, who was wrapping up his time at Stonehill, used the back of a rake to smooth the dark soil. Logan walked steadily behind the dibbler, its wheel leaving holes in the ground, spaced a perfect six inches apart. Cliff held a flat against his waist, bending close to the ground as he used his free hand to detach soil blocks and drop them in every other hole.

"You can drop," Ian said, motioning that I should mimic Cliff's movements. I breathed a silent sigh of relief; hoeing was not something I'd quite gotten the hang of. I picked up a flat and attempted to prop it against my body as I walked. The well-developed root structure of the seedlings made it difficult to separate them.

"You can do it like that if you want," Dylan said, eyeing my awkward stance. "But Cliff's like Superman over here. I think his way is way too hard." He suggested I place the flat on the ground and use both hands to pull out soil blocks, moving it forward every minute or so. I wanted to be able to do it Cliff's way, wanted to prove that I was strong enough, but it just wasn't going to happen—at least not that day. I heaved my flat onto the ground and started working.

By midmorning, my back ached from crouching over the seedlings. The ground was wet from the previous night's rain and everyone was in their Hellies, bright orange and deep forest-green waterproof overalls made for hard work. Ian had promised to buy me a pair for my birthday after an afternoon of rock picking in the rain left me soaked and miserable, but we hadn't found the time to go shopping.

I was wearing a pair of Seven jeans an ex-boyfriend purchased for me. He'd taken me to a mall, convinced, after I wore the same skirt twice in the matter of a week, that I needed new clothes. I had tried on every cut of denim available until he nodded in approval and charged the $170 on his credit card. The jeans were a few years old by now, and the relationship seemed like a lifetime ago. They threatened deconstruction, threadbare in the knees, the belt loops beat up by hundreds of upward tugs. And now they were covered in dirt and grass stains. I liked farming in them; thinking about the life they had come from made me laugh. On top I wore a white camisole, long since sacrificed to stains. It was still a little uncomfortable and unfamiliar, but I was beginning to feel like Stonehill was my place of employment—that the farm crew were my co-workers. I realized that everything I had assumed about what shape my life would take was wrong, all wrong. I didn't want a nine-to-five or fancy clothes and painted nails or restaurant meals. I wanted this, and it was extremely exciting that I had landed smack-dab in the middle of it.

Around eleven an unfamiliar truck pulled into the field. "Arianne!" Cliff exclaimed and ran to meet her, enveloping her tiny frame in an enormous hug. I continued to work, concentrating on properly burying each seedling. Arianne exchanged hellos with everyone as she changed into her overalls and quickly joined the group. I felt suddenly shy, especially when the conversation turned to an online dating site the farmers had all, apparently, created profiles for.

"What about you, Ian?" Arianne asked. "Are you dating anyone?"

Jack chuckled heartily and everyone laughed, made whooping sounds. I picked up my flat and walked a few steps forward to reposition myself for the next round of planting. I didn't say a word, but my posture, the way I sucked in my cheeks, betrayed everything.

"I see," Arianne said with a knowing grin and a wink. Ian kept quiet, burrowing into the ground with his left hand, using his right one to stuff a seedling into the spot.

We switched jobs frequently so those hoeing didn't suffer from fatigued backs, and the thighs of those dropping and planting weren't too sore. I avoided the hoe for as long as I could, but when it was my turn to pick it up, I shyly watched Arianne use hers before trying my own. She was short and small, but had no trouble wielding it. I took a breath and asked her how she did it, and if she ever found it as difficult as I did. She smiled graciously and told me that it all got easier with time. I watched as she worked for a minute, relying on bent legs rather than a hunched back, and moving her feet forward in a rhythm that worked with, not against, the hoe. Plus, she choked up on the handle, gripping it closer to the ground than I had been. It reminded me of my first days in culinary school, when my instructor encouraged us to hold our knives at the blade, rather than timidly by the handle. I mimicked Arianne's stance and began uprooting weeds. It instantly felt easier.

We were late to lunch, to Dylan's chagrin. "It would have been warm," he said with a weary sigh, "if everyone was here on time." He'd made pizzas from homemade flatbread and canned tomatoes, sausage, and sautéed onions, and everyone jockeyed for the prime pieces, the favorite being middle portions with less crust and more meat. The dough was pillowy and chewy, with good texture and give. There was leftover coffee from breakfast, since poured into a jar and refrigerated, and we divided it up among us, pouring in streams of milk and handfuls of ice cubes.

Twenty-one rows of vegetables made it into the ground that day, and by the time the sun went down, I had finally become comfortable with the hoe.

DESPITE ONLY TECHNICALLY WORKING PART-TIME ON THE FARM, I found myself creating reasons to be there. I returned from doing laundry and writing at my apartment early and eagerly on Wednesdays, my day off, and hung around with Ian while he did his weekend chores, asking him questions about caring for livestock and building electric fences as we completed the tasks together. I was still writing, however sporadically, but it didn't hold my attention anymore; not in the way working on the farm did. Living alone began to feel too quiet and unstructured in comparison to the comings and goings of the crew. And while I wasn't making much money at

Stonehill, I was spending far less. Being there just felt easier than being away. It felt better.

"I really think you should take your time off," he constantly reminded me. "You can work your life away, but what will that give you? Back problems and relationship problems. Take your Wednesdays off," he repeated, more adamant this time.

I wasn't too worried about the back problems, but didn't want to jeopardize our budding love life. I started forcing myself off the farm each Wednesday, although I did spend the majority of my time baking cakes, dessert breads, and breakfast pastries for the crew.

I experimented with treats like a barely sweet chocolate loaf bread and vanilla bean pots de crème, working the farm's eggs and milk into my store-bought flour and butter. It was all well received, but the biggest hit with the farmers was a simple pear tart. One morning, sitting impatiently in front of a blank Word document on my computer, the curser blinking judgmentally, I sighed and gave it up. My newspaper column wasn't going to be written that day, no matter how intently I stared at the screen. So I closed the laptop and began pulling ingredients for a tart from my cupboards. It was a dessert I had made many, many times, with whatever ingredients I had on hand, or whatever was in season. It had been studded, on various occasions, with tangy red raspberries, fragrant cracked hazelnuts, and sweet stone fruits like peaches and plums, halved and nestled in a brown-butter filling. This time I reached for two pears that stood ripening on my countertop. Their necks sloped gracefully, the skin flecked with brown spots. I sliced them into thin pieces, fanning them out in a circular pattern and grating fresh ginger over the top. My father called as I whisked together the filling, and teased that he was going to come grab it before I could bring it to Stonehill. I smiled into the phone: My parents used to be the sole benefactors of my baking projects.

I returned to the farm early that evening, so I could whip cream with sugar and cinnamon. I had divided the tart into twelve small pieces, and the crew fought good-naturedly over who would get the extra slices. "Just wait until strawberries come in," I said. "Then this'll be *really* good."

· · ·

On a particularly hot Saturday in early June, I trailed along with Ian as he topped off the organic grain mixture in the broiler chickens' mobile coops. At 4:30 p.m., the sun was still mercilessly hot and my shoulders had begun to burn.

"Do you want to wear my shirt? Would that help?" Ian asked, already beginning to unbutton his thin thrift-store find. He peeled the fabric from his back and I sighed at the reveal of his shoulders.

"I will never get used to how good you look," I said, pulling my white tank top over my head and handing it to him. "Thanks for the shirt. You should wear mine in exchange." I ended the thought with a giggle, and he smiled back goofily.

"Sometimes I think you're like an eager kitten," he said. "The littlest things excite you, and I swear you can make a game out of anything." He paused. "It's sweet. I really like that about you." As I worked the buttons of his shirt, he shimmied into my top, the same faded white tank I wore during the first transplant. It ended two inches above his navel and clung to his skin, stretching across his chest.

"Oh, god, you look ridiculous." I dissolved into laughter and sank onto the ground to steady myself as he posed, hands on his hips. "You have to promise me you'll wear that for the rest of the afternoon."

"That seems like," he said, picking up the tool belt from the ground, "an awfully long time to make promises for."

"Yes," I said, standing on my toes to reach his mouth. "But it'll be entirely worth it." As we walked across the field, I grinned at the sight of the barns on the other side of the road. They captured the late-afternoon light, and the broken-down equipment along the fence glimmered in the sun, too. The farm was a very pretty place, in a messy sort of way—that is to say, if you didn't mind clutter, there was a lot to be dazzled by. My father had taken to visiting once a week, picking up a jar or two of milk and dropping off dried fruit and teas from my mother. "I like Stonehill," he told me, "but it kind of looks like a dump." I disagreed, thinking that the wooden bushels and plows in states of disrepair gave it an authentic sort of flair.

Once the chickens were properly watered and fed, Ian and I walked back down the hill and along the road. A car slowed and pulled up next to us. "Here we go," I said, poking him in his ribs, very visible through the tight material of my tank.

An elderly woman rolled down her window and looked at us quizzically. "You move the chickens?" she said in broken English. I was unsure of how to answer her. Had we moved them? I wasn't yet familiar enough with the farm to answer authoritatively.

"Yes, they're in their mobile coop," Ian answered her slowly.

"Why?" her brow was furrowed.

"Well they have lots of nice pasture to eat now. They can eat grass and bugs and worms *and* the organic grain we were feeding them. It's better this way," he explained and chatted with her for a few minutes before she finally rolled up her window and drove away.

"What was that about?"

"She used to bring the hens food," he said, shaking his head with a kind laugh. I wondered out loud what she thought of our shirts and Ian just shrugged. "I guess we'll never know."

I MADE DINNER THAT NIGHT, PAN-FRIED SAUSAGE LINKS AND A GREEN salad from a mesclun mix. In a small-mouthed jar I combined a spoonful of Dijon mustard, a few generous cracks of black pepper, apple cider vinegar, and olive oil, with a sprinkling of chopped rosemary. I screwed on the top and shook vigorously, pouring it over the greens. "Ta-da!"

We ate outside on mismatched plates with ancient forks, soaking in the last beams of light before the sun disappeared. I could hear the cows in the distance and smiled as Lizzie, Hazel and Jack's dog, bounded past us in search of something fun to chase.

We were both tired that night, but after our showers and once we were settled into bed, Ian pulled me close, our hips meeting together under the sheet.

"Ugh," I groaned in mock annoyance. "You *always* want to have sex with me. It's so irritating." We both laughed, knowing full well that it was I who always wanted to have sex, I who usually initiated the advances. "Well okay," I said, opening my mouth to accept his kiss.

"But you should know that this is completely selfless and I won't enjoy a moment of it." His hand moved to my thighs and I shifted, opening my legs to him as well.

"Yes, completely selfless," he said, and dove under the covers.

THE NEXT NIGHT, HE SAT AT HIS DESK WRITING A LETTER AS I SCRIBBLED in my journal on the bed. I glanced up at him and felt my heart swell then contract. Turning back to my notebook, I wrote:

> Sometimes I feel a certain and tangible distance coming from Ian. I'm unsure as to why and how to remedy it. Or why I always feel remedying it is my job. It's such a funny little line; he is so giving, so full and deep, and then like that—like a snap—he closes up, making it difficult to access him, his heart, mind. Whatever fears, anger, sadness or doubts that are living in him are a mystery to me. All I know is that he is treating me differently, with less patience, and a bit like an annoyance, if I may be so frank. This is hard because it makes me feel weak, at fault, & I know he desires little more than a strong & confident partner. Perhaps he is testing me after all.
>
> He came home earlier tonight after chores. Stripped down naked & imitated the way the pigs lolled around in a stream of hose water. His eyes brighten so endearingly when he story-tells, his body moves like an acrobat trying equally to impress & express.
>
> Oh, how could this not be the perfect match for me!

"Ro, I want to talk to you about something," he said, setting his pen down. I set mine down as well and steeled myself; I had been here before. "You're such a good person," he started, moving to the bed to sit with me. "You're smart, and a good writer and funny. And we have a really fulfilling sex life." I nodded. "And I know we talked about this a couple of months ago, but I really haven't moved forward in my thinking. I wonder if you still feel more strongly about me than I do you."

Fuck. I chewed the inside of my cheek. "Go on."

"And it feels like you might, actually . . ." His voice slowed down. He swallowed hard. "Like you might love me?"

My heart dropped. I did; I did love him. I had realized it that week, and had been holding it inside, close to my heart, afraid of sharing it and being met with rejection. I did love him. "I do fucking love you," I said, my voice cracking and giving way to fat, salty tears that pooled at the corners of my eyes. "You're right."

"Hey, hey," he said, rubbing my back with his palm. "I don't know if this is really something to even worry about. Maybe it's not. I don't even know what this means."

"Right," I said, rubbing at my eyes with my knuckles. "I mean, I think it's completely normal—and okay—for two people to fall at different rates." I felt exhausted. "But what *are* you feeling about me?" I was confused and wounded.

He sighed. "I guess I don't feel passionate about you; not like I *need* you. It's just easy and good and comfortable."

"Have you ever felt that for someone before?" I asked, already fearing the answer. "Have you ever felt passionate for someone?"

"Yes," he responded. "But maybe this is just how it is when it's actually right." I pressed my eye sockets into my knees. "Because none of those relationships have actually lasted. Maybe this is different because it's supposed to last."

"I think so," I said, more to myself than to him. "Yeah," I repeated, meeting his gaze with bleary eyes. "That's what I think, too."

"Well, we don't need to figure it all out right now," he said, and even though I wanted to, I nodded and suggested we just go to sleep. I was wearing one of his old T-shirts, and I pulled it up over my head, tossing it on the ground beside the bed.

"Ready?" I asked, turning my back to him so that I fit up against him like a spoon. He wrapped his arms tightly around me and his skin felt warm on mine. I realized I hadn't entirely convinced myself that things would be all right, but didn't want to relay that to him. There was only room for one of us to be unsure, I reasoned, and revealing my insecurity would do nothing to help matters. I reached up and grasped his hands with mine. "But we will figure it out, right?"

"We will, Ro," Ian said, kissing the top of my ear. "Maybe not this week, but we will."

LATE MAY, EARLY JUNE

As Jack had warned, it is very difficult to run a farm if you're in the business of raising pet animals. So I tried to remain cognizant, as I fawned over the baby chicks, that they'd soon grow into chickens that would be processed for meat. I felt a particular attachment to the batch of birds we had visited on my birthday, but I also had to admit that the fact there were three-hundred of them made it a little easier to consider the idea.

For the first chicken slaughter of the year, the meat birds, or broilers, as they're called, have only been on the farm for eight weeks and no one has grown sick of them yet. Around week three, they cease being sweet-looking chicks and begin to look more alien, but there's still a fondness for their patchy fuzz. No one has become tired of pulling the mobile coops ten feet forward every morning, straining their shoulders with the awkward bulk and heft. No one has grown weary of finding a bird dead when opening up the coop—as a result of heart attack, most likely—and walking it over to the pigs to fling it into their paddock and hear the crunch of delicate bones.

No, no one has grown tired of any of that yet. At a place like Stonehill, where the farmers have been eating beef shanks and ground pork for the better part of the winter; mashed rutabaga and potatoes too many ways, everyone is just excited to spend a day outside, working together as a crew. Everyone is just excited to get to eat chicken.

The slaughter was scheduled for a Monday. The week before, Jack called a meeting at lunch, steering the chatter from idle observation and tawdry jokes to the logistics of the upcoming slaughter. "The question is"—he directed the question at everyone but was really asking Cliff and Ian—"how do we want to do it this year?"

I chased my beet greens around the plate with the tines of my fork, sweeping them through the pool of balsamic vinegar that gathered in the middle of the porcelain. A lengthy discussion ensued about the pros and cons of sticking a knife through the chicken's brain to stun it before slitting its throat. After a short but congenial debate, it was decided that we'd forego the brain sticking and, in the interest of efficiency and time, merely slit their necks on either side of the esophagus.

Of course, I wouldn't be doing the slicing. Jack was to kill; that was accepted without question. "I'd really like to have you guys," he motioned to Cliff and Ian, "on the evisceration line." Ian nodded dutifully and Cliff did, too. Lara, being Jack's right-hand woman, would also clean the chickens of their internal organs. Toby would as well.

Logan agreed to take up his post at the scalder and plucker, and Cliff's father, who was to visit that week, would be stationed by the cooling tubs, slicing off the feet and twisting off the necks of newly de-feathered birds.

"What do you want to do, Ro?"

I shrugged and took a sip of my milk. "I'd like to learn how to eviscerate," I said, not really sure if that was true. "But I really just want to be helpful. Put me wherever."

"What about—" Jack leaned back in his chair and crossed his arms in front of his chest. "What about if you spend some time on the evisceration line and then bounce back and forth to the butcher shop? Since distribution is kind of your thing, you can work on draining, cooling, weighing, and packaging the birds." That suited me fine; I was happy to have a job that reflected my specific role in the grand scheme of things.

"Can we all agree"—Ian leaned back, too, opening his legs and slouching a bit in his chair—"that we won't eat chicken on Monday?"

There was a murmur of agreement, and I asked why.

"It's just too much. It smells really fucking bad; you'll see. After having your hand in their cavities all morning, you're just not in the mood to eat one."

I thought that I might disagree. I had never been through a chicken slaughter before, so of course I didn't know for sure. Regardless, I was pleasantly surprised at how nonchalant I felt about the whole thing.

JACK AND LARA WOKE EARLY ON MONDAY, EARLIER THAN USUAL, TO collect the chickens in the dark. Jack had parked the trailer in the field the night before, so all they had to do was ferry the birds from their coops to the trailer and drive it over to the concrete pad behind the barn where the aluminum killing cones—hollow, inverted pyramids that tapered at the bottom, maintaining enough width to fit a chicken's neck—were located. Lara confessed to us later that she had woken far earlier than necessary, excitement and nerves prompting her to get up around three.

The rest of the crew woke up early, too, and hurried to complete the chore list before starting slaughter at 6:30. We'd kill a small batch to eviscerate and cool before breakfast. Toby milked the cows and put them back out to pasture, then poured eight gallons of thick, late-springtime milk into half-gallon jars and transferred them to a cooler to chill quickly. Ian and Shae brought in the horses, picked their feet and groomed them, while Cliff made the rounds to the pigs, laying hens, brood cows, and steers. My job was to make breakfast and keep it warm, be sure it was ready when needed.

Eggs seemed an odd choice in light of the "no chicken" rule, but I couldn't remember a morning we didn't eat them in some form or another, so I pulled a carton from the fridge, its top askew as a result of the monster double-yolk eggs that sat alongside the cracked and dirty ones. Fried eggs would become drastically overcooked if left to warm in the oven, and scrambled eggs would go from soft and pillowy to unappealingly dry gobs. A couple of frittatas seemed the most prudent choice, so I started chopping onions and garlic, and warmed two cast-iron pans over the stove top. A quart jar of lard stood open next to the oven, a spoon sticking in it, its slender handle slick with fat. I scooped out two large blobs and tapped the spoon against the side of the pan. As soon as the lard hit the heat, it sizzled and skidded along the surface.

I piled the aromatics onto the blade of my knife and transferred them to the pans, then used a wooden spoon to stir them around, coating them with lard. Two generous pinches of salt and pepper went in as well. As the onions and garlic cooked down, I unwrapped a package of loose breakfast sausage from last week's distribution. Loose was always preferable; I knew Ian didn't like the casings, and normally made it a point to squeeze the meat from them before cooking. This just made things easier, streamlined the process.

I divided the whole lot between the two pans and used the spoon to break it up into bite-size pieces as it browned. The sage in the sausage filled the kitchen with a heady, slightly sweet scent, and I took a moment to stretch my back and enjoy it before removing the pans from the heat, wrapping their handles with towels and transferring them to the wooden prep table. I cracked twenty eggs into a bowl (three of them contained double yolks) and used a fork to break up the yellow, smiling as I thought of Logan's methodology. "If you beat the eggs before you add any milk or cream," he'd told Ian the other day, "the yolks won't get lost in the opacity."

I made certain all of the yolks were properly incorporated before shaking a full half-gallon jar of milk and streaming a cup or so into the bowl. I threw in more pepper and salt for good measure, along with some dried red chiles that I crumpled between my fingers. I beat everything together with the fork, then poured it over the sausage, garlic, and onions. The lard and rendered fat from the sausage rose to the top of the mixture, slick and oily. I placed the pans in the oven.

When I arrived on the farm in February, the farmers made their coffee in a large French press, but the crew had grown so big that this method seemed comically inefficient. As a solution, we merely stirred coarse grounds into a pot of just-boiled water, let them sit for four minutes, then strained them twice through a broken sieve, and kept the liquid warm on a back burner. We served ourselves with a small metal ladle that, when left in the pot, became very hot and caused a good deal of cursing most mornings.

I had brought an electric coffee grinder with me to the farm, but there was a manual burr grinder in the kitchen already, owned by Logan, who said he once tried to use it to make peanut butter when he was a young boy. I liked using the burr grinder, holding it against my stomach and twisting the crank as quickly as I could. In my initial attempt with it—after the first night I stayed over at the farm with Ian—I had held it too high and laughed at how cumbersome and awkward it felt. I grew to love it though, partly because, with the amount of coffee needed, my arms always felt good and sore long before I had gotten enough grounds.

We had greens, too, from an abundant harvest. More than twenty bushels of spinach, mustard greens, and arugula had been cut from the field on Thursday, and our CSA members—try though they did—couldn't fit all of it into their reusable grocery bags. We stuffed the leftovers into a clean, clear plastic trash bag and donated it to a local food pantry, saving a good bushel or so for ourselves. I now tossed handfuls of spinach into a blue plastic bowl, the only one large enough to hold a salad that would feed everyone, then frowned, remembering something Ian had said after the first salad of the year. I had combined spinach and shallots, dressed it all with apple cider vinegar, mustard, and olive oil, and waited for the swooning to start.

"It was real good," he told me later, "but I always think that greens should be cut or torn smaller in a salad. The spinach was maybe just a little too big in this one. It was awkward. But good. It tasted good."

Staring at the mound of raw spinach in the blue bowl now, I dumped it all out on the table and tore at it with my hands, making sure each leaf was small enough to eat without folding it over with one's tongue, that each stem was snipped short. I had learned this in culinary school—that salad greens should be bite-size—but, to me, that had seemed too fussy for farm life. It had surprised me that Ian disagreed. I returned the spinach to the bowl and tossed in handfuls of raisins, then whipped up a vinaigrette in a half-pint jar. I checked the frittata by sticking a knife in the middle, then giving it a shake. It was still a bit wobbly, but seemed mostly done, so I turned the oven down to 170 degrees, covered the salad with a towel, wiped my hands on my jeans, and checked my watch. It was 6:20 a.m.

Pulling on my barn boots in the mudroom, I could hear heavy metal music blasting from the barnyard as I ran down the gravel path alongside the road and took a sharp left turn past the milk house. Cliff was using a hose with a spray nozzle to wash down the plastic folding tables that we sometimes brought to the farmhouse and set up under the maple tree for outdoor dining. Logan was testing the temperature of the scalder with a thermometer and Jack was in the butcher shop, sharpening knives against a whetstone. The trailer bustled with activity. I took a few steps closer and, underneath the strains of Rage Against the Machine, could hear the squawks and squeaks of the birds, the flapping of their wings.

Everyone was wearing their Hellies—again—and I rolled my eyes inward at my loose, high-waisted Levi's jeans, my black T-shirt with the command EAT LOCAL written across the chest in green. When I was cooking at Stonehill, I felt increasingly comfortable, like I was doing exactly what I ought to be, and that I had ownership of the role. But here, in the middle of the barnyard, surrounded by such unfamiliarity, I felt confused and anxious that farming was actually the right choice for me. I felt like an interloper, until Ian caught my eye and smiled kindly beneath the brim of his pale blue hat.

I expected some kind of ceremonial start, but when it was time to begin, Jack merely opened the trailer, grabbed a bird, and set it upside-down in the first cone. The chicken flailed madly until Jack pulled its head through the opening, and then it grew completely still, as though it were in shock, denial, or perhaps even acceptance. He repeated this, filling all of the cones, then killed each chicken, working until the birds were truly motionless and the area was covered in red blood. He set the knife down before he reached into each cone to grab the dead bird and set it down on the table on which we had made lard months earlier. Logan scalded every carcass, then ran them all through the plucker, a funny-looking machine that quickly stripped the chickens of their feathers. He proceeded to drop them into washtubs filled with cold water. Cliff's father made quick work of their heads and feet, then the evisceration crew cleaned up the innards. The esophagus and intestines were discarded, but we kept the liver, gizzard, and heart. A volunteer was stationed at the end of the assembly line and cleaned them all. Once the birds were relieved of their organs, a small slit was cut in the flap of flesh under their stomach, and the legs were tucked in tidily. Each chicken was sprayed with a hose—both its exterior and internal cavity—and dropped into a second large tub of cold water to cool quickly.

I wish I could say I felt a strong emotional, visceral reaction to the whole procedure—I very much wanted to—but all I could think, as I watched the birds go from live to dead to finally, quite positively dead, was how very efficient it all was, and how we were doing a good job of getting things done. The most striking thing, I suppose, was the blood. It covered the ground and tables in bright red splashes everywhere you looked. The killing cones looked like something out of a horror scene, and I guess, for the chickens, they were.

It was too soon to begin loading the birds into milk crates and bringing them to the walk-in cooler in the butcher shop, so I stood in between Cliff and Ian on the evisceration line. Cliff had offered to teach Hazel and me how to clean them, so we both picked up a bird and watched closely as he explained how everything fit together. He showed us how to swipe our index finger along the neck, detaching the esophagus from the flesh, how to fit our hand into the cavity of the bird and bring it back out with a palmful of intestine, gallbladder, liver. He made an incision with his knife on the flap of skin, explaining how to tuck the legs into it, and then he told us we were ready to try.

I began by completing a neck swipe, but things got a little hairy after that. Confused about the order of events, or, more likely, where things were actually located inside the chicken, I dug around with my index and middle finger, searching until I wrapped them around something firm and fleshy. I grasped onto it and yanked, hard, then came up with a heart through the small opening that was the chicken's neck. "Is this okay? Is this right?"

"Jesus Christ, girl," Toby said, chuckling. "You pulled that chicken's heart out through its fucking neck. Watch out, Ian."

Cliff laughed. "Wow," he said. "I guess you could do it that way, but . . ." I grinned and tossed the heart into the metal tray filled with pinkish water. After a few more chickens I began to get the hang of it, and I soon found my way around the process, working efficiently if not quickly. And then it was time for breakfast.

The eggs were still warm, and I was thankful that I had made two pans: everyone was very hungry. I cut one large triangle and stuck a spatula underneath it to let everyone know that they could cut their own, and that big pieces were okay. The kitchen was crowded as everyone jockeyed for position around the coffee warming on the stove top and the food on the prep table. I piled my own plate high with salad and put a small saucepot of milk on the front burner. As it warmed, I whisked it vigorously, working my wrist as tiny, frothy bubbles dotted the surface. Ian had once told me that cutting coffee with milk was so much more enjoyable if you warmed it first, and I had to agree. I poured the milk between our two mugs and used a large spoon to dollop the froth over the top. He was halfway through his meal when I handed him the coffee. "Oh, man. Thank you." He took it from me, letting his fingers touch mine as I passed it on. "Real good, Ro," he said, and ate another bite of salad as I noticed with pride that he didn't have to fold a single leaf of spinach.

No one lingered over breakfast, and I understood that while sometimes farmers could cultivate a real sense of appreciation and adoration for a homemade meal, it was just as often eaten in a rush. I supposed, taking the first sip of my makeshift latte, that was just one more difference between real farmers and myself. To my mind, the whole point of it all was the meal. I turned the mug around in my hands, so the chip in its lip faced away from me, and leaned up against the door as I waited for the flurry of activity around the frittata to clear. *Well*, I considered, *we don't have to agree on everything.*

After we ate, I washed the dishes and joined the crew outside. Having eviscerated enough chickens for the day—or ever, I figured— I got to work transferring them to the butcher shop. I pulled the now-cooled chickens from the water and loaded them in the plastic milk crates that had been scrubbed clean earlier that morning. I hoisted the crate up against my body, resting it on my right hip as I opened the door to the butcher shop, and again when I reached the cooler. I set each chicken right-side up on a metal rack and went back outside for more. While each batch of birds sat cooling, I rinsed livers under cold water until it ran clear, then stuffed them into quart and pint jars, screwed on tops, and repeated the process with the hearts. Jack was planning on making a sausage from the gizzards, so once they were clean, I just packed them in large plastic bags and secured the ends with a twist-tie. When the cooling tubs got too full to add more chickens, someone would holler at me, and I'd emerge from the butcher shop.

Ferrying chickens was physical work, and wet, too. By mid-morning, my arms were slick with cold water and a thin layer of chicken slime, and my pants were positively soaking. But it was hot out, and I didn't much mind.

We wrapped up at around two that afternoon and did a bare-minimum cleanup before tumbling into the house for lunch. Shae had cooked, preferring not to be a part of the slaughter, and at the end of the day I had to admit I was very grateful for a meal that, as requested, did not involve chicken.

JUNE

A full-diet, draft-powered farm tends to hold a certain sort of magnetism for young, agriculturally conscious folk—or at least Stonehill did—and as spring edged toward summer, it seemed like the steady trickle of daily volunteers had turned into a deluge. Cliff had been coordinating with some friends, old co-workers, acquaintances, and even a few strangers about week- or month-long stints on the farm: if they weeded, harvested, fed livestock, and helped kill chickens, we'd give them a place to sleep (that place might be a patch of grass underneath a big maple tree, but they could certainly have it) and feed them at mealtime. As our dining table grew more and more packed, finally shoving whoever arrived latest for lunch onto the couch or wooden crates set up along a wall, I grew a little curious about the sustainability of it all, for both the farmers and the volunteers.

We weren't paying for the extra work, but the kitchen was going through a lot more food than it had in the spring. Cooking dinner for the crew became a large-scale production: Planning on chicken? Better roast three. Hankering for potatoes? Mashing a large pot's the way to go. Throwing together a salad? Plan on two big fistfuls of arugula per farmer. There were leftovers, sometimes, but most often I watched worriedly as everyone served themselves, fretting that there wouldn't be enough black bean soup, that the pork chops wouldn't stretch as far as I'd originally intended. Whenever in doubt, I made a large pot of short grain brown rice, figuring that the starch would be a sufficient caloric filler.

"Would you farm," Cliff had asked Lara before she came to work in official capacity, "if all you could eat were peanut butter and jelly sandwiches?" She had responded immediately with an "absolutely not," and I figured that most everyone felt similarly. We weren't just in it for the eats, but they were, at the end of it all, a pretty big part of the appeal. And so I tried to keep that in mind as I grumbled about the inconvenience of pulling meat from in between the third chicken's rib cage, or vigorously whisking together a pot of béchamel sauce that would easily feed my family four times over. If we didn't have good food, what was the point?

I enjoyed cooking most on the weekends, when I got to create food for just Ian and myself. "I love how happy this makes you," he would say, beaming over a summer squash galette or rice with homemade yogurt and curry powder. "It is so nice watching you do your thing." We ate outside on the ground in the greenhouse, surrounded by seedlings, or else on our bed in just pajama pants and bare feet. We ate with our fingers and never used napkins, wiping our hands on each other while laughing. We feasted on delicious dishes, sharing everything, then reclined back and let our bodies digest for a few minutes before attempting to move.

MOST VOLUNTEERS CAME WITH LITTLE MORE THAN A FEW PAIRS OF work clothes and a nice outfit for town errands, a few good books and perhaps a guitar, but Ethan, an eager young man in his early twenties, arrived with the back of his beat-up old car bursting with bottled edible concoctions and experiments; experiments that soon lined the countertops and the back of the farm fridge. He was an idealistic sort, one who spent a full day wiping his name clean from "Google's reach," so the inclination toward homemade and fermented foods didn't surprise me, and I supported it—the fermentation, at least. I just didn't want to support it in the already cluttered farmhouse kitchen.

"What is this?" I asked him one day as I rummaged in the crisper for radishes, preparing to make lunch. He drank the glass of milk he'd just poured, gulping it down in one large swig, never taking the rim of the cup from his mouth. I watched his Adam's apple bob.

"Kombucha," he said, letting another pint of milk slosh into his glass.

I frowned. "And this?"

"Uh, I think that one's kraut." I pointed to another, its rim mottled with what looked like fuzzy mold. "Ha! Honestly, I'm not even sure about that one," he said, and I sighed. He seemed unperturbed.

"Do you mind if I move them"—I paused, looking around the

kitchen for an open space that wouldn't be in my way as I chopped—". . . somewhere?"

He immediately blushed, and his thin, gangly limbs went a little weak, realizing perhaps for the first time that while his presence was welcome, his fermentations may not be entirely so. "Oh, fuck, I'm sorry," he said with such genuine inflection that I immediately felt guilty for scolding him. "Are they taking up too much space? I'm so sorry. Move them anywhere you want."

I smiled sheepishly, trying to coax kindness back into the room and my heart. "No, I'm sorry. I guess I'm just a little particular about how I like the kitchen to look," I said, rubbing the back of my neck, wondering if it was inappropriate to air frustrations with a volunteer. "I guess I'm just feeling a little bit overwhelmed by all the work to do and by all of the people here. It can be . . . challenging to feel like you're always entertaining, never *home*. Does that make sense?"

"I know what will help," Ethan said, hoisting himself onto a stack of empty plastic tubs that had been emptied of arugula and spinach the week prior and not yet made it back to the barn. His weight immediately toppled the stack and he went crashing down onto the floor. I looked worried but he just stood up and fixed the stack. "I'll roast coffee beans when I come back, and you can have an afternoon cuppa."

"That's so sweet, Ethan," I said. "You roast beans? You have them here?"

"Yeah!" he said, rummaging around in the various boxes and bags he had deposited on the prep table against the wall. To make room I grabbed a metal bowl that contained, for some reason, two cups of golden beets and a few carrots, all going soft. I stuffed them in the refrigerator to keep them from going bad. "See?" He opened a burlap sack of green coffee beans and pulled out a handful, letting them fall through his fingers. "I buy them wholesale from a guy online."

"That's pretty cool," I said, sticking my hand in and running my fingers through the beans. They felt like tiny pebbles worn smooth from a lifetime's worth of high and low tides. "Well, sure. I'd love a coffee."

"I don't have a roaster, but I just do it in a stockpot. Sometimes I take them too far, and they get oily and burnt-tasting, but that's only sometimes." I nodded encouragingly. "You know," he said thoughtfully, "you'll make a good mom someday. You're fun and silly, but you're stern, too." He picked up the plastic tubs and held them in front of his body. "After I finish livestock chores for Jack I'll come back and show you how I do it!"

"Thanks. And thanks for taking those." I nodded my head toward his tower of plastic tubs and lobbed the top off a radish. He smiled and slipped out the backdoor into the mudroom. I followed him out with the intention of closing the door in his wake, but the air entertained a delicate breeze, and I stepped out farther into the sunlight to let it cool my shoulders. I watched as Ethan took off across the old winter paddock, running as he went, the tubs bouncing in front of him. Halfway across the field, his foot snagged a rock and he tumbled face-first onto the grass and dirt, the containers flying every which way.

"I'm okay!" he called, waving from the ground. "I'm okay!" I gave him a thumbs-up and retreated back inside to preheat the oven.

KAYLEIGH AND AMANDA, TWO SISTERS WHO HAD SPENT THE BETTER part of the last summer at Stonehill, had returned, too, and it was clear to see why everyone was glad for it. They were hard workers— not farmers by trade, but available for the summer and willing to tackle any task—and we soon realized that we'd be hard up for hands in the field without them. Some days they weeded from after breakfast until dinnertime, stopping only for periodic five-minute breaks in the shade to sip from an enormous thermos full of crushed ice and water. They were both tall, with long, thick hair, and worked in basketball shorts and T-shirts or tank tops, sneakers with high socks and baseball caps, slathering on sunscreen at regular intervals.

In that way, they seemed different from everyone else: I rarely, if ever, noticed the core farm crew applying SPF lotion. Lara always worked in a brimmed bird-watching hat with a string that hung down below her chin—she gave me an old one that didn't quite fit her, a gesture for which I was very thankful at high noon most days—and covered her shoulders and back with sheer button-down tops. Ian wore a hat, too, either a faded army green cap or a straw hat that looked about eighty years old. He also dressed in button-downs; at least until he took them off, as he did most days, driving his team of horses in just sneakers, cargo work pants, and a belt that had once belonged to his father. I acquired quite a tan myself, my shoulders and chest burnished a deep golden color, made all the more prominent by the pale mark on my wrist that became visible whenever I removed my watch. "Not gonna lie, Ro," Toby said one day as we prepped a few rows in the vegetable field together. I was raking the soil after he hoed it. "You're looking a little Mexican these days." I touched the skin on my cheek. It was warm from the sun, and I wondered if I should be more cautious about protecting myself after all.

When I wasn't readying the barn for distribution or cooking meals, I joined Kayleigh, Ethan, and Amanda out in the field. My weeding education had slowed a bit from its quick start a few months earlier—with so much vegetable washing to do, I found myself more often at the tubs with a scrub brush in hand than out in the brassicas with a hoe. The volunteers, in contrast, knew the tools well and were efficient, cheery workers.

But Stonehill was my home, and they were merely visiting. I held this knowledge close to my heart, calling it to mind whenever I felt insecure about my role, or how I fit in. I had a room, a job, and a boyfriend at the farm. Plus, all of my books were there. How could it *not* be home? Ian and I had spoken tentatively about the concept of home in a specific place, and while we both agreed that neither of us would stay at Stonehill forever—that seemed an awfully long time—it was quite a nice place to settle into for a few years. I kept telling Ian that I wanted to hang some of my photos next to his in our bedroom, but I just hadn't gotten around to it.

In fact, I hadn't done much to make our bedroom feel more like my home since I moved there a few weeks earlier. Farm workers didn't receive room and board until they were officially full-time, but with all of the work I had been doing, it seemed impossible to get everything done without being a constant presence at Stonehill. Ian and I discussed it and decided that it just made sense if I moved in with him. He seemed a little anxious about sharing his space with me—"This is all happening really fast," Shae had warned me, and, no doubt, him—but in the end he acquiesced: how was I going to learn to be a farmer if I didn't live on a farm?

And so I spent a weekend driving to and from my apartment to Stonehill, not bothering to properly pack my furniture, clothes, and trinkets—it seemed unnecessary. I just tossed everything in big crates and shoved a few sweaters in between the fragile things. Ian was working, so I brought everything up the stairs to his room by myself, except for a big wooden trunk, which Cliff, who was passing by, helped me lift and carry. When I finally finished moving everything, I stood in the middle of the room, surrounded by my things all over the floor and Ian's things all over the walls and on the shelves, and I thought, "Yes, I think this will work quite nicely."

ONE HOT, DRY AFTERNOON I JOINED THE VOLUNTEERS OUT BY THE herbs in the western corner of the vegetable field. "Okay," Kayleigh said, smoothing out a small piece of paper and reading from it. "According to Ian's notes, we have to do the Brussels sprouts, the cabbage, and the tomatoes before we take on the herbs." I leaned on the handle of my hoe and listened, watching Ian with Duke and Bear across the field. "So this morning we knocked out the Brussels and cabbage—holy cow; there were a ton of weeds up in there—but the tomatoes are just a mess. I honestly feel like that'll take us days."

"Mm." I nodded. "You're probably right." A nasty carpet of bindweed had taken root between the tomatoes. It was a stubborn plant with roots that could be, as Cliff had recalled Arianne saying once, "As thick as a man's arm!"

"So what if we do the herbs right now and just get them out of the way?" No one responded. I was hesitant to override Ian's orders, but it *would* feel good to accomplish a full task before sundown. "It'll be quicker," Kayleigh said, tempting us as she lingered on the sound of the last word.

"Oh, all right," I said. "I'll take the blame if we get in trouble."

"Why would we get in trouble?" Amanda said, gently working the sharp end of her hoe in a rocking motion along a row of basil. "I mean, all the weeding needs to get done—why does it matter what order we do it in?"

"I guess some things are priority," I answered, taking up my post in a row of purple-tipped Thai basil a few feet over. "I mean, hell if I know what's what. But he's . . . particular." I winked, to insinuate I meant no harm, and thought about properly sized spinach leaves as I began annihilating the milkweed and thistle that crept dangerously close to the herbs.

After an hour, Amanda begged off to do some scything on the hill above the vegetable field, which was covered in weeds. It was best to get rid of those before they went to seed and scattered their progeny all over the damn field, Jack had explained. That would be ideal. Ideal and realistic didn't always match up in the farming world, though, and some of them had indeed already gone to seed, so better not to wait a minute longer. "Do you mind sparing an extra body?" Jack had asked Ian, acknowledging the fact that Amanda was scheduled to work in vegetables that afternoon.

"No, that's important, too," Ian acquiesced. "Plus, it's nice for volunteers to be able to do different jobs." A few days earlier, as we fell asleep, he had expressed worry and a bit of guilt that the volunteers' time had been so concentrated in the vegetable field. "I love having the extra help," he had said, lying on his back and offering his right arm to me. I took it and began running my fingernails over it in light circles. He shuddered with pleasure. "*Oh, so good.* But that's just it. They should be extra help. We shouldn't be relying on our volunteers for labor."

I scratched at his bicep and dragged my fingers down over his elbow and back up again, considering the very real and terrifying logistics of managing a business, of operating a farm, of having a life.

OWNING A FARM, RUNNING A BUSINESS, WAS SOMETHING IAN OFTEN daydreamed about and he had been actively working toward finding his own farmland for years. He knew he wanted to be close to Saratoga—half an hour or less, he said, because when you were in the height of busy season, forty-five minutes was just too much travel time—and while he hadn't yet scouted a property that was both close in proximity and an attractive price, he worked hard at visualizing what the land would and could produce, figuring out the sticky details of it all.

He envisioned something small—smaller than Stonehill—but built on similar principles and with much of the same livestock and produce. He wanted cows, too, for raw milk, and planned on doing the majority of the labor with himself, a few seasonal apprentices, and his friends and family. Everyone, it seemed, had a role and a place on his farm: Shae would help run the whole operation, and people I had yet to meet—friends from his childhood and teenage years—would be involved, too. Jamie would build the infrastructure, Jonah and Marianna would help grow things, and so on and so forth until every one of his friends had a job to do and a title to cherish.

"What about me?" I asked one evening as we drove to Saratoga for a weekend away. "How would I fit in?" He didn't seem to be in the mood to daydream, so I barreled on ahead without him. "I'd like to write—to be doing it more than I am now—so maybe I'd divide my time a little better. Maybe eighty percent farming, twenty spent writing? But that'd be tied up together, really; it'd all be tied up together, what with creating recipes for publication and cooking food on the farm for friends, for family and volunteers . . . for us." I paused and snuck a glance. His face betrayed no emotion, and I couldn't tell if he was annoyed, or anxious, or just bored. "I want to make time to do all of the things that I think are important here, but just don't always have the time for."

"Like what?" he wanted to know.

"Like making butter. Rendering lard. Baking all of our bread from scratch, and with a sourdough starter. Yogurt, cheese, all that stuff."

"Why don't you feel you have enough time for it now?"

I shrugged and pulled at a cuticle. "I guess I feel like I'm really busy with distribution."

He considered this. "So how could we change that? Would you

want to do distribution on Friday, instead of Thursday? So you have the whole week to work on farm and homemaking jobs?"

"Yeah!" I said, considering the idea. "That's actually really smart. And maybe just do away with farmstand. Instead of selling product to the public *and* having a CSA, just price the CSA accordingly—properly—and you won't have to sell through a separate vehicle."

"That's the hard part," Ian said, "figuring out how much you need to grow and raise and produce, and how much to charge for it, while making sure it's all still manageable." He started to run some numbers, and I checked out, visualizing an on-farm restaurant or, better yet, a once-monthly affair open to all and any.

"What about a pop-up restaurant?" I asked aloud, and Ian thought about it.

"That could work. What are you thinking? Dinner?"

"Well, sure. But not always; lunch sometimes, or even breakfast. I could do wine pairing, even with breakfast—come on, you know that would be fun—well, with champagne, at least. It could be one price for the general public, and a discounted price for the CSA members, and . . ." I was on a roll. "And I could do seasonal dishes that really make people think. You know, that help them understand what eating locally is actually all about. None of this bell-pepper-in-December bullshit I see these days." I took a breath. "Like, a sweet potato and bacon hash. We'd make the bacon, of course; and serve it with toast fried in lard, with a hole cut out of the middle and a fried egg in that!" I frowned. "But we'd have to find a way to make it worth the price tag, make it highbrow." I thought some more. "So we throw a hollandaise sauce on there. Fresh chives. Done. Easy. Maybe twenty? Thirty seats? Twenty-five. I catered a fancy three-course meal for sixteen people last year; certainly I can make some real food for a slightly bigger crowd. Champagne and . . . well, not orange juice, because fuck me if that's local, but . . . beet juice? No! Beet-infused *vodka* for an amazing Bloody Mary." I looked at Ian, my eyes shining, and he looked thoughtful and I felt hopeful. "What do you think?"

"I think," he said, slowly, considering his words carefully, "that could work."

JULY

An old friend of Shae and Ian's was getting married in California, so they decided to take a whole week off and explore the coast while they were there. It wasn't discussed, but we all assumed I'd stay on the farm, so I did. Suddenly, the tiny room Ian and I shared felt large and empty. My boxes of books were still crammed in every corner, my laundry basket full of folded clothes, my pictures and posters and *things* bursting out of their containers. Somehow, without two bodies in the space the chaos seemed very quiet and uncluttered.

The first night he was gone, I laid in the middle of the bed, my head on his pillow, my body splayed out over the whole mattress. I couldn't sleep. Even in the heat of new summer, we slept closely, our bodies tangled together, sticky flesh touching at various points. Having the bed to myself seemed frightening—I felt too alone and exposed.

I reached for my phone, then put it back down. I picked it up again and typed a message to Ian. "I miss you," it said, and my finger hovered over the SEND button for a few moments before I deleted the whole thing and placed the device back on its nightstand perch.

Ian's words from the night before stung in my ears. We were standing at the window of our bedroom in an embrace after he finished packing. "I'm going to miss you," I had said, a small pout in my voice. He had frowned and let his grip on me go. "What? Isn't that okay?" I was confused and a little hurt.

"Yes. I guess it's just . . ." His voice trailed off and I let go. "I mean, I'm going to be gone for a week. Will we *really* miss each other?"

"I will," I said, feeling foolish.

"Okay. And I don't want to discount that," he said, patience and annoyance fighting for prominence in his tone. "But it really is just a week and I think it will also be good for us to spend time apart. I think it's good for couples; it's normal."

"Well, I'm not going to miss you *that* much," I muttered, flopping on the bed and kicking his T-shirts off the quilt with my foot.

But as I lay on our mattress the next night, I did miss him. He had left early that morning—before I woke—sliding out of bed in the middle of the night. I knew this because he had left a letter for me on our writing desk, along with a bouquet of wildflowers arranged in an empty beer bottle.

The letter started out in black ink that quickly became spotty and faded, then continued on in orange marker. He wrote about his excitement for the week to come—the wedding with friends, the California coast, the time off the farm. He also wrote about his reluctance to leave in the height of the busiest season, and his feelings of guilt for doing so. He explained that although he knew we would have fun if I had come along, it was good I was staying at home; it was good to have time apart and that he hoped I found joy in my independence and in the week's work. It was important I stayed to help with chores and organize the pickup. Besides, the invitation to the wedding had come before he knew me. So, really, there was no reason for me to come at all. I suspected he was a little excited about the time away from me, and I tried not to take it too personally—an endeavor that seemed at once silly and awfully difficult.

Thinking of independence and joy and what really brought those things, I finally fell asleep. I woke in the middle of the night to the sound of my telephone buzzing. I had just missed a call from Ian. "Mm." I rolled over sleepily and unplugged the charger. He had left a voicemail, and as I listened, I cozied my body a little deeper under the sheet and quilt.

"Hey," the message began, followed by a giggle. I smiled, trying to imagine what he was laughing at—himself, or friends, as they walked the streets of San Francisco. Either way, he sounded happy, and a little drunk.

He started again. "Hey. So we just left the bar, a bar, some bar, and I was hoping you would pick up." He paused. "But then I was happy you *didn't* pick up, because it's really late. Oh, man, you're going to be waking up soon, and—oh." He sighed and I could hear the grin in his breath. "We just left this bar, and now we're on our way to get a snack at this—this taqueria." He laughed again; there must have been something funny about the taqueria and I wondered what it was.

"Anyway." His voice transitioned into something softer, gentler, more sensual. I instinctively moved my hand to my inner thigh, fluttering my fingers over the fabric of my underwear. "Anyway, I was just thinking about you, about how much I want you." There was an insistence in his tone, and I arched my back a little, imagining him beside me.

"And by the time you get this, you'll be up and it'll be morning, and I'll be sleeping but I just wanted you to know. Just know that wherever you are when you hear this, and wherever I am . . . I'm wanting you."

I ENJOYED THE REST OF THE WORKWEEK, BUT ANY TIME AWAY FROM the vegetables, the kitchen, or the barns felt aimless. After a long day of hand-weeding basil plants and hoeing the brassicas with our volunteers, I would wash and comb my hair, slide into a pair of jeans I had cut into shorts—my favorites—and finish my day alone. It felt odd, the process of unwinding from the day without someone to speak with. I had grown used to chattering with Ian every night, griping about tasks gone wrong as we stood in the shower together, troubleshooting co-worker conflicts as we rubbed raw shea butter onto each other's sunburned backs. We talked through teeth brushing, and I always laughed at the fact that he dutifully flossed Monday through Friday but gave himself a break on the weekends. "You can't be virtuous all the time," he would say.

The time alone felt unpunctuated, and by Friday, as I worked my wet hair into a braid, I tried to speak aloud about my day in hopes of actually finalizing it. "I really love hoeing, now that I've got the hang of it," I said to Ian's jade plant. "There's something about it that feels so satisfying, even though my arms become sore after just moments. It's real work—and I love how my body, when pushed, is able to handle it."

"But I was a little embarrassed today," I said, focusing my attention on our pile of yoga mats. "I was trying to sharpen the hoe at the toolshed when Jack and Ethan drove by on the tractor. Jack saw me using the steel incorrectly—*But how could I have known? No one ever told me!*

I thought with indignation—and screeched the tractor to a halt, literally jumping off it and running to rescue me from my ignorance."

I grew flustered at this memory. He showed me the correct way to hold the steel against the edge of the hoe, but he had done so with what I perceived to be an air of condescension and disbelief at my stupidity. "If you're going to sharpen it, I mean," he had said, "you should know how to do it right."

"Okay," was all I could muster in the moment.

"Um, thanks!" I called after him as he ran back to the tractor where Ethan was waiting and watching with a face of kind indifference.

I sighed at the memory, wishing Ian was there to boost my confidence, but I couldn't help but wonder if he would have sided with Jack, and decided it was best to keep that story to myself, after all. I tied an elastic band around my braid and slipped on my sandals. Logan had made lamb burgers with a raw kohlrabi slaw for dinner, and I didn't want to be late.

IAN ARRIVED HOME JUST BEFORE MIDNIGHT THE NEXT WEDNESDAY night. I was feeling antsy and encouraged—despite my unrest at the time alone, the last week had been peppered with quiet phone calls, whispered words and proclamations of security, forward motion. He sent a few emails, my favorite being a short, simple few lines that read:

> So much to catch you up on. Redwoods—so big, beautiful, old, calm, sun dappled. Fun drives with great friends. Surfing and wetsuits and oysters. Amazing. You'd love it. I'll show you pictures. In the meantime, you should know:
> I keep thinking about being with you. Smelling you. Pulling into you and up against you. You're beautiful.

I read it again and again, wishing it were written on paper so I could pull the words close to my chest and clutch them tightly with my fingers. I was not sure what had changed—I only knew that, somewhere between the taqueria and the redwoods, something had.

After spending over a week on my own, I had settled into a bit of a routine. One evening, I washed down the bedroom and bathroom walls and floors with cloth rags, a homemade solution of vinegar and water, then flung open the windows to let in fresh air and light. I did all of this in nylon biking shorts and a lacy green bra, thrilling at the impracticality of non-work clothing, loving the feeling of being free and uncontained by wool socks and boots and pants and shirts and watches and hats. I had taken to eating dinner and breakfast in bed on the days I didn't meet the crew for mealtimes, feeling absolutely luxurious on Saturday when I ordered in Mexican and ate it naked in bed with a beer. It occurred to me that I never did these things with Ian around—that is to say, whatever it was I felt like doing at that moment—always seeming to check with him first. Always afraid to suggest something he didn't want.

THE NIGHT IAN CAME HOME, I SAT WRITING IN MY JOURNAL, SIPPING a glass of juniper-heavy gin mixed with ginger beer and chilled with plenty of ice stolen from Toby's stash in the milk house fridge. I promised myself to be a little more mindful of my needs and wants as I considered Ian's. I figured the shift in attitude would be good for both of us. *But why*, I wrote, chewing on the cap of my black felt pen, *do I feel it's necessary to behave like this in the first place?* I pushed my notebook away and considered it—really thought about things—and then pulled back the book to write: *I think, if I'm being really honest— and I should be—I feel an enormous pressure to be exactly who he wants. His uncertainty has made me paranoid, as though harvesting spinach faster than anyone else might tip the scales in my favor; as though over-salting a quart of butter might end it all with a definitive finality.*

I was on the verge of sleep when I heard a car pull up underneath the catalpa tree outside our window. The door shut with a definitive thud and my breath caught in my throat. I suddenly felt very nervous. I turned my head to the side, exposing my neck, and squeezed my eyes shut until I heard the door to our bedroom open. He was home. Ian crouched down next to the bed and I let my eyelids open slowly, fluttering once or twice. "Hi," I said, my voice breathy, my heart seizing and releasing in my chest.

He stroked my hair back over the crown of my head with his hand. After just a few days away from the farm his palm and fingertips seemed softer and smoother. I felt, curiously, that I was meeting him for the very first time—and perhaps, in a way, I was. His gaze met mine, and we both looked at each other for a few moments, quietly, before reaching out. "Hi, Ro," he said, and cupped my chin, turning my face to meet his.

A FEW WEEKS LATER, IAN'S FRIEND DEVON ARRIVED ON THE FARM IN a cloud of dust kicked up by his motorcycle. Devon was a free spirit and a wanderer; he was fresh off a tour of India and Thailand, and had spent some time before that working at North Farm. Months ago, when Ian told me all about his friends, he mentioned that Devon had built fence posts for the paddocks there. With no other frame of reference, and the big task of keeping all of his friends straight, I referred to Devon as "Fence Post Guy" up until and a few days after his arrival.

We were all eating dinner under the big maple tree in the front yard, the young dairy cows grazing a few feet away. Much to our next-door neighbor's annoyance, the calves had been munching their way through the grass all summer. I thought it was nice to have them around, provided you watched your step as you navigated the lawn on the way to mealtime. The lack of rain meant the grass's growth had slowed to a devastating crawl, and the animals were becoming resourceful. Once, mid-meal, Cliff looked up and laughed heartily, noting that Portia (or Porsche, depending on who you asked) was gnawing on a three-foot-tall thistle.

The dry spell had one nice plus: we didn't have to spend mealtime cooped up around the tiny table in the dusty living room. We ate breakfast, lunch, and dinner around one of the chicken slaughter tables, except for Fridays, when I snatched it up at around eleven and carted it off to the distribution space to use at the farmstand.

The day Devon showed up, while we ate dinner in the balmy heat, his bike slowed to a soft roar as he passed the yard. Ian leapt up from the table, taking off like a shot toward the barnyard. Everyone else laughed and continued eating; I stood up and walked back to the kitchen to put together a plate for Devon. I was carrying it outside when they arrived, both strutting with their chests out. Ian looked younger, somehow, even more confident than he usually did. Devon wore his hair in a topknot and his facial hair was groomed into an impressive moustache that, given the right amount of attention and product, could be coaxed into a handlebar style. He wore a leather jacket and grey ribbed tank top over his broad shoulders and very thin waist, and his skin shone with sweat and perhaps a few days' worth of life on the road. I set the plate down on the table and wiped my hands on the apron I was wearing, a sheer vintage thing found in a shop in Saratoga, patterned all over with tiny pink flowers and trimmed in a pale green. Ian had given it to me, along with one from California. I secured it around my waist, tying a bow above my navel.

"Fence post guy!" I said, shaking his hand. "I've heard quite a bit about you."

"Oh you have?" he said, raising an eyebrow and tossing a look at Ian.

"Oh, yes," I said with a wink. "Pretty much everything you could discover about a person, I already know."

"That's enough out of you," Ian said, hands on his hips. I smiled, pleased with myself, and settled back into my chair. I was going to like having Devon around, I thought. I wasn't necessarily attracted to him, but he did make me feel flirtatious, aware of my sexuality.

After dinner, Devon and Ian planned to take a walk around the farm and set up the tent where he'd be sleeping, so I retreated to our bedroom to do a few yoga poses and shower. Devon wanted to sleep outdoors, in between the greenhouse and farmhouse, and I couldn't help but wonder if setting up inside the greenhouse among the hundreds of tiny seedlings might be a nicer experience. (A volunteer, Kyle, would later try it and report that, due to raging winds that ferociously shook the plastic, no, it was not entirely "nice".)

The next day, Devon joined Ian and me in the vegetable field to pick green and wax beans. There were over six-hundred feet of beans to tackle, making picking either an all-hands-on-deck or all-day affair. We brought out as many five-gallon buckets as we could find, loading them on a garden cart and pulling it behind us. We settled into the rows, each of us with a bucket at our side, and began picking. We knelt close enough to talk, leap-frogging one another when we reached a line in the dirt or a pile of rocks left by the person directly in front of us. We were in search of perfect specimens—nothing too thin and short, but not monstrous or too-far gone, either. "You should always be tasting them," Ian said. "Especially when you see one that looks different from the rest." He held up a bean that was a little brown and blotchy around the edges. "Taste it," he said, chewing a bite and then swallowing reluctantly, tossing the rest out into the furrow with a look of disgust, "and you'll know if it's good or bad next time you see one like it." I snapped into one and chewed. Fresh beans have an intensely satisfying and refreshing juicy quality, making them, I have always thought, just as desirable for workday snacking as fresh strawberries and sweet peas. Our CSA members were on the fence about wax beans. ("It's the name," one of our most dedicated members, Neve, explained. "Something about the name.") Once we filled a bucket of beans, we walked to the edge of the row where the cart sat, expectantly, and dropped the buckets' contents into a plastic tub, then reclosed it and covered it with a sheet that had been brought to the field damp with cold water, but was now dry and hot.

The two men had a lot to say, and I enjoyed listening to them, experiencing this other part of Ian that his friend knew. Though I expected the conversation to veer toward Devon's recent travels, they instead talked about a woman he had loved and was no longer with. I asked a few questions, but couldn't really think of anything worthwhile to say and stayed mostly quiet. As we moved down the row, their conversation turned toward the Midwest, where the two of them had met, when Ian was in graduate school for his degree in rural sociology, an academic concentration I hadn't even known existed before meeting him.

I was paying scant attention, wanting to allow them the time to catch up independent of me, and also chewing over a bit of financial trouble I had run into: my laptop had broken, and I didn't have enough money to pay for a replacement. At that point, my freelance writing career was but a distant memory, hidden somewhere among the hay gathered in my pockets, but I didn't want to give up the idea that I could pick it up again someday. In light of my financial anxiety, I had called my father a few evenings earlier to ask his advice. I had expected a lecture in practicality and the difficulty of making a living in agriculture. Instead, as I walked around the perimeter of the vegetable field with my cell phone pressed to my ear, he told me that he was proud of me. "I've seen you grow so much over the last few months," he said, and I felt a little shy. "So I'm not worried about your finances—you'll make it work; I believe that. But don't forget what you're really good at, sweetie. Don't forget about all of the work you've done as a writer."

"What do you think, Anne?" Ian asked, and I was brought back to the present, cocking my head to the side and regarding him curiously. "Ro. *Ro*. What do you think, Ro?" He corrected himself and I gave him a funny look.

"I'm sorry, can you repeat the question? I wasn't really paying attention," I said, leaving out the fact that I had, though, heard the slip and reference to his old girlfriend. Devon chomped down on a bean, and I watched it get smaller as it disappeared into his mouth with a series of quick crunches.

I waited for the rest of the day to see if Ian would bring up the gaffe but he didn't, so I addressed it that night in bed.

"I'm sorry," he said. "It was just one of those things—we were talking about grad school, and since I dated Anne during that time . . . I don't know. It was just one of those weird things. I'm sorry."

I felt a little annoyed, but took the opportunity as a chance to show what I hoped would be a heartening display of acceptance, calmness, and security. "It's totally fine, baby," I said, turning on my side and placing my palms together, sliding my hands under my cheek. "I get it! And hey"—I smiled wickedly—"At least it wasn't during sex. That'd be weird, right?"

"Yeah," he said. "That'd be weird."

. . .

We had been talking about sneaking off into the rows of popcorn ever since Ian's trip to California, and I made no bones about letting him know how much I wanted to. The stalks were tall and full, their leaves thick, encouraging obscurity. We were also growing sweet corn, Spring Treat and Silver Queen, but something about the popcorn had a certain allure. Something about it seemed like just the right amount of kitsch for a barnyard romp, an activity for which, Ian complained, yanking my arms down from around his neck, I was always ready.

But one Friday evening, he surprised me after farmstand. I was sitting on the bed, adding up sales with an old scientific calculator, the kind I used in eighth-grade math class, when he told me that he had a treat in store. I looked up and blinked.

"It's not like, I mean, it's not a real surprise, exactly," he said, closing the flap to his shoulder bag and straightening his back. "You'll know where we're going," he said, his voice trailing off before picking back up again. "But you don't know what I have planned."

"Ooh, I do love surprises," I said giddily, rubbing my hands together. "Do I have to close my eyes?"

He considered it. "Maybe when we get outside."

"Do I have to bring anything?"

"Just you."

I stood and slid into my sandals, offered him my hand and closed my eyes, squeezing them tightly shut for extra emphasis.

"You didn't have to—you don't have to close them yet," he said.

"I know, but I want to," I said with a laugh. I was excited.

He guided me down the staircase, my right hand skimming the banister as we went. I heard him open the big wooden door, and we paused as he slipped on his shoes, too. I gripped his hand and we walked down the three wooden steps in front of the house. I waited as he latched the door shut, listening for the click. I'd gotten us into trouble a couple of times the week earlier for being careless when I closed it. "You really have to be more mindful," Beth had said in a tone that let me know if she had been the type to wag her finger, she would have done so vigorously. "I've noticed this door just blowing in the wind twice recently!" Her arm swooped and her voice billowed on the word "blow," drawing it out to sound like what it was.

Ian guided me across the yard and took a right. I heard a car fly by and knew that we were on the side of the road, walking the short distance to the vegetable field. "We're stopping here," Ian said, and I paused momentarily before hearing a very delicate *snap*. Then he tugged my hand and we picked the pace back up. The slope of the ground declined, and I knew he had cut off the road, choosing the path by the stream instead. He didn't speak when we reached the field, just pulsed his grip on my hand and pulled me along what I presumed was the outermost row of vegetables, filled with dill plants that had gone to seed. I could smell them.

I kept my eyes closed through the entire walk, even once we reached the popcorn and the leaves slapped gently at my arms and neck as I trailed behind Ian. My hand was still in his, but he let it go slack and slide out when he stopped moving. I stood too, on suddenly unsteady legs, teetering a bit. "Wait one moment," he said, and I did. Then, "Okay, kneel down and open your eyes."

My knees hit something soft and man-made, and I was surprised not to feel soil settling into my toes. I let my eyes open slowly and smiled. We were sitting on his red striped blanket from Kenya and between us lay a bottle of Sauvignon Blanc, two jars, and a pile of what looked like wildflowers and weeds. "How very romantic," I sighed.

"So first, we're going to have a little wine," Ian said, pouring some out. "I don't know if this is any good—I hope it is—I just picked it out and didn't know." I swirled the liquid around in the jar and stuck my nose in the glass. It smelled pleasant, like very fresh hay and tart limes.

"Cheers," I said. It was good, if a little warm.

"And then, you're going to take off all of your clothes and lie back on the blanket." He waited a beat. "When you're ready."

I was ready, so I pulled my tank top and once-white jogging bra up over my head, shimmied out of my cargo pants and, lastly, a little shyly, took off my underwear, my right foot catching at the end. Ian helped pull it off, but didn't place his hands on me, simply set it aside onto the blanket. He seemed to be in no rush, and I wondered what he had in store. I lay back then, feeling awkward and exposed, turned over onto my side, propping my face up with my palm.

"This is dill weed," he said, handing me a flower, its stem ending in a fresh break. "And this is a zinnia—well, you know that," he said, handing me a coral-colored flower I recognized from the field behind the machine shop, full of flowers and you-pick cherry tomatoes. Earlier that summer, he had stolen the first one that opened, presenting it to me with a proud grin. This zinnia was the same color, although its petals were smaller and tighter. "Black-eyed Susan, and dwarf sunflower," he said, handing them over as well. "Common wildflower—a weed, really—and Queen Anne's lace." I held each flower in my hand like a makeshift bouquet, and looked at Ian expectantly. "Memorize what they look like," he said. "Memorize what they feel like." I held each one individually, considering their petals and leaves, their dark green stems and bright pollen centers.

"Okay," I said, setting them back down.

"Okay. Now lie back and close your eyes." I did, and waited. "I'm going to touch you with each plant," he said, and a pulsing of anticipation ran through me. "You have to guess which one I'm using each time." A breeze fluttered the stalks, and I shivered despite the heat-heavy late evening air.

I nodded.

He was quiet and still for a few moments before making contact with my skin. I giggled and squirmed. "That tickles!" Short, soft petals grazed my abdomen just above my hipbone, and I knew immediately what it was. "Zinnia," I said, confidently. The flower traced its way up around my breast, making lazy, swooping circles.

"Very good." Ian kissed my neck, just below the ear. "And this?"

There was more surface area on this flower, and its fronds touched my rib cage in a round shape. "Queen Anne's lace?" I wagered.

"No, dill," he answered, and did not kiss me. "Now try this."

"Oh, that's Queen Anne's lace," I said, feeling something similar to the last, but slightly scratchier. "That's a giveaway."

"Good job anyway." He kissed my collarbone.

"Sunflower!" I said almost immediately on the next one, and guessed the wildflower, too, each time receiving a kiss, gentle and restrained. Once we ran out of flowers, I opened my eyes and reached my hand up to caress his jawline.

"I won't forget about dill, ever again. Not as long as I live," I promised, moving my palm over my chest and pressing down on my heart.

"Be sure that you don't," he said and, grabbing at my waist with both hands, proceeded to make certain I never would.

AUGUST

August was delicious, if a little more sparse than we had been hoping for. We had sweet corn—finally, sweet corn—and celery, plenty of tomatoes, and chicken, pork, and beef. The brassica situation was looking bleak: "We may not," Ian said, his brow furrowed, "have broccoli and cauliflower at all this year." There was cabbage, thankfully, small, tight heads of it, plus zucchini and yellow summer squash. Much to our members' chagrin, our cucumber situation was sorely lacking. We barely had any, and as I walked up and down the rows, I noted that most of the plants were completely withered. A day's harvest yielded seven, maybe ten, short, stubby cucumbers. I tossed them in a flat with the summer squash during distribution and hoped that people would find the assortment charming rather than tragic. I always used multiple colors of chalk and cheery punctuation when labeling the vegetables we had fewest of ("summer squash AND CUKES!!!" seemed less tragic than "more of the stuff you're sick of, plus enough cucumbers for the first three members that arrive"). We did harvest a surplus of green beans a few weeks in a row, encouraging members to take those home and pickle them in lieu of traditional dill cucumber pickles. "You can pickle carrots, too," I said, "and beets." We had a lot of beets.

We would be harvesting radishes in the next few weeks, but in the meantime, Ian explained, the crops needed to be thinned. "If we had done this earlier," he said, "the radishes would probably have had more room to size up. But we're doing it now, and we'll see how they do." The ones I pulled from the ground were about the size of my fist.

"How big will they get?" I asked, the black Spanish radish and aptly named pink Misato Rose already impressing me in comparison to my radish frame of reference, comprised of the small pink variety found in grocery stores.

"At North," Ian said, "we harvested some that were this big." He held his hands apart and spread his fingers wide, mimicking the size and shape of a large grapefruit. Larger root crops stayed firm longer, and with the long winter ahead, a turnip as big as your head was a very good thing. ("Good soil. That's what you get, I guess," Lara had said thoughtfully, "when you grow crops in the same place for nine years.")

IT HAD BEEN ALMOST TWO YEARS SINCE CLIFF AND HIS COW MINNIE moved to Stonehill Farm, and Lara was organizing a party to commemorate and celebrate the occasion. She had emailed all of our CSA members and called Cliff's family and friends, planning a secret party with grilled chicken, a keg from a local brewery, and the word "potluck" written explicitly on the invitation. The party was scheduled for a Friday after farmstand, and I grinned inwardly that Thursday, as many of our members winked at me knowingly, filling their mesh and canvas bags with extra carrots, tomatoes, and black beans.

Lara and I planned to spend Wednesday afternoon running errands. Even though I was officially a part-time employee, I put in around fifty to sixty hours a week. Lara, who worked even more, felt guilty about taking time in the middle of the day, but once we had escaped the farm, driving with the windows down and the radio on, we both relaxed. Besides, Cliff was so busy, we doubted he'd even notice we were gone. We picked up the keg, lingering at the bar to try a glass of Golden Dragon, a new beer that the brewmaster had concocted using pounds of our Thai basil in a quest to brew with as many local ingredients as he could. It was a sweet, successfully herbaceous beer that tasted cold, crisp, and very refreshing. After that, we swung by a few craft stores to pick up decorations.

A friend of the farm arrived early on the day of the party, her eye and flair for decorating sorely needed. She had a knack for making barnyard kitsch look quaint, and as I put away the last of the produce from farmstand and Toby sanitized the milking equipment, she and the rest of the crew turned the concrete pad behind the barn into a charming party space. Tablecloths of all different patterns and sizes covered our tables, and an abundance of chairs seemed to have appeared overnight, the seven or eight wooden folding ones from the farmhouse supplemented by many unfamiliar ones. They had been borrowed from friends and CSA members, dropped off when Cliff wasn't looking. I strung tiny lights, which reminded me of Christmas, save the fact they were in tones of gold, brown, and orange, along the wall that bordered the butcher shop so they'd illuminate the concrete pad with a soft glow when the sun set. Jack set up a grill at the end of the pad and began lighting charcoal.

"The chicken's in the walk-in," I called to him. I had quartered fourteen birds earlier that week, placing them in large hotel pans and wrapping them with plastic.

"Ha! I know," he called back. "I had to hide them because they were out in the open. If Cliff had come in . . ."

"Oh, shoot!" I said. I hadn't even considered that.

"Naw, it's cool. I don't think he did."

To get Cliff away from Stonehill, his cousins had talked him into taking the afternoon off to enjoy "one last boat ride" on the lake before summer's end. It had turned out to be a perfect afternoon, hot and bright. Lara planned on taking him on a walk around the farm upon his return, strolling up the lane through the dairy paddocks, and smack-dab into the party. So far, everything was going according to plan. Guests began arriving in a steady stream, and soon the barnyard was full of laughter, chatter, and food. Jack churned out chickens as fast as they would cook, and our members had done our produce proud. The tables overflowed with delicious dishes like eggplant puréed with tahini and spiked with cilantro, and a black bean and corn salad seasoned with nutty-sweet sunflower oil, plus more desserts than we'd ever devour in one night: decadent brownies with thick, sweet cream icing, rustic apple pie with a crimped crust, lumpy chocolate chip cookies scented with vanilla. Wine and beer were poured and drunk out of assorted sizes of mason jars. My pint-size glass smelled more like vinegar and dill than Campari, but I had grown used to that sort of thing.

Toby got a text from Lara: She and Cliff were at the end of the lane, still out of our line of vision, but they'd be arriving soon. We herded all of the guests into the pocket of space next to the milking parlor and the farm crew grabbed Minnie, a rope tied loosely around her neck, and began walking out to meet the two of them as they approached. At the last moment, she turned around, situated her rear to face the lane, and refused to budge. We all chuckled knowingly and let her be.

"What . . . What!?" Cliff said, placing his fingers on his temples and shaking his head as he approached.

"Happy two-year anniversary!" we shouted, wrapping him and one another in a tangle of arms and hands.

"Ho-ly cow," he said, and clapped Minnie's side. Lara glowed beside him; she looked beautiful and very happy.

"Did you know? Could you tell it was Minnie?"

Lara laughed. "You know what he said? As we were walking up the lane and saw her in the distance, he thought at first it was a horse. But then, as we got closer, he said 'That's Minnie . . .'"

". . . I'd know that cow's butt anywhere!" he finished.

Shots of Jäegermeister were poured into our jars, and we all clinked glasses. "To Stonehill. To Farming. To two years; to many more. To you. To us." I noticed Cliff's mother and father looking on quietly, and I could feel their pride from across the barnyard.

LATER THAT EVENING, AFTER EATING OUR FILL AND CHATTING WITH friends and members, Ian and I escaped the crowd. "Shh." He turned around as soon as we were out of sight, and pressed his index finger to my lips. I licked it and dissolved into giggles. "You can't be so loud," he teased, then lowered his face to meet mine. "And you're a goof." We kissed feverishly for a few minutes before continuing to trip our way through the barnyard.

My glass was filled with a half-pint of wine, something white and dry; I no longer cared what it was, just that it tasted good on a Friday after work. As I attempted to find my footing, a small wave of it sloshed out of my jar, dripping onto my skin. I stuck the fleshy part of my hand, from between my index finger and thumb, into my mouth and sucked off most of the wine, wiping the rest of it in the folds of my dress.

Behind us, we heard the faint laughter of our friends and the farm community. The path was illuminated by the dim glow of candles and twinkling strings of lights from the barn, but the moon, which hung ripe and bright in the sky, did most of the work.

Ian held my hand as we navigated the thistles, rocks, and cow shit on our way to the greenhouse. Wearing flip-flops with my party dress, I hadn't felt so fancy in ages. When we reached the plastic-wrapped structure behind the farmhouse, the noise from the party seemed almost a memory. I tiptoed inside, crouching down to come nose-to-nose with the seedlings poking through dark soil in heavy wooden boxes. "Look at this one," I said, pointing to a box that contained a few small and patchy basil plants.

Ian investigated. "Fucking rats. Fucking flea beetles." The tender, sweet herbs were favored, it turned out, as much by flea beetles as by humans, and the leaves were chewed through with what looked like hundreds of tiny pin pricks. The rats had burrowed in the damp soil, unearthing some of the surviving seedlings and making a general mess. "I'll have to set traps. And maybe row cover."

I wanted to bring him back to the moment, to assuage and eliminate any negativity. I wanted to be light. "Hey," I said, "remember when I spilled the package of Jericho all over that flat? Remember how many seedlings popped up?

"You're very bad," he said, pulling me closer to him at the waist. I could feel him through his thick cotton pants, and I pressed my fingers into the space where his neck met his back. "Come here." I took his hand and we walked back outside the greenhouse, kissing again, his tongue pushing my mouth open.

Wordlessly, he turned me around and bent me at the waist over the two-ton woven plastic bag of organic compost, lifting the skirt of my floral-patterned dress as he did so. I sighed with pleasure and, at the same time, suppressed a small laugh: I couldn't help but think of what a friend said earlier that summer, when he saw a picture of Ian. He had rolled his eyes and nudged me with his elbow. "See why you like to farm."

. . .

I HAD LONG-STANDING PLANS TO VISIT MY SISTER IN COLORADO AT the end of the month. Determined to show Ian I was *independent*, and eager to get off the farm for a week, I booked my flight, swallowing hard as I paid $400 for my ticket, and began packing hiking sneakers and zip-up athletic jackets. Sasha had been teaching Spanish in an elementary school in Vail for a couple of years, and the Colorado lifestyle and fresh air suited her.

"I think it'll be good for you, to come out here," she said. "I know you have clean air on the farm and all, but it's hard to enjoy it while you're working. We'll have fun—do the hot springs and see a concert at Red Rocks and *definitely* go on a hike or two." The more I thought about it, the more excited I got. My parents and I were close, but in recent years Sasha and I had drifted apart. We both had a habit of diving into our own lives, focusing on whatever was directly in front of us, and we always seemed to put "keeping in touch" on the bottom of our to-do lists. So while I wanted to show Ian that I had a life outside of him, I also wanted to prove it to myself.

The week before I left, we spent some more time talking about our relationship. The day-to-day was exciting and romantic and heavy and hot, but in the darkest corners of the night, I could feel him pull away from me, sensed the way he tripped and stumbled over his words when I looked at him longingly. His gestures were grand but, he reminded me, he was really trying to commit himself to me. After dinner one evening. Ian again expressed his continual doubt, and for the first time, I couldn't find it in myself to respond. I was tired of feeling inadequate and insecure, exhausted from the up-and-down. Instead of hurriedly fighting for his affection, I simply sat in silence and let myself be sad because, honestly, I figured, what else was there to do? I hoped he would come to a certain and confident realization, an assurance and excitement about us, our future, me—but I had no idea how to bring him to that point, or if I even could.

We walked out to meet the horses in their paddock the next morning, and halfway through the field, the lead lines and halters around my shoulder seemed too heavy to bear. We hadn't spoken a word to one another, but at that point I paused, mid-walk, and said through a thick catch in my throat, "I need to stop for a minute."

"Okay," he said calmly, and stood beside me as I sank to the ground, letting the halters slide down my arm. We were both quiet for a few minutes, until I could sense his unrest, his desire to get a move-on and complete the morning's chores.

"I just wish," I said, "I just wish I knew if you were going to break my heart. Because if you were, I would leave." My eyelids felt very heavy, and my shoulders hurt.

"Do you really mean that?" he asked. "Because I think it is always worth it. This"—he motioned to himself and then to me—"is always worth it." He frowned. "It seems unfair to place that kind of pressure on a relationship. It seems foolish—to me, I don't know—not to see the value in what something is . . . even if it isn't forever."

I would have none of it. "But why kiss me the way you do? Why hold me the way you do? Why sleep with me *at all*?"

"Because I do care about you. I do—love you." I drew in my breath and looked at him, my lashes wet.

"You do?" It was the first time he had said it.

"Yeah, I do, Ro. I'm confused, and I'm not going to deny that, but I do love you and I want you to know that."

With a deep sigh, I slung the halters back over my arm and stood, trying to look cheery, or at least cheerier than I had. "Well, then, onward and upward," I said, and we went to collect the horses.

I LAY AWAKE THAT NIGHT, GNAWING AT THE SIDE OF MY THUMBNAIL. We had made love twice that afternoon. I napped from four to five, luxurious and lazy in the deep sunlight, and when I woke, I felt his presence. He was sitting in the chair at my favorite window, the one in the corner by the catalpa tree, smiling and studying the way I slept or perhaps just the way he felt about me. He moved seamlessly from the desk to the bed, settling his body on top of mine. His mouth met my skin while I was still hazy, but I immediately experienced a familiar rush in my chest, a crystalline tingling that felt like wind chimes. He moved along my body, sliding his stomach up mine, meeting my gaze with his. I felt almost certain that my heart was going to lurch into my stomach, or else shatter into a thousand small pieces.

"Put me inside you," he instructed and as I did I felt a shiver of pleasure. As we moved, his body became slick with sweat. I kissed him and he tasted like hard work and hot sunshine. I felt at once satiated and very sad.

"I want this forever," I said, and he responded with a very firm kiss, one that knocked our teeth together.

MY FLIGHT TO COLORADO WAS DELAYED, AND INSTEAD OF LEAVING early Saturday morning, I was rescheduled to head out on Sunday. Ian and Devon, who was still visiting, had volunteered to man the Stonehill stand at the weekly farmers' market in town. The farmers' market was a project we had signed up for in response to Toby's goading—one which we immediately regretted.

Toby *loved* farmers' markets, and had a lot of experience working them from his time at his first farm. He had even studied farmers' markets in college, learning what drew customers in and what moved produce. He knew just how to arrange vegetables to make them look enticing and attractive, and kept a spray bottle full of water for misting. The basil and eggplants looked particularly nice dappled with water droplets, and it also kept them pert. He was always quick with a good-natured joke, a warm smile, or, for young children, an extra-sweet cherry tomato or kid-size carrot. A charmer when it came to selling product, Toby knocked it out of the park—or rather, he would have, had the market been more conducive to pushing produce.

"It's a freakin' craft fair," he said after his first Saturday in town underneath the red tent we kept tucked away in the shop. "There's, like, one or two other farmers there. The rest of it is homemade flip-flops and cookies and jams," he grumbled, unpacking the chalkboard signs he'd borrowed from the distribution area.

I met him in the barnyard to help him unpack and opened the door to his silver truck to grab the tablecloths. I smacked his shoulder. "Yeah, but how *are* the cookies?"

"What?"

I lifted up the evidence, a plastic bag full of crumbs, and he ducked his head in mock sheepishness. "It's a long time to sit there," he said indignantly, hauling a folding chair from the bed and leaning it against the egg-washing table that rested against one of the barn walls.

It *was* a long time to sit there, as I learned a few weeks later when Ian and I pinch-hit for Toby, who desperately wanted and deserved a morning off. We packed up Toby's truck with everything we'd need, plus more, just in case: the blue plastic tubs of every produce variety we planned on selling, and a cooler full of freshly washed eggs in cartons. We piled in two folding chairs and two of the plastic tables, along with tablecloths to cover them, wooden flats and woven baskets for displaying vegetables, blocks to set them on for a tiered effect, a wad of extra cash for breaking twenties (which Ian folded and stuck in the chest pocket of his pale blue button-down), a calculator, Cliff's business cards, the chalkboard signs and plenty of chalk, a spray bottle filled with cold water, a big half gallon of drinking water, the tent and its stakes, order forms for whole chickens, and bouquets of fresh flowers tucked into bottles and jars of assorted shapes and sizes.

"It's no wonder Toby complains about this," I said, jiggling the passenger-side truck handle to open the sticky door. "It's a hell of a lot of work for a day off." We arrived at the market half an hour before it started, but residents and out-of-towners there for a summer on the lake were already strolling the sidewalks, clutching iced coffees and walking very small dogs. As Ian worked to pitch and secure the tent, I began hauling the load from the truck, parked twenty yards away, and when I finished that I wrote the prices for each vegetable on the chalkboards. Together we dressed the table, arranging the produce attractively. And then we waited. We both sat back on the folding chairs, sipping coffee cut with milk that we'd poured into a thermos. The sun had already been up for hours, and so had we, tiptoeing around the kitchen as we packed together snacks for the long day ahead.

Our first customers were a middle-aged couple who inquired politely about how we grew the vegetables (no pesticides, ever, and all harvested just two days prior), where the farm was located (oh, about seven miles down the road), and how long we'd been farming there (we had both been at Stonehill about a half-year, but it wasn't our place; it belonged to a friend). They graciously accepted the samples of Sun Gold tomatoes, fresh basil, and carrots we offered, but in the end just purchased a dozen eggs for $3.50 and tucked the carton away before strolling up the sidewalk to the stand for Alfalfa, the farm down the road from Stonehill known for their sheep's cheese and Galloway beef.

The next customer was an older woman, walking by herself, who asked if Ian and I owned the farm. I smiled at the thought and, to my surprise, so did he. "No," I answered, propping my elbows on the table and placing my chin on intertwined fingers. "We just work there." When she left, a few pounds of tomatoes in her bag, I turned to Ian. "How funny—she thought it was ours."

"I might be more inclined to sit here if it was!" Ian said, and offered his cheek to me. I kissed it and he kissed mine in return and we settled back into the cool metal of our chairs.

It wasn't that we weren't eager to connect with new customers or share Stonehill's bounty, but spending a whole day working when "time off" was so precious felt like a big imposition. For the first half of the day Ian and I chatted cheerily with customers, but by the time noon rolled around, we were both cranky and anxious to pack up. I hoped that Ian and Devon would have a better experience while I was in Colorado. I had a feeling they'd enjoy themselves—even if they didn't sell too many vegetables.

Now that I had an extra day before my flight, I decided to use the morning to scrub all of the extra produce tubs and hose down the distribution space. I could have written to friends or visited my parents, or just sat quietly and read, but those sorts of tasks had all begun to seem obnoxiously cumbersome. They just seemed to take so much energy out of me, if you were speaking in terms of my emotional and mental reserves. Farm work tired me out, but expending physical energy seemed, in a way, easier than making an emotional effort.

The sun was already hot, and I felt feisty as Devon walked by, carrying an armful of flats to pack into the truck for the market. I turned the hose from the tub I was rinsing to him; the stream of water hit him square in the chest, and he startled. "Jesus!" he said, but if he was upset, his voice didn't relay it.

I grinned wickedly, daring him to retaliate; daring Ian to catch me flirting. "Whoops."

"Oh, I'll get you back, Bilow," Devon said, pulling his tank top out from his chest and squeezing as he wrung it out.

"I look forward to it," I said, pointing the nozzle in Ian's direction and raising an eyebrow as he entered the barnyard. He just pointed a finger at me and shook his head *no*, and I lowered the hose. "Fine, but don't think you're getting off so easily," I said, and continued scrubbing.

I wrote to Ian every day while in Colorado, on hand-painted greeting cards and on pages ripped from my journal, labeling the return address with my name and locations like "At a very high altitude," "9,000 feet & surrounded by trees," and "Still up in the clouds." I told him that I missed him; that I wished he were with me. I told him about the local, organic deli where I enjoyed a turkey and cranberry sandwich after a hike up the mountains in Breckenridge. I told him about the air quality and the very blue skies, and I told him again that I missed him. I told him that I often felt breathless here, but that it was the sort of thing I imagined one could get used to if one spent enough time.

Sasha and I went rafting on the Arkansas River, a tourist must-do when in Colorado. We flirted with the tour guides, all young men with either crew cuts or messy hair, and when they explained the various strengths and skills required of each seat on the raft, my sister pointed to the two of us and said, "Where should *we* sit? She has strong arms—she's a farmer—and I have strong legs because I mountain bike." I looked down at my arms and admitted happily that they did indeed look strong. They were a golden tan, the soft hairs bleached blond from the sun. My biceps were toned, and fat blue veins protruded from my forearms. I was proud of them, and flexed my right one the way Ian had taught me, pulling my wrist in a fist toward my shoulder while also resisting it, pushing it away. Ian may have taught me how to do it, but the muscles were all mine.

By the end of my trip, I felt closer than ever to Sasha, like we had somehow made up for lost time and that we'd both be better at being friends once we parted ways. But I was also ready to come home. Although my parents had volunteered to pick me up from the airport late that Sunday and deliver me to the farm, I asked Ian to do it. He wore his brown Dickies, and the green and red flannel button-down that I liked so much. He must have recently showered, as his hair looked wet and he wore his glasses.

He popped open the trunk and I crammed my enormous duffel bag in it, then came around the passenger side and slid in. "Hi," I said breathlessly, reaching across the middle and kissing him. He kissed back. "I'm here. You came!"

"I'm here," he said, and patted my knee as we drove off toward the farm.

LATE AUGUST

Because Stonehill functioned as a year-round CSA, the crops grown and offered in the summer and early fall months were chosen, in part, because of their preservation-friendly qualities. Swiss chard could be quickly blanched and frozen, packed into tight softball shapes, as could spinach, and with time and patience, bags of sweet corn and edamame. Carrots, green beans, and beets could all be pickled, cabbage turned into kraut, and tomatoes simmered into sauce. Week after week, we encouraged the CSA members to take these steps at home, while struggling to find the time to do it ourselves.

The farm was busier than ever when I arrived back from Colorado, with Lara spearheading the tomato project, spending days in the kitchen canning Amish Paste, Cosmonaut, Moskvich, Pink Brandywine, and my favorite, Cherokee Purple. The Cherokee were firm and meaty, with a deep burgundy interior and a less acidic taste than other varieties. I liked to bite into them like apples, eating everything down to the stem. Lara ended up with more than sixty canned quarts of crushed tomatoes, sauce, and purée, a number I found impressive, but she just wrung her hands and looked at the pantry worriedly and sighed. "It's not enough."

The trouble with late summer is that, while there's so much delicious, fresh, raw food ripe for preserving, there's very little time to actually do so, since you spent your days planting, weeding, and harvesting said food.

Hazel painstakingly picked all of the Sun Gold and Juliet cherry tomatoes that were splitting at the seams, and simmered them down into a ketchup spiked with curry, a treat she quickly learned to guard closely. The crew would go through half a pint, easy, on fried eggs and potatoes, if left unmonitored.

In the slightly less frenetic hours before and after lunch and dinner, Logan and I ran big chef's knives down ears of corn, the prep table quickly becoming a blanket of pale yellow kernels. We had done a little research on the best way to preserve the grain, and while some sources swore that a quick dip in boiling water would better capture the summery, just-picked flavor, we both rolled our eyes and simply scooped up the kernels with our palms and poured them into zippered plastic bags. "If I'm going to cook with frozen corn in the winter," I said, picking silk from the cobs, "it'll be in eggs, or a soup, and I hardly think we'll notice a minor flavor discrepancy."

I loved soybeans and was thrilled to be growing them. To harvest, we simply sliced off the stalks and wheeled them in from the field in a garden cart, which I left parked at the entrance to the barn throughout distribution, encouraging members to take their share and more. In the kitchen, I picked bean pods off the stalk one by one, inspecting the questionable-looking specimens to determine whether they were truly unsalvageable. Most times, I placed them in a "keep" pile, a few brownish-black discolorations not enough to deter me. Those I did blanch and shock, then spread out on tea towels across the table, countertop and stove top, until they dried and were packed into bags and frozen.

As I rummaged through the dozen bags of beans I added to the freezer, I understood what Lara had meant. The meals I cooked earlier that year, back in March and April, relied heavily on preserved food, and while summer made me feel like we'd have produce forever, the farmers knew better. There were a few bags of frozen vegetables in the stand freezer in the distribution space, which also contained the remaining quarts of maple syrup; a few jars of chicken stock; whole chickens with slight deformities, like a broken wing or ripped skin on the breast; and a handful of small bags of gizzards from the first slaughter, which would probably not get used but seemed too much effort to clear away. I was never quite sure of what, exactly, was in the four chest freezers, despite attempting to maintain some semblance of order for the CSA pickup. One was reserved exclusively for broiler chickens, but beyond that, it was anyone's guess what lived in the other three. Pork sausage, steak, and ground beef never stuck around long enough to be frozen—our CSA members snatched it up as soon as it hit the wooden bushels stacked inside—but if you rooted around, you could probably find a Boston butt or a top round, and you could definitely find pork tongue, lamb heart, pork hocks, and beef shanks.

I was also pretty positive there was a whole frozen turkey or two somewhere at the bottom of one of them.

The small stand freezer in the farmhouse kitchen was a hopeless mess of ice chips, half-full bottles of gin, and squished half-gallons of ice cream that were purchased from the convenience dairy in a neighboring town and then hoarded until the rest of the crew discovered them with a fist pump and a "Yes!" I reminded myself how happy I had been to find a mess of zucchini bags, some loaves of quick breads, and packages of goat liver and venison steaks back in April when everyone groaned at the sight of steamed beets. I was determined to make a better go of things this year and tried to convince myself that no matter how busy life seemed in the height of summer, I'd be damn happy for warm-weather vegetables in January.

In the newsletter each week, I implored our members to take extra food to preserve, insisting they consider life without greens come the first snow. We had so much chard in the fields that we offered a full bushel of the stuff to anyone who wanted it, crammed full with big leaves and colorful stalks.

The distribution space being small and shared, it didn't quite lend itself to a visual display of the abundance we pulled in from the field, so I stored blue plastic tubs of backup vegetables in the walk-in cooler, running to and from the temporary shop and shuttling them back and forth throughout the afternoon and evening. I could hardly keep the carrots stocked, the traditional orange Mokum being a favorite of the juicers in the group, the Purple Haze prized in salads for their royal-hued exterior and bright orange core. Arugula, head lettuce, and spinach all went quickly, especially since, once June ended, the more popular greens didn't grow with the fervor of early spring. The chard couldn't have been more robust, but it was a hard sell in a season when everyone craves fresh, raw salad.

The CSA was advertised as free choice, and we encouraged people to take what they'd eat for the week. If you planned on consuming two whole chickens, we reasoned, you should take them. Big kale fan? Grab a whole bunch! We always urged members to try new foods, and while many shied away from the "weird" vegetables and organ meats, some were brave adventurers. Caroline and Shane, a young couple, would often rummage around in the freezer until they found something interesting.

"How would you cook this?" Shane asked one week, pulling out a paper-wrapped veal tongue.

"Oh, babe, really?" Caroline said, looking over from the bushel of green beans.

I laughed and ran into the butcher shop to ask Jack. I had some ideas, but knew that I couldn't speak on offal with the eloquence he could.

Distribution began at 4:00 p.m. and ended at 7:00, although a handful of cars always seemed to arrive outside the door by 3:50. After a few uncomfortable encounters with members who began showing up at 3:45, 3:40, poking their heads into the barn, causing Jack and I to bristle as we ran around the space with a broom, a wet rag, a butcher's knife, I sweetly asked everyone to *please* wait in their cars until four o'clock on the dot. The next week, no one set foot in the space until five after.

One rare Thursday, I found myself ready early. Shoving my hands into my pockets, I surveyed the barn. The tables were open and covered in bright red tablecloths, bordering the south side of the barn. Wooden flats of tomatoes, small and slightly hard eggplants, pert basil, feathery dill, and tangles of parsley and cilantro sat on top. When Toby helped me wash herbs, he lovingly bunched and laid them in the burlap-lined box in tidy rows. I tried it once, but quickly grew frustrated and bored and eventually gave up, tossing them all in at once and fluffing them with my hands to reach high above the box.

In the middle of the space, a big wooden structure held fourteen bushels of vegetables, including four bushels of carrots—two of each variety. Those I had also tossed in haphazardly, learning a lesson in time management early in May after attempting to point each and every one of their tips downward. We topped them in the field, simply twisting off the greens and spreading them back over the dirt to decompose. At the top of the display was a bushel of arugula and another of tangy, astringent sorrel. I had a backup plastic tub for each in the walk-in, but that was it. "Limit enough for one nice meal," I had written on the chalkboard sign underneath the arugula. The lemony sorrel, being an acquired taste, I wasn't quite so worried about. On the other side of the structure I had arranged bushels of beets, both red and golden, along with beet greens, scallions, and onions. I loved the taste of scallions, sharp and assertive, but their preparation was, by far, the biggest time suck on Thursday. We used scissors to first snip off their small white roots, then peeled back any brown or wilting outer layers before arranging them in flats and spraying them with a gentle stream of water and letting them drip dry. I typically preferred to work alone, to be quiet with my thoughts as I washed vegetables, but when it came time to tackle scallions, I begged for an extra set of hands.

Ian was always busy orchestrating the harvest, but once the morning's frenzy wound down, he would swing by the barnyard and check to make sure things were coming along. He didn't love trimming and cleaning scallions, but he always helped me with the chore, working quickly while I scrubbed the dirt from bunches of beets.

"I wonder how we can make this more efficient," he said that Thursday before distribution started. I looked up from the tub. He sat on one of the folding chairs, yanking off the brown exteriors to reveal bright green shoots.

"I don't know if that's possible," I said as I set a plastic flat on top of two bushels for him. He arranged the trimmed scallions on it in a single layer. "Here." I handed him the hose and watched as he sprayed off the dirt. "I mean, short of having more people."

"Yeah, maybe that's the solution." He piled the clean scallions in his hand and shook them once before placing them in a burlap-lined wooden flat, fanning them out over the sides. "But we should also get a better station set up. That would definitely help. We need a good sorting table, and a pressure washer wouldn't hurt."

I nodded. Since my return from Colorado, all Ian and I seemed to have time or energy to talk about was farming. We were moving forward together in that we hadn't discussed his doubt and anxiety recently, but I couldn't help but wonder if that wasn't just because bringing up such an emotional landmine took more effort than either of us had energy for.

The large metal table that stood against the wall separating the space from the butcher shop was covered in a sheet patterned with faded daisies—I had picked it up at the local thrift store earlier that summer—and on top of it sat extra products for sale from local farms: jars of sweet wildflower and dark, funky, buckwheat honey, dried mushrooms and garlic powder, black bean salsa and rhubarb sauce, baking mixes for gluten-free breads, plus jars of our own lard and bouquets of wildflowers, picked and arranged, most weeks, by Ian. He had come around the corner an hour prior with two vases behind his back. He set one on the table and the second in my hands as he planted a kiss on my forehead.

The milk house was clean and ready for customers, its concrete floor scrubbed by Toby earlier that afternoon, the return bushels empty and ready for half-gallons and empty egg cartons. A faint breeze cut through the otherwise thick, hazy air, and fat white clouds dotted the sky. I took a swig of water from my jar and retied the blue plaid button-down shirttails that hung at my waist, re-rolled the sleeves up around my elbows. My pants were streaked with kitchen grease and sweat, but I smelled all right and had gathered my hair into a plump ballerina bun on top of my head. I hoped I looked presentable enough, by farm standards anyway.

I opened the valve to the hose and sprayed it until the water felt cold on my wrist, then showered the vegetables with a blast. They glistened in the sunlight, the eggplants taking on a nice sheen. As I coiled the hose back around itself, I heard the screen door to the milk house shut. I peered around the corner to see who had come in and immediately smiled. It was Tracy, a small woman with a big smile and strong-looking arms. She was a favorite among the farm crew, due in part to her sweet letters of gratitude for the vegetables, meat, milk, and eggs, but also because of her willingness and eagerness to take home the less-popular cuts of meat: the chicken hearts and beef shanks, the lard and the tougher portions that required slow cooking.

She set her empty milk jars into a bushel with a clink and smiled at me from underneath the brim of her hat. I made a mental note to bring extra bushels into the milk house—these would fill up quickly. We used the hefty rectangular wooden crates, made sturdy with wooden slats on each side, for everything from displaying vegetables to collecting bottle returns to chairs when we had extra guests for dinner.

"Hi!" I said, standing aside so she could step into the distribution space. "We have eggplant today!"

"I saw on the chalkboard," she said, her voice full of appreciation. "And tomatoes—I've been loving cooking with them," she said. I smiled back.

"Oh, thanks, by the way," I said, gesturing to a cardboard box under the table, "for the crock." Tracy had recently purchased an authentic German fermenting crock, which she used to churn out batches of sauerkraut and a funky, garlicky concoction called kraut-chi, and she had offered to lend it to me so I could make my own. I desperately wanted to—admittedly, Ethan's ferments had inspired me—but between the early morning harvests and afternoons spent pulling bindweed from the rows of tomato, I just hadn't had the time. If I was honest with myself, I probably wouldn't. "Thank you so much," I repeated. "I'll help you carry it out to your car after you shop."

By that time, a few more members had trickled in: Garrett, with his long white ponytail; Christie, stylish in a cropped hairstyle and frosted pink lips; and Meagan, tall and blond, dressed in yoga pants and trailing her two small kids, the oldest of which was already gnawing on the fat end of a carrot. I brought out my stash of extra chalk and set it on the concrete pad outside the barn, smiling as the kids drew pictures of robots, cows, and rainbows. I tried not to remember that just days prior, we had hosed chicken guts from the very same place.

"Hi, all!" I said, plastering an enormous smile on my face and spreading my arms out like wings. "Isn't it an absolutely stunning day? Sure, we could go for some rain," I said, tossing my head at the lone bushel of arugula, "but gosh-darn-it if it isn't the most beautiful weather right now." Every time distribution started, I felt the day's stresses fade away and I relaxed into my role. I loved nothing more than talking about food, and the enthusiasm and curiosity of our members encouraged me to share cooking techniques and recipe ideas. I didn't always feel like a "real" farmer, but surrounded by a community of people who wanted to eat well and cook creatively, I was in my element.

"It's a little hot, I'd think, for you guys," said Meagan, inspecting a Brandywine tomato before placing it gently in her reusable grocery bag.

"Well, yeah," I admitted. "But we had lunch at the lake today." There was a conspiratorial giggle in my tone, as I recalled the stacks of plates and silverware I held in my lap, the containers of shredded pork and iceberg salad with buttermilk dressing on the floor between my feet in the front seat of Ian's car.

He had driven the seven miles from the farm to the lake—Lara and I as passengers, Cliff and the rest of the crew in his Subaru—with the windows up and the air conditioner off. "It's delayed pleasure! It'll feel that much better when we get to jump in the lake," he explained as Lara and I fanned ourselves and made faces, our necks and cheeks growing red.

"Yeah," I said, banging my fists on the dashboard in mock desperation. "But it's miserable now!" After we had all dove—or jumped—into the lake, we ate the salad and meat with steamed beets and red wine vinegar, a shower of dill and chives, and then laid back and absorbed the sun before returning to the farm and pulling on our pants, boots, and wool socks.

"So don't feel too bad bad for us." I winked at Meagan. "We may work hard, but we do find ways to have fun."

"How much arugula is enough for one meal?" Neve asked, drawing my attention away. She frowned, fluffing the greens with her hand, pulling them from the bushel and letting them fall back down in gentle cascades. I paused. I was always thrown for a loop when it came to questions like these. Who was I to say, really, how much one person—or one family—would eat? If it were me, I'd cart home a full bushel of kale each week. I couldn't help feeling a little guilty when I placed restrictions on greens.

"Mmm, maybe like that?" I said, pointing when Neve had piled two big handfuls of the spicy rocket into a plastic bag. She stuck her bottom lip out a bit, and I nodded. It was just about the perfect amount for one salad, but considering we encouraged members to take what they'd eat for the week, and it was high summer, we were all craving more than a weekly salad. "I know. We're all waiting for rain. Right, Cliff?"

Cliff had just walked into the distribution space from the milk house, his black work slacks looking sharp in contrast to the tattered heavy metal T-shirt he sported. "Oh, man," he said, touching the tips of his fingers together in front of his chest. "We could really use some."

"But you guys irrigate?" Meagan picked up her smallest child, who was inspecting a golden beet in the way another child might consider a hamburger.

Cliff and I both shook our heads.

"Really?"

"Really," Cliff said.

"Really," I echoed, thinking back to the weekend prior when, desperate for precipitation but with none in the forecast, we decided to take matters into our own hands. The winter squash—acorn, butternut, delicata, and pie pumpkins—were rapidly shriveling and wilting, and Ian had wrung his hands worriedly before deciding to do a little makeshift irrigating. He connected length after length of hose and screwed on the showerhead attachment from the greenhouse, walking up and down the two-hundred-foot rows and dousing each individual plant with a stream before moving on to the next.

"Do you think it will help?" I had asked when I came to relieve him in the field, already hot and pulling my tank top up over my head, looping it over my shoulder.

"I don't know. I honestly don't." He handed me the hose and gave me detailed instructions about how long to hose each plant, how far away I should position the head. He watched me water a few, gave corrections, then left to check on the horses.

"Maybe we will next year," Cliff said, back at distribution.

"That'd be good," Neve replied, sneaking an extra handful of arugula and folding a few pieces into her mouth.

Soon after, Tracy wrapped up her shopping and waved me over. "So good to see you."

I grinned at her. "You too. Let me carry the crock out to your car."

"You don't mind? You're not too busy?"

I was, sort of, but I always felt too busy. And I wanted to do this for her. "I don't mind in the least," I said, hoisting the cardboard box that contained the heavy ceramic pot into my arms, each hand reaching for—but not quite meeting—the middle underneath. "I'll be right back," I called to Toby and Cliff as we carried our packages over the threshold into the milk house and then out the door. "If anyone asks." And, to Tracy: "Remind me which car is yours?"

She was just about to describe it to me when I felt a terrible lurch and movement in the cardboard. "Oh, *fuck!*" I shouted as the weight of the crock sunk out the bottom of the box. It hit the ground and shattered all over the gravel, if not in a thousand pieces, in nine hundred and ninety-nine.

We both stood still as statues for a moment before finally looking up at each other. "I'm so sorry," I said at the same time Tracy asked if I was all right, our words riding over one another. We repeated ourselves and spoke over each other again.

"I am so sorry," I repeated a third time, this time my voice obstructed by tears. "And I'm sorry I'm crying." I jammed at my eyes with the back of my hand, clearing the blur enough to see that Tracy was fighting back tears of her own. "Oh, no. I feel miserable," I said. "You were so generous to have lent it to me, and I . . . I'll pay for it, of course. Tell me how much. Just tell me how much."

"No." Tracy grabbed hold of my bicep. "No, that's not it. I just . . . I can't ask you to pay for this, not when I know how little you make and how hard you work."

I didn't know exactly how much a genuine German crock cost, but I suspected it was quite a bit (one-and-a-half week's pay on the farm, it turned out).

"Don't be crazy," I said, placing my own hand on her arm and shaking her tiny body back and forth. "That's insane. I borrowed it, I broke it. It was an accident, but it happened in my hands. I should have been holding the box better. Let me do this."

"Let me think about it," she responded. "If you do, I will make you kraut every week."

"Not necessary," I said, bending down to pick up shattered pieces of clay. "But I will happily accept it." We both laughed through our tears, looking at one another with a new curiosity: *Who was this woman with equally easy tear ducts?* And, *could she be a friend?*

THE PARKING LOT RETURNED TO ITS NORMAL LEVEL OF MESS AND chaos, with what was left of the broken crock packed in the back of Tracy's car, and I stepped back into distribution, which in my absence had gone from busy to utterly frantic. Toby was transporting extra milk jars from the butcher shop walk-in to the fridge in the milk house, and Cliff was patiently going over a customer's invoice. The arugula bushel sat empty, save for a few squished pieces clinging to its outer edges, the flat of basil looked tragically picked over, and the tomatoes were all but gone, except for the few ugly ones lingering between green and ripe. I waved hello to a few members who caught my eye, then darted down to the temporary shop. It wasn't fair that people who came later got slim pickings, and I wanted to restock the produce as quickly as possible. Stacking the tubs of arugula and basil on top of a third one filled halfway full with summer squash, I lifted them with a grunt. The bottom tub fell even with my thighs, and the top reached a few inches over my head. I slammed my backside into the door to close it on my way out, and as I did so, I heard a smack and a crash.

"You have got to be kidding me," I grumbled under my breath, setting the tubs on the concrete floor and turning to inspect what had broken. A quart jar of congealed lard, having sat on top of the cooling unit outside the walk-in for weeks—for what reason, I wasn't sure— had finally succumbed to gravity, thanks, no doubt, to my forceful slam of the door. The jar had broken into many pieces and the lard, slightly warm and melting, seeped out onto the concrete, dripping into the dirt pathway in the middle of the room. "Well this'll be great for the rat problem," I said, picking the tubs back up and marching upstairs. I'd deal with it later: right now, there were people to feed.

SUMMER

SHAVED CABBAGE, KOHLRABI, AND CARROT SLAW

Raw, raw, raw. All I crave in the summer are vegetables in their purest states. The trick for a fine raw slaw is to shave the vegetables as thinly as you can. Here, I eschew the traditional mayonnaise-based sauce in favor of a garlicky, peppery vinaigrette. Allowing the vegetables to marinate in the dressing for a few hours will serve you well, as they'll break down a bit and absorb much more flavor. This recipe requires a few cheats—fermented plum vinegar, sesame oil, and tahini, which are, of course, not local. But I find it's well worth the splurge.

· SERVES EIGHT TO TEN ·

2 cups grated savoy or napa cabbage

2 cups grated carrot

1 cup peeled and grated kohlrabi

2 tablespoons finely chopped garlic

¼ cup apple cider vinegar

1 teaspoon ume (fermented plum) vinegar

1 tablespoon tahini

½ teaspoon ground black pepper

¼ cup extra-virgin olive oil

¼ cup toasted sesame oil

¼ cup finely chopped fresh parsley

Salt, optional

Finely shave the vegetables, using either a box grater or the grater attachment of a food processor.

[CONTINUED]

In a large mixing bowl, whisk together the garlic, vinegars, tahini, and pepper. Slowly stream in the oils, whisking the whole time. Add the cut vegetables and use a spoon to coat them completely with the vinaigrette. Taste, and adjust seasoning if desired (I find the ume vinegar imparts enough of a salty taste for me, but you may certainly add salt).

Let marinate for at least one hour, preferably more, and finish with fresh parsley when it's time to serve. I think this tastes best at room temperature.

MAPLE AND BACON CORNBREAD

At Stonehill, we ate cornbread until we were blue in the face—largely because I made it so very often. To my mind, it's a go-to dish that's impossible to resist: easy to pull together, equally at home in a sweet or savory application, and the perfect vehicle for the young farmers' favorite food group: butter. Here I doctor it up with cumin and hot chiles. We dried our own Thai hot chiles and I would just crumble them right into the batter, but if you don't have whole chiles on hand, a dash of red pepper flakes will do just fine.

· SERVES EIGHT TO TEN ·

6 strips fatty bacon

1¼ cups bread flour

1 cup cornmeal

½ teaspoon baking soda

1 teaspoon baking powder

1 teaspoon salt

2 dried red chiles, crumbled

1 teaspoon ground cumin

Salt and pepper

2 eggs

1½ cups buttermilk*

¼ cup plus 1 tablespoon maple syrup

4 tablespoons (½ stick) butter, melted

Preheat the oven to 375°F.

Heat a 9- to 10½-inch cast-iron pan over medium-low. Add the bacon and cook very slowly, until the fat is rendered and the meat is crisp, 15 minutes, lowering the heat if the bacon begins to crisp too quickly. Remove the bacon and place it on a paper towel to cool, then crumble it into pieces. Take the pan off the heat to let it cool slightly.

[CONTINUED]

Meanwhile, in a large mixing bowl, combine the flour, cornmeal, baking soda and powder, salt and pepper to taste, chiles, and cumin. Mix well until combined.

In a separate bowl, combine the eggs, buttermilk, ¼ cup maple syrup, and melted butter, plus any residual rendered bacon fat (leaving a little in the pan). Beat well with a fork, then add to the dry ingredients. Stir in the bacon bits, and mix with a wooden spoon until just combined.

Use a towel to rub the pan down with the leftover bacon grease (be sure to get both the bottom and the sides), then pour the batter into the prepared pan. Bake for 25 to 30 minutes, until lightly browned and a knife inserted into the middle comes out clean. Drizzle the remaining tablespoon of maple syrup over the top while still warm. Let cool before eating.

*If you don't have buttermilk on hand—and I never do—you can combine 1 tablespoon lemon juice with 1 cup whole milk. Let sit for 10 minutes, then whisk to combine. Proceed as directed.

PAN-SEARED STRIP STEAK

I'm no grill master, but the real reason I like to pan-sear my steaks is for the chance to baste them in butter. To go the completely homemade route, you can use the Honey Butter recipe on page 73, and omit the honey. If you're nervous about cooking to temperature, invest in a simple meat thermometer.

· SERVES TWO ·

1 tablespoon lard or neutral oil, like canola

2 strip steaks

Salt and pepper

2 tablespoons butter

Let the steaks sit at room temperature for 30 minutes before cooking. When ready, season generously with salt and pepper to taste.

Heat a large cast-iron skillet over high and add the lard or oil. Let it melt completely, then add the steaks. Sear until they reach desired doneness, 4 to 5 minutes per side. In the last minute of cooking, add the butter and let it melt, then use a large spoon to baste the steaks constantly with the melted butter. Keep in mind that the steaks will continue to cook for a minute or so once removed from the heat.

Let them rest for a few minutes before serving. Sometimes, while the steaks are resting, I add fresh, raw greens to the hot pan and let them wilt and mop up the juice before finishing everything off with a squeeze of lemon.

BLISTERED TOMATO GRATIN

Summer tomatoes are beautiful raw, and although they don't need help, things certainly don't have to be bad to be better. This is a fairly simple preparation with relatively few ingredients, so be sure you're using high quality product. Homemade breadcrumbs are a must.

• SERVES SIX TO EIGHT AS A SIDE DISH •

3 tablespoons olive oil, divided

4 large firm, ripe, round tomatoes. (Feel free to play around with varieties; I'm partial to Cherokee Purple.)

Salt and pepper

6 cloves garlic, peeled and smashed

1 cup freshly torn bread crumbs, in pieces roughly the size of a thumbnail

⅓ cup grated aged Cheddar cheese

1 tablespoon finely chopped dill

Preheat the oven to 425°F.

Rub the bottom and sides of a casserole dish with 1 tablespoon olive oil and set aside. Slice the tomatoes ¼-inch thick (a serrated knife works best for this) and arrange them, slightly overlapping, in the prepared dish. Season with salt and pepper to taste.

Meanwhile, heat the remaining olive oil in a skillet over medium-high heat for 1 to 2 minutes. Add the garlic, then remove the pan from the heat; leaving it too long on the flame will cause the garlic to burn. Immediately stir in the breadcrumbs and drizzle the mixture all over the tomatoes. Sprinkle the cheese on top.

Bake on a rack in the upper third of the oven for 15 minutes, until the cheese is browned and bubbling. Remove from the oven and scatter the dill over the top. Serve while warm.

FALL

SEPTEMBER

The first hint of cooler weather snuck in with September, and as the nights dipped down in temperature, I found myself baking bread with much more enthusiasm and greater routine. I began spiking the loaves with flax seeds and oats, the combination of nutty grains and toasted seeds adding a comforting depth. Bread was best loved at dinner, when it could be used to mop up sauce or soup, but if there was any left over, it went straight into the next morning's meal.

When I cooked breakfast, I'd slice the loaf as thinly as I could, stretching it to feed as many of us as I assumed would be present that morning. I had brought a few of my culinary school knives to the farm, including a tragic mockery of a bread knife. It couldn't have been duller—or more dangerous—and you really had to put your back into the process of sawing slices apart. Once you reached the heel, if it was smaller than two inches, *forget it*. No bread, no matter how crusty and chewy, was worth hacked-off finger nubs. When it got down to the butt end, it was best to just run it through the nine-pound tub of organic peanut butter (provided someone had made it to the grocery store that month) or hope the salted sweet cream butter had been sitting out at room temperature, rendering it soft and spreadable. You should just eat the evidence and pretend that it had never existed.

I'd place all the cut pieces on an ancient, perpetually grease-streaked cookie sheet, drizzle a bit of olive oil over each slice, holding the enormous jug as gingerly as I could, and mete out Scrooge-like dribbles over the bread. Then I'd turn them over and rub them into the pan, coating both sides with fat, pinching salt and black pepper between my thumb and index finger a foot above the table and releasing it in a shower. As the bread baked in the oven, cranked to a temperature I hoped was around 425 degrees but was never quite sure, considering that the oven's calibration was about 100 to 200 degrees off, I sautéed loose breakfast sausage if we had it (ground pork doctored with chile flakes if we didn't) and fried eggs on a stove top griddle. If I timed everything just right, I'd have already slid a fried egg onto each piece of bread and be in the process of scooping spoonfuls of pork over everything when the farmers arrived. Sometimes I slathered the toasts with Dijon mustard, or mayonnaise, or a combination of both, and if there were fresh greens—peppery arugula being a favorite—those went on, too. It was an open-faced sandwich to savor, though we always inhaled them, already hungry from the morning's chores.

If we were lucky enough to have a whole, unadulterated loaf at breakfast, I just set it on the table with all of the correct accoutrements and let people make their own choices. We always had assorted jams to go with the butter, but left to my own devices, I often heated lard in a small cast-iron pan and fried a thick piece in it, pressing down on the bread with a fork to encourage an aggressively browned crust, to let the fat seep into every crevice.

More often than not, though, we ate oatmeal. When I placed the CSA's order from the grain farm up the road, I was mindful to ask Tanya for a five-pound bag of rolled oats for the farmhouse as well. For a time, we experimented with thirteen-pound orders, but it took us longer to eat our way through it than the oats stayed fresh, and I found myself using exorbitant amounts of butter and maple syrup in batches of granola concocted just to use up the flakes before they went rancid.

Funnily enough, oats were not a favorite of everyone on the farm. Toby almost never touched them, save one time I drowned mine in a sea of cream, maple syrup, and broken walnuts, and he tried a small bite before deciding that no, he'd had it right all along; he didn't like oatmeal in any form. Lara claimed an oat-overdose for her lack of enthusiasm for them. Those of us who did eat oats were particular about how we did it. I got huffy and irritated if they were pre-seasoned or sweetened, preferring instead to stir in my own butter, cinnamon, what-have-you. Logan always made an enormous batch, then packed it into two-pound plastic tubs to be reheated throughout the week, a practice I disliked so much that I pretended the pre-cooked concrete slab of oatmeal simply didn't exist, making a fresh batch of just enough every time. It was wasteful, and I felt a small tinge of guilt whenever I did this, but apparently not a big enough one to stop. Ian liked his oatmeal savory, and mixed in with whatever else he happened to be eating. A firm believer in distinct boundaries between foods, I watched, flustered and distressed as he filled his favorite ceramic bowl with oats, barley, miso, a few flakes of butter, fried eggs, sweet potato hash; all of the other food on the table that morning.

"You should try it," he encouraged periodically. "You, with all the food rules." I always shook my head violently and shuddered, scooping up a raisin or bit of dried fig taken from my personal stash with the tip of my spoon, though eventually I did get in the habit of adding a few teaspoons of salty-sweet adzuki bean miso and enjoyed that all right.

Our hens periodically stopped laying enough eggs to feed both our CSA members and ourselves, and on the occasions that we didn't have any for the house, I had to get a little creative. Sausage was frequent (although overuse was frowned upon by Jack, who painstakingly stuffed each link). Bacon was a luxury, typically relegated to the fatty ends that, when dealt with patiently, rendered a gorgeous amount of grease but resulted in little more than bacon bits. I was always happy to eat just oats and cream for breakfast, but felt a sense of responsibility to the rest of the farmers to produce rib-sticking morning meals.

If I was feeling particularly domestic, I'd tie on one of my aprons from Ian and whip up a batch of oatmeal muffins. I had made them so many times that I had the recipe memorized. It called for buttermilk, but when that wasn't available—we didn't make butter near as often as we should have—I poured a bit of bottled lemon juice into a measuring cup of cream-heavy milk and let it sit until the dairy took on buttermilk's characteristically tangy flavor. That got poured over rolled oats and mixed with dry ingredients before I dolloped it into the twelve-cup muffin tin that I had greased with butter, or lard, or bacon grease, or whatever. I liked their size when they came out of the oven, properly small, the size of my fist and no bigger, and I liked how they greedily absorbed a pat of butter, tolerated a smear of orange marmalade.

Once or twice I made scones, but the amount of butter required for them seemed wasteful, and at the end of it all, it was a lot of dirty food processor parts for twelve humble pastries. As I carefully wiped the blade of the machine clean, I vowed never to take another scone for granted, and also promised to make them for myself weekly if I ever left the farm.

We tried to stay on top of the extra pantry items we needed that were not grown on the farm, but no one had taken ownership of that role, and we usually just watched our supplies dwindle, assuming someone else would replenish them. Once, due to an ordering oversight on my part, our pantry was plumb out of oats and flour, and there wasn't an egg to be found on the farm. I felt particularly guilty, as Logan had offered to make breakfast that morning so I could spend a little extra time picking the horses' feet. He roasted two chickens and shredded the meat into homemade stock along with potatoes and a shower of chives and scallion. "This smells good, but I don't really like chicken for breakfast," I said, mixing crunchy peanut butter together with a handful of dates. I took a bite and immediately felt my mouth seal itself shut. "I don't really, either." Logan shrugged. "But I didn't know what else to do."

It's important for a farmer to eat a good breakfast. This is especially true if you happen to be a farmer at Stonehill in September, because you're exhausted. You're still dealing with the post-summer obligations: moving beef, killing chickens (thankfully, it is your last month of doing so), harvesting, possibly still planting or at least cover-cropping, feeding pigs (you are always feeding pigs), hell, maybe you're even still making hay. But now you're also readying yourself for the winter, creating room in your walk-in coolers and having the first go at washing and storing root vegetables, realizing that you should have preserved more and hoping to god that your members did. And plus, at this point—in September—you're just exhausted. You're sick of farming, and want a break. At least that's how I felt.

"I'm freaking beat," Toby said one afternoon after milking, kicking his boots off and flopping on the couch.

I was in the kitchen, pounding boneless pork cutlets into thin sheets and dredging them through flour, eggs, and homemade bread crumbs. I rinsed my hands and wiped them on my apron, sinking down onto the cushion next to him.

"Are you feeling kind of, just, over it?" I asked.

"Yeah. Like, we're so busy all the time and I just want to take a break but I feel guilty whenever I do. What about you?" He slid down deeper into the couch.

"I still love the work," I said, pulling my feet up on the cushions and crossing my legs. "But I might be getting burned out. And"— I paused, slightly embarrassed by what I was about to say— "I think I'm jealous of the fact that you guys all get to work together."

"What do you mean?" Toby asked.

"Vegetable harvests and transplants, weeding and seeding," I said. "That's always a big thing. Like, with a crew. And I feel like I'm always just washing carrots by myself, or stuck here, in the kitchen."

"Really?" he looked concerned. "But you love this, Ro. The kitchen is your thing."

"Yeah," I said, playing with the hem of my apron. "Sometimes I wonder what I'm doing and if it's right. Maybe I'm just sick of *this* kitchen. It's so messy. And chaotic. I miss cooking in a restaurant sometimes. They have all the good equipment." I waited a beat. "And dishwashers."

Toby had spent some time as a line cook before coming to Stonehill, and he nodded now. "Dishwashers," he said, "would be nice." We both laughed at what felt like a secret joke, but then he grew serious. "Really, though, try not to forget how much you like cooking. Try not to get disillusioned. You're twenty-five. It's too early for that shit."

"You're right," I said, and smashed my face into his bicep as I hugged him.

Not one for affection or sentimentality, Toby peeled me from his arm. "All right, all right," he said. "Whatever."

There are only two entries in my journal from that September, one dated September 1 that reads:

Things Ian is teaching me: how to drive horses, be kind, look up when I walk.

And another, slightly longer but pointedly more apathetic ramble from the eleventh:

Good god, am I exhausted. I have intentions of writing; I just never seem to have the energy to do it. All I can think about is long, uninterrupted sleep. It's so close . . . I can touch it with my fingertips.

Bear kicked me. I have a bruise, it's swollen & it hurts. Charity dinner was a hit. Ian is good to me. We got a new greenhouse; the truck driver took a branch out with his cab. My head feels heavy. I love winter squashes. And green, leafy things. I hate this toothpaste. I need to make time to write thank-yous to many people. I need to make time for people.

THE CHARITY DINNER ALLUDES TO A BRIEF GLIMPSE INTO MY pre-farm life. I had donated a private dinner for eight to an annual gala put on by the Syracuse University basketball coach. It was my second time contributing, and that year the couple who won the prize lived just a few miles from the farm, in a twist of convenient serendipity. I did all the prep work, and Ian helped me execute, plate, and serve the meal in their home. I had pitched the dinner as a celebration of seasonal harvest, and made roasted chicken. I broiled the wings with maple syrup and served them as an appetizer, along with steamed vegetables and a garlic aioli, mashed parsnip and celeriac with fresh herbs, a toasted kasha salad with bitter greens, and, for dessert, a classic gingerbread cake with poached figs and cinnamon cream that I had agitated into a slightly thick cloud.

As the guests lingered over coffee, Ian and I soaped up the dishes. We were both quiet, and I felt a sense of pride. I missed cooking in a more formal setting, I realized, for people who considered an elaborate meal to be a treat, and not pretentious. I had enjoyed arranging food on a plate and presenting it, and I longed for the chance to thoughtfully compose a meal from start to finish and spend days, instead of hours, preparing it. I thought of Ian's and my earlier discussion about pop-up farm dinners, and I wondered if I might institute something like that at Stonehill. There had to be a better way to tie in who I had been with who I was becoming.

As to Bear kicking me, well, that happened, too, and it hurt a lot. Logan and I were retrieving him and the other horses from their paddock adjacent to the vegetable field one morning when it happened. I'm still unsure as to how it occurred—apart from me not being cautious, that is—but thankfully I was facing away from the horses, so when Bear wound up and made contact with me, it was on the fattest part of my calf, rather than square on my shin. The blow was so intense that I immediately fell to the ground, letting the lead lines slip from my hands as both he and Duke galloped off in the opposite direction, thankfully still in their paddock. At the time, Logan was gathering Pat and Pearl, and Lara was moving the beef to fresh pasture. Neither one saw the kick happen, but both saw me go down and came rushing over to check if I was all right.

"I'm okay," I said, gasping for air in short, shallow breaths. "I just need to sit down."

"Do you want me to bring in all four horses?" Logan asked generously.

I felt stubborn. Surely, saying yes would reveal something flawed about my character. "No. I want to do it, but I need a minute." A minute turned into seven; finally my breathing normalized and I was able to stand. I walked Duke and Bear back to their stalls with a limp, and I realized at once that I was very lucky that he had only gotten my calf, and that I would certainly have quite a bruise to show off.

ON WEDNESDAYS AND THURSDAYS IN SEPTEMBER, ONCE MORNING chores were completed and breakfast was consumed, any extra hands we could glean from other jobs worked on the arduous task of harvesting. So much produce came in from the field: lettuces and other greens, root vegetables, herbs, gritty leeks with long graceful necks, squash, peppers, and tomatoes, plus melons, if you were lucky, which we sometimes were, with both watermelons and cantaloupe-type ones. My favorite, and a surprise treat for our members, was the Peace, a variety with juicy flesh just like a watermelon, except for the fact that it was buttercup yellow.

I spent less time in the field than most, typically harvesting enough to fill a garden cart's load, then wheeling it back across the street to my washing station, where I stayed put for the rest of the day, sticking my hands into the tubs of cold water that felt, depending on the day in September, gloriously cool or mercilessly chilly. On one particularly nice morning—sunny, but not too hot—as I swirled muddy spinach leaves around in their third tub of clean water (I finally understood the allure behind bagged designer lettuce that boasted being "triple washed"), I was feeling a bit sorry for myself again, isolated from the crew and alone with just my thoughts and NPR, when Lara rolled a cart piled high with celery into the barnyard. She stopped by the tub and plunged her arms in up to her elbows, lifting handfuls of spinach and swishing them around. They caught a glimmer of light and the water twinkled. "I could do this all day," she said with a dreamy sigh, and for the first time that month, I was thankful that I got to.

EARLY OCTOBER

As the tree line turned an intense shade of red, Ian's and my frenzied routine settled into something a little more relaxed. We still had plenty to do, from harvesting vegetables to processing sides of pork and beef, but something about the work seemed less urgent than it had just a month earlier, and we began allowing ourselves to wake up a little later. In the height of summer, Ian had set his alarm clock for 4:45 a.m., getting up to perform his stretching routine before ambling out the door. I followed shortly after, willing myself to ignore my excitement about the day and sleep just a little more.

But in October, we didn't set the alarm until five-thirty, or even six on some days. I still tended to wake up around five, and would turn over, watching Ian's chest rise and fall as he slept. When the radio switched on Ian would quickly silence it. He was wont to rise as soon as he woke, but that month we'd both burrow down into the covers, pulling each other close and kissing with our heads beneath the quilt.

"What does your day look like?" I'd say, and he'd tick off a to-do list before asking me the same question. I always answered in meals, rather than chores or tasks, hoping he'd be just as excited as I was about the prospect of half-moons of delicata squash drizzled in brown butter for breakfast, and thin minute beef steaks for lunch, seared quickly so they retained their pink interior. And then we'd kiss some more and pull one another even closer, tangling up the blankets until we realized how late it had gotten and admitted that we really should begin the day.

The day, as it happened, was largely spent harvesting storage crops. A year-round CSA has to provide food to its members even in the coldest months so it was imperative, especially since we didn't have a heated hoop house, that we store enough root crops to last us and our community through the darkest corners of winter. Unfortunately, our yields were coming up shorter than we'd hoped. We packed just four large bags of kohlrabi, and the celeriac situation didn't look much better. I began to tuck away creative ideas for beets and carrots, a chocolate beet cake sounding the most enticing, if the least practical.

We'd been harvesting summer leeks for weeks, and the fervor with which our CSA members snatched them up made me feel relieved that we had plenty of winter storage leeks to pull up from the ground. I always felt a smack of guilt when I had to utter the words "That's the last of it, sorry," and was pleased that I wouldn't have to break the bad news about leeks—for another few months, at least.

The first day of the leek harvest was a bitter cold Wednesday afternoon, and as Ian and I crouched in the field together, pulling them from the ground, I felt my fingers go from chilly to cold to numb. I hadn't yet purchased insulated pants or overalls, and worked in just my faded Levi's over knit tights, a tank top, thermal shirt, sweatshirt, and jacket. I crammed my hair into a hat that I pulled down over my ears, but every exposed part of my body felt the dropping temperature.

"Try not to get any mud on them," Ian said, then, glancing at the brown-streaked leeks I'd laid out next to me, waiting patiently for their roots to be lobbed off with one of the harvest knives. He noted my pained look and eye roll, then corrected his request: "Try for as little mud as possible. I don't remember leek harvest ever being this dirty at North." I gathered a bunch in my arms and walked them over to the growing pile by the cart. His features displayed a concerned look.

"Maybe because the soil is wet?" I offered. Their fat white bottoms were quite muddy, which wouldn't be a problem, but the soil had also sneakily worked itself into the folds and fronds of their dark green tops, which would prove a little trickier to clean.

"Hey," Ian said quietly, motioning with his knife toward the base of the hill behind the vegetable field. "Look."

"Oh," I said softly, watching Duke canter back and forth between the north and south ends of his paddock. Ian opened up each day's paddock, which was the area fenced in for grazing, each time he moved them to fresh pasture, and the horses were left with a large area, almost the full length of the vegetable field. Each time he neared the edge of the paddock, Duke turned on a dime, effortlessly reversing the direction of his body, never stopping, always carrying on. It looked as though he was running a race, and maybe Bear thought so as well, because he joined in then, galloping along with Duke, a bit clumsier, more ambling, but still majestic and strong in a very obvious way. "They look incredibly powerful," I observed.

"I wonder what he's feeling," Ian said, his eyes still on Duke. We both watched them take another few laps before turning back to the leeks. Ian breathed in deeply. "It must be amazing to be able to run that fast, to be that strong."

Although it was chilly, things were only going to get colder, and I knew that spending the time to wash vegetables now was preferable to attempting to scrub frozen mud away in January. The leek harvest took far longer than we had been expecting (those sorts of jobs always did), so we gave up for the day, carted a heavy load back to the barnyard, and debated what to do. Starting a washing and bagging session at five that night seemed unwise. It was already dark, and I had to make dinner for the crew, which had dwindled back down to our core group. Meals were quieter again, as the summer crew departed in stages. We sent Shae off with a dinner at which speeches were made, and on Amanda and Kayleigh's last day Toby drove into town early to pick up orange juice and doughnuts. Ethan left, taking his jars with him, and I had to say I was sad to see our countertops so empty.

Back at the barn, Lara and Ian debated what to do with the already-harvested leeks, before they finally decided to bunch all of the bushels together and then cover them with as many sheets as we could find, plus an enormous, heavy canvas that smelled like hay and musk.

"If they freeze," Ian said, considering the lumpy canvas, "it's probably not that big of a deal. They froze at North all the time. We'd take them out for distribution and they'd be completely hard. But no one ever complained."

I liked leeks more than any of the root vegetables. Ian asserted that you could use them as you would an onion, and he was right, but my favorite thing to do was slice them in half length-wise and broil them in butter, then drizzle them with a vinaigrette made with lots of mustard, black pepper, and apple cider vinegar. It was easy to eat two or three good-size leeks that way, and I always took an extra one for my plate so I could surprise Ian with it once everyone else had gone back for another round. "Hey, Ro, why don't you save food for me?" Toby asked once, to which I smiled sweetly and replied, matter-of-factly, "Because I'm not sleeping with you." Ian's ears turned red, but we all had a good laugh.

WHEN WE WEREN'T HARVESTING VEGETABLES, IAN WAS ADAMANT THAT the horses be worked as much as possible throughout the fall and winter—there was no sense in merely feeding them and letting them slip out of shape, after all, when you can get some perfectly good jobs done. Both Lara and I expressed interest in learning how to drive a team, and it seemed natural that Cliff teach her and Ian teach me.

I had been walking Duke and Bear in from pasture all summer, practicing holding their lead lines with just the right amount of pressure. I walked forward, a horse on either side of me, and I tried to keep both of them just behind my shoulders. They didn't lag often, and most days I found myself yanking on the rope and pleading, "Easy, easy, *easy*."

"You have to be assertive," Ian said over and over again as I struggled to make them react on my first command. "You're supposed to be telling them to do what you want, not asking them." I nodded. "You have to control them with your voice, because if something goes wrong, you're just not strong enough to stop them from doing something—physically, I mean. I'm not, either. No one really is." I rubbed my biceps with my palms and considered what "something going wrong" might look like. They were so sweet and loving in their stalls, lowering their big heads down to meet mine, letting me plant kisses on their noses, that I couldn't imagine a situation in which they became dangerous. But deep down, I knew better.

A few weeks later a construction crew arrived to renovate the old machine shop, gutting it completely while keeping the heart of it.

With the foreman, Clark, came his dog, a nervous and aggressive mutt who made Hank and Lizzie, Stonehill's dogs, look on warily. Ian and I were bringing the horses out to pasture for the afternoon, walking them down the lane to their paddock. Ian led in front, Pat and Pearl in either hand, and I trailed with Duke and Bear. Halfway down the path, I felt the lines tighten with tension in my hands, and seconds later, heard a loud, snapping bark. Clark's dog had followed us out from the barn and his presence had not gone unnoticed by the horses. Sandwiched between Duke and Bear and feeling them become increasingly agitated, I let the line go loose and yanked it back, hard. "EASY," I yelled, my voice as strong as I could make it. "Easy. Easy." I felt their hooves begin to prance and their bodies move closer to mine, and I suddenly understood that I could get trampled. I let go of the lines, feeling the rope slip out of my hands—just like that— and they bolted away to the left, away from the dog. Jack had been building a fence in the field and began to run after them. Wordlessly, Ian handed me Pat's and Pearl's lines and he ran, too. I watched helplessly, holding onto the girls, who were quiet and calm, and watched as Duke and Bear slowed to trots, then all but gave up and began grazing the lush, thick grass. I exhaled, only then realizing that I had been holding my breath. My entire body felt locked.

High-tensile fence bordered the pasture, so there wasn't much danger of the horses escaping the field and making for the fifty-miles-per-hour road, but that detail felt inconsequential. The fact of the matter was that I had lost control of two important, strong animals, and that it could have been a lot more dangerous—for everyone involved.

"It's okay," Ian said as we walked back to the barn to prep their stalls and sweep out the loose hay. "I mean, I want to understand what happened, but I also know that at some point, all you can do is let go. I get that. I'm glad you weren't hurt. I'm relieved." He sounded very tired.

I was tired, too. I considered the order of events. "I don't know, really, what happened. I guess I just wasn't as assertive as soon as I should have been. And that dog . . . "

"Yeah, the dog was bad. I'm going to talk to Clark about that." He quickly resorted back to teacher mode. "But is there anything you could have done differently?"

We entered the barn from the big garage door. "I could probably . . . no, could definitely have been more attentive to the environment before it even happened." I hung the halters on their nail hooks. "But I really thought I was. The dog took me by surprise as much as it did them."

Ian seemed frustrated. It was always a sore subject when the horses misbehaved. "Well, sometimes it's just shitty like this." He began to reach for Pat's water bucket, and I put my hand over his.

"Let me do this," I said. "I'll prep their stalls. I want to."

"Are you sure?"

"Yes." I was sure. I wanted a moment of quiet to reflect, to really consider his question—could I have done anything differently?—and to calm my nerves before roasting chickens and frying potatoes for the crew's dinner. Ian kissed my mouth briefly but kindly, then stalked off in the direction of the machine shop. The next day, and every one after that, Clark's dog was tied to a post in the truck barn, barking insistently at anyone who passed by.

I GOT BETTER AT CONTROLLING THE HORSES, BUT I FOUND THE NUANCE of actually driving them maddening. Whether they were hitched to a spring tine, a drag, or a disc—all pieces of equipment used for cultivating the fields—I struggled to keep it together, to anticipate the horses' movements and preemptively nip them, move in a logical pattern, not hit rocks, and, on top of all that, walk in *straight lines*. I just couldn't seem to do it.

"Maybe . . ." Ian started to say one afternoon after an hour of my zigs and zags over the soil. We were in the field closest to the stream and woods, bordering the western-most treeline, where we had tried to grow bitter greens—escarole and pan di zucchero—before deer nipped off all the heads. The cabbage was doing all right, and the summer squash flourished, but it had been, all in all, a devastating failure for the head lettuce we'd planted. "Maybe I should just be quiet and not say anything—let you drive for a few passes, and then we'll connect after that," Ian suggested. We were spring-tining, overturning the soil to ready it for planting, and walking behind the implement rather than driving; it should have been easier for me, but I still found it confusing and overwhelming.

"Yeah, maybe," I said, already doubting my abilities. "Let's give it a go." I walked the horses in a large figure-eight pattern, focusing so intently on keeping Duke's right side in line that I forgot to actually drive the team. It wasn't until Ian spoke up that I realized the team was pulling on the reins, and I was letting them.

"Okay, stop in maybe five seconds," he said, and I counted slowly before pulling the lines back and articulating my command. He laughed impatiently and shook his head. "First, I think we have different ways of counting time."

"What do you mean?" I gathered the lines in my left hand and used my right to wipe beads of sweat off my upper lip.

"Well, to me that was nine or ten seconds."

"Oh." There was a silence, and Duke tried to move ahead. "Easy," I said, yanking on the lines. He stopped.

"So how do you think that went?" Ian wanted to know.

"Um," I said. "I mean, I think I could have done better with being anticipatory. I feel like I'm good at correcting them, but . . ."

"Right," he said. "You should communicate what you want before they make the mistake. So you don't have to correct."

"I think it's just a lot to think about," I said, realizing that I was holding a fair amount of tension and frustration in my lower abdomen. I pushed my hips forward and tucked in my belly. I complained sometimes about the way my stomach protruded over my waistband, and he was convinced the problem was just in the way I stood. "Good posture is something you develop," he had said, adding, "I find it really attractive." When pressed by me on how he acquired it himself, he shrugged. "I guess I learned it through yoga, and just, I don't know, being conscious of it." I scrutinized and corrected myself in the bathroom mirror each night as we brushed our teeth.

My posture was noticeably poor after the last pass in the field. With my hands still tight around the lines, I stretched my shoulders and lengthened my neck. "But," I said, "I really do believe that the majority of this stuff becomes easier with time and practice. Like, I just have to keep doing it, and soon I won't have to think about what pattern I'm supposed to be walking in."

"Right," Ian said. "And maybe . . . " He thought for a moment. "Maybe you, Cliff, Lara, and I could switch once in a while. It might be helpful to have Cliff teach you."

"Yeah. Duke, *quit*." I smacked his rear with the line, a bit too timidly, but he got the message and stepped away from Bear, who seemed to be paying him no mind anyway.

"I know I could be more patient with you," Ian admitted. "I think that when you get upset, I slip into relationship mode and think of you as my girlfriend instead of my co-worker."

"Well, I *am* both," I said.

"Right, but not in this moment." I shifted my weight and was quiet. "Okay," he said. "Another few passes?" I sighed deeply and rolled my shoulders back as I tightened my grip around the lines.

"Sure."

LATE OCTOBER

After putting everything out on the table as the crew assembled for lunch, I started getting ready to head out. "There's roasted squash with garam masala, black bean soup with chiles and the rest of that chicken stock, plus some loose sausage I cooked up with sage." I felt a little guilty about leaving in the middle of the day—especially on a day when there was so much to do. Since it was Friday, Cliff would have to sit in for me at farmstand.

"If someone could wash the dishes when you're done . . ." I mumbled into the collar of my flannel shirt. It wasn't so much an official request as it was a belief that someone would, eventually, soap up and rinse off the plates, drinking jars, and silverware. If the sink got full enough, someone would do it.

Ian had grabbed his favorite bowl from the shelf and was about to ladle soup into it when I gave him a pleading look. He'd already held me tight that morning, stroking my hair and wishing me luck; there was no practical reason he should give me another send-off.

But I was nervous. We had been discussing birth control for months, and I had finally settled on the copper IUD. I was adamant I didn't want a hormonal form of control—"I'm crazy enough," I joked, and Ian laughed but also agreed—and although he still wrestled with doubt over his commitment to our relationship, we had been monogamous from the start and we didn't seem to be making any moves for the worse. After talking with a few women who had the device, it seemed like the right choice. "This is for both of us, obviously," I had said to him in the shower on the evening we'd finally said *yes*, thinking about how nice it'd feel to be a little freer, a little less worried. "But really, it's my decision."

"I know." Ian handed over the soap. "And I respect you for that."

"It hurt like hell," a friend warned. "But my boyfriend brought me tea in bed all weekend while I watched movies. So in that way it was kind of nice. It feels good to be pampered, you know?"

It did sound nice. Ian and I had planned to visit his parents in Lake Placid that weekend; I was excited to share him with just his family for three whole days, and couldn't wait to enjoy the foliage on the drive up.

Now, I nodded my head toward the door and fished my sweatshirt out of my cubby. I needed to take a shower before my appointment. I doubted the gynecologist would care if I was perfectly groomed, but I was never so cognizant of the scent of stale dairy and pig shit as when I left the farm. Ian followed me out. "What's up?"

I balled the grey zip-up hoodie into a wad and shoved my face into it. It smelled like hay. "I'm nervous," I said, rocking my body toward him.

He sighed and pulled a strained look. "I know. I wish I could go with you, but . . ." His gaze drifted out to the truck barn, where a broken cultivator sat. He had offered to fix it for a friend who farmed an hour away, but it had sat, untouched, for weeks.

"No, no," I said, dropping the sweatshirt to the ground and lightly pounding my fists on his chest. "I know you're busy. There's so much to do." I rested my head on his shoulder and waited for him to envelop me. "There's always too much to do," I said, finally giving up and wrapping my arms around his waist instead.

"You'll be fine," he said. "It'll be over before you know it." I looked up at him with an eye roll. *Oh, really?* "If anything happens—if you need anything—you know you can call me, Ro."

"I know," I said, but he looked anxious and I could tell that he was nervous about everything he had to accomplish before we left for his parents' place. "But you have a lot on your plate. I'll survive." I may have been hoping for a little coddling, but I couldn't help but admire his work ethic, the way he refused to relax until his to-do list was completely checked-off.

I ARRIVED AT THE DOCTOR'S OFFICE LATE AND RUSHED THROUGH MY paperwork. I just wanted to be in and out, to go home and pack and escape from Stonehill for the weekend. There never seemed to be enough time to do everything. Lara had once said, over the summer, that she tended to neglect her friendships until harvest is over, then pick back up with correspondence, emails, letters, and visits. But it was already mid-October, and, just like the month before, I couldn't seem to find the time to call my parents, let alone connect with long-lost girlfriends.

"How much, exactly, is this going to hurt?" I asked the doctor as she washed her hands. "And how long do I have to wait to have sex?"

She smiled gently. "Most people wait about five to seven days," she explained. "And it will hurt, quite a bit, but it's quick." I spread my legs apart, letting my heels rest in the stirrups. My thick woolen socks had a hole in the right big toe, and I felt embarrassed by it. "I'm going to numb you, first. That might be the worst part." A searing hot pain immediately shot through my body, as if an iron poker had been marinating in a campfire for a good half hour before being inserted into my vaginal canal.

"Ah, *fuck*," I said, squeezing my fists together and letting my nails dig into my palms. "Fuck," I repeated, a little quieter.

She smiled sympathetically. "Okay, now the actual device and we're done." I grimaced. It wasn't that I needed Ian to be there—I'd been through worse without him, and could certainly handle this on my own. But I couldn't help but feel a tinge of annoyance that he wasn't. This was for both of us, after all. I closed my eyes and pictured rust-red trees reflected on the lake. *Soon.*

"Okay! All done," my doctor said.

"Gah!" I said, shuddering. "What now?"

"A lot of women experience cramping and discomfort for a few days, so take it easy. Do you have someone to drive you home?" I pulled at a loose thread on my faded cotton gown and avoided eye contact. "Really?" she asked. "Well, be careful."

The drive *was* difficult, and I grew frustrated that I was having such a hard time pushing through the physical pain with just my courage and gumption. Back at the farm, I packed hiking shoes, jeans, and a few cozy sweaters, before collapsing into bed where I stayed for an hour. I had told Cliff I'd probably be able to dive back into work after the procedure, but there was no way in hell I was going to sit in a drafty barn for the rest of the afternoon, selling radishes and potatoes at the farmstand. I felt a surge of guilt when I untangled myself from the quilt and peeked out the window. A glut of cars crowded the entrance of the barn. Cliff must be slammed. Maybe I could go relieve him for just a bit, I thought, but ultimately talked myself out of it.

By the time Ian put away the cultivator and tools, fed the horses and wrapped up for the day, my entire uterus felt inflamed. My abdominal muscles throbbed and my belly was swollen to twice its normal size. I changed out of my jeans and pulled on a pair of sweatpants with a more forgiving waistline. "How are you doing?" he asked, pulling his T-shirt off over his head and sliding out of his wool pants.

"Not so great," I said, situating my face into an apologetic mask. "I'm pretty bloated, and the cramping is . . . bad."

"Oh, Ro. I'm sorry," he said, standing over the bed in his tattered boxer shorts. "Can I do anything?"

"No, no," I repeated for the second time that day. "I think I'll live. Go get clean so we can get out of here."

"Okay," he said, and walked to the bathroom. I massaged my stomach in gentle circles to the sound of his crooning coming from the shower.

Things were better, gentler, kinder in the car—they always were once we left Stonehill. Despite my growing discomfort, I was happy to be away from the pressures and responsibilities of farm life. Ian relaxed into the mood, too.

"I feel pretty shitty, babe," I admitted.

"I'm sorry. Thank you for doing this," he said softly. This time, unclouded by the threat of animal chores and vegetable responsibilities, his concern seemed genuine. He reached his hand across the divide and grabbed mine. Our fingers intertwined and rested in my lap, his thumb casually rubbing my knuckle.

My smile was a cross between something sweet and a little sad. "Of course. I'll do anything for us," I said, testing the waters. His grip grew a little slack, but he didn't say anything. I pressed harder. "I love you."

"Love you, too," he said, and accelerated into the passing lane.

· · ·

WE ARRIVED AT LAKE PLACID LATE THAT NIGHT, AFTER HIS PARENTS had already gone to bed, and slept soundly. In the morning, he woke early to jump in the lake. "I don't think I'm in," I said, rubbing my foot against my calf, feeling the scratchy warmth of my ballet-pink legwarmers.

"You don't have to," he said, grabbing a towel and kissing my forehead. I snuggled deeper under the quilt and waited for him to come back, dripping wet and full of laughter.

"Let me cook you breakfast," he said when he returned. My heart swelled.

"Really? You don't have to."

"Yes, of course," he said, looking a little hurt. "I can do it."

I settled onto a step on the porch and pulled a blanket tighter around my shoulders. Outside felt a little chilly, but the sky already boasted a brilliant shade of blue and the hill across the way looked positively aglow with a mélange of orange, yellow, red. I sipped my coffee slowly and lit a cigarette. The tobacco rushed to my head and made me feel slightly dizzy.

The swelling in my belly had decreased significantly, and the fire between my legs had simmered down to glowing coals. The smell of paprika wafted from the kitchen, and I could hear the comforting clink and clang of pans being removed from their shelves and set on the stove top. I felt calmer than I had in ages as I gazed out at the old wooden swing and leaves littering the paved road.

Fifteen minutes later, Ian brought out two plates. Two fried eggs on his, one on mine, plus what looked like a hash of some sort.

"Mm," I said, sticking my nose closer to the food as he set it down in front of me. "It smells amazing. What is it?"

He explained how he'd cut potatoes in a small dice and sautéed them in butter, salt, pepper, paprika, and cumin before adding chopped celery and celery leaves. "I think next time I should put those in at the last minute." I picked up a leaf with my fork. It was crispy and singed, black around the edges. Popping it into my mouth, I shook my head.

"No, I actually think they're perfect as is," I said. He rolled his eyes, unconvinced.

I ate hungrily, and when I was done I gave him my plate to pile on a few more spoonfuls of potato. Something about the combination of flavors, or just the fact that he had cooked it, made this the best thing I'd eaten in weeks. After breakfast, we sat and talked with his mother, who was writing letters in the dining room. Ian updated her on all the farm goings-on, and I talked about a new writing project I had in the works: I was detailing a day in my life at Stonehill in a diary-style article for *Edible Finger Lakes*.

Later that morning, we met Ian's childhood friend Jamie for a hike. Jamie was renting a place on the lake for the summer, doing handyman work for a handful of wealthy clients. We climbed up a mountain with a breathtaking view of Lake Placid, stopping at the top to rest and catch our breath. A butterfly with either a hurt wing or little ambition flitted lazily from Ian's thumb to a rock to my knee and back again. We watched it for ten minutes, barely moving. I sat as still as I could, worried that the slightest movement would disturb it. I just wanted to make it feel safe.

On the walk back down, I picked up a few choice leaves, perfectly dried in brilliant hues of red. "Ooh!" I squealed. "These are perfect."

"Perfect for what?" Jamie wanted to know.

Ian rolled his eyes.

"I have this *thing*," I said, a twinkle in mine. "I collect the most beautiful fall leaves wherever I go."

"What do you do with them?" Jamie asked.

"Um," I blushed.

"Yeah, exactly," Ian said. "Right now, there's about twenty crusty leaves on my dresser at Stonehill."

"I'll find a place for them soon," I said, rubbing the biggest one between my thumb and forefinger.

We stopped at Jamie's lake house to check out the view from his deck. I set my leaf collection on his ottoman and stretched out on the floor, my eyes closed and hands resting on my stomach as he and Ian chatted about a girl he was seeing. "I don't know," I heard Jamie say as

I squeezed my eyes shut more tightly. "I just don't want what she wants. Marriage, kids, all that. And she's young, in her twenties. I told her that, and we decided that it's just not gonna work. But we can't seem to stop." I draped my forearm over my eyes. "I'll call her and invite her over for breakfast, like 'Hey, I'm making waffles; you wanna come over?' and she will and we'll have fucking great waffles and fucking incredible sex."

Ian laughed. "It sounds like it's working for you both right now." I bit my tongue, skeptical that she was finding it so breezy and relaxed. It's difficult when one person is more deeply invested than the other.

We walked back to Ian's car and stopped at a convenience store for a six-pack of hard cider. As I handed Ian a wad of bills to pay for half, Jamie gasped. "Oh, Ro, you forgot your leaves at my place."

"Meh," I said, a little disappointed, a small shrug in my shoulders.

"It's okay," Ian responded, counting out the bills and handing them to the cashier. "She really only likes the act of finding them." I frowned at his dismissal, but wondered if he was right.

That night, Ian and I lay together in bed, stuck together like two animals seeking warmth. He gently kissed the skin beneath my ear, swiping strands of hair away from my neck. I turned around and met his lips with mine. We kissed deeply, moving our bodies together until we had to stop or move forward.

"Is it okay?" he asked, setting his hand over my abdomen as I pulled off my underwear.

"I think so, yes," I said. It had been a little over a day. "Just be gentle?" I was tender and sore but thankful to receive him, reluctant to pass up this moment. Afterward, I let the stars blur into yellow-blue streaks of light across the black sky as my eyes closed. I felt comfortable, even if not entirely so.

SQUASH BISQUE WITH CANDIED SEEDS

Two types of squash make this soup special: classic butternut, and a colorful thin-skinned variety called delicata that's extra sweet and cooks quickly. The seeds are the best part, so don't discard them.

· SERVES EIGHT TO TEN ·

FOR THE SQUASH BISQUE:

3 tablespoons butter, divided

2 cups cubed delicata squash, skin left on and cut into ½-inch cubes

Salt and pepper

1 cup roughly chopped onion

1 tablespoon dried ground ginger

¼ teaspoon ground clove

1 cup roughly chopped carrot

1 cup roughly chopped celery

3 cups peeled, roughly chopped butternut squash

6 cups vegetable stock

⅓ cup cream

FOR THE CANDIED SEEDS:

3 tablespoons sugar

Pinch of salt

Reserved squash seeds from butternut and delicata squash

[CONTINUED]

Preheat the oven to 375°F.

Melt 1 tablespoon butter and pour it over the delicata squash cubes, then season well with salt and pepper to taste. Roast in the preheated oven, stirring once or twice, until soft and golden brown, 35 to 40 minutes. Reduce oven heat to its lowest temperature and keep warm.

Meanwhile, in a large pot heat the remaining butter over medium heat and add the onion, ginger, and clove, plus generous amounts of salt and pepper. Sauté until soft and translucent, 6 to 7 minutes. Add the carrot and celery and sauté until softened, 5 to 6 more minutes. Add the chopped butternut squash and cover with stock. Cover the pot and bring to a boil, then reduce to a lively simmer, stirring occasionally, until vegetables are very tender, 35 to 40 minutes.

Working in batches in a food processor or blender (or using an immersion blender directly in the pot), purée the soup until creamy and very smooth. Return to the pot, and stir in the cream. Gently reheat and season to taste.

To make the candied seeds, rinse the reserved seeds, removing any squash flesh. Spread them out on a kitchen towel and pat to dry.

In a heavy skillet, moisten the sugar and salt with a drizzle of water, just enough to make the sugar the texture of wet sand. Over medium-high heat, stir constantly until the water is almost entirely evaporated. At this point, you've almost made a caramel. Add in the seeds and continue to stir as the sugar turns from crystals into a liquid syrup. Immediately remove from the heat and spread on a nonstick or greased baking sheet. Let cool for a minute or two before breaking the seeds apart into bite-size pieces.

To serve, ladle soup into bowls and top with a few spoonfuls of roasted delicata squash and a few pieces of candied seeds.

SIMPLE MARINATED BEETS

My mother isn't fond of beets, so I rarely ate them growing up. What a treat it was to discover them as an adult! I grew bored, however, of the same old "orange, goat cheese, and walnuts" preparation and, on the farm, decided to take things on a slightly more savory route. The roasting time is a bit of a commitment, but I think it's worthwhile to cook them slowly and gently.

· SERVES FOUR TO SIX ·

8 to 10 beets, roughly the size of a baseball

4 cups water or vegetable stock

3 tablespoons sunflower seed oil

3 whole scallions, finely chopped

1 tablespoon finely chopped garlic

1 teaspoon finely grated horseradish root

Salt and pepper

Crème fraîche or plain yogurt

Preheat the oven to 375°F.

Rinse and scrub the beets under cold water, leaving the skins on. Cut off the tail of each beet and discard. Place the beets in a roasting pan and cover with the water or vegetable stock (water is certainly fine; I tend to have a great deal of vegetable stock on hand, so I use that for additional flavor). Cover tightly with foil, and place in the oven. Roast for 1½ hours, shaking the pan occasionally, until the beets are tender. To test, stick a paring knife into one and lift up. If the beet slides off easily, it's done. If not, it needs more time.

Remove the beets from the liquid and set in a bowl to cool. Once cool enough to handle, use an old kitchen towel (one you won't mind getting stained) to rub off their skins. They should slide off easily. Discard the skins, slice off the beet tops, and discard those, too.

[CONTINUED]

Cut the beets into quarters, or eighths if they are large, and place in a mixing bowl.

Drizzle the sunflower oil over the beets, along with the scallions, garlic, horseradish, salt, and black pepper. Toss to coat, and let sit at room temperature for one hour before serving.

To eat, top with crème fraîche or yogurt and more black pepper.

BUTTERNUT AND BROWNED BUTTER PIE

I wish I had the patience and precision of a trained baker—alas, my attention span is too short for such things. I love this recipe because it calls for a press-in crust: just mix together melted butter and flour, then smash it up the sides of the pan. I've been riffing on an old Bon Appétit *crust recipe for years, making some tweaks here and there—it's virtually foolproof. The filling is, I believe, creamier than pumpkin. Maple syrup stands in for sugar here, giving the finished tart more complexity and depth. I made this frequently at Stonehill, especially in the coldest winter months, when it served as a nice excuse to spend a little extra time in a warm kitchen.*

· SERVES EIGHT TO TEN ·

FOR THE FILLING:

3 cups peeled, cubed butternut squash

6 tablespoons butter, divided

Pinch of salt

¼ cup maple syrup

2 large eggs

¾ cup whole milk

½ teaspoon almond extract

FOR THE CRUST:

7 tablespoons (¾ stick plus 1 tablespoon) butter, melted

¼ cup maple syrup

1¼ cups whole wheat pastry flour

Pinch of salt

¼ teaspoon ground ginger

Preheat the oven to 375°F.

Place the squash on a rimmed baking sheet with 2 tablespoons butter, then place in the preheated oven. Once the butter has

[CONTINUED]

melted, stir to coat the squash with it and place it back in the oven. Bake 35 to 40 minutes, until the squash is tender.

Meanwhile, begin making the crust: Pour the 7 tablespoons of melted butter into a medium mixing bowl. Add ¼ cup maple syrup and whisk to combine. In a large bowl, blend together the pastry flour, salt, and ginger, then use a wooden spoon to stir in the butter and syrup mixture. The dough will be wet and greasy.

Using your fingers, press the dough into a 9-inch glass pie pan so it is uniform thickness and reaches slightly over the edges of the pan. Trim any shaggy edges, then use your thumb and forefinger to crimp the ends. Bake 18 minutes, until puffed and lightly golden. Remove from the oven and let cool slightly. Maintain oven temperature.

Once the squash is cooked, begin to assemble the filling. Melt 4 tablespoons butter in a skillet over medium heat, stirring occasionally, until the milk solids have begun to brown and smell nutty. Set aside to cool slightly. In the bowl of a food processor, combine the cooked squash, browned butter, ¼ cup maple syrup, eggs, milk, and almond extract. Purée to combine.

Spread the filling into the prepared crust, smoothing the top evenly. Lower the oven temperature to 350°F and bake 25 to 30 minutes, until the filling has just set. If the crust begins to brown too much, cover with aluminum foil. Let cool completely before serving.

PORK CHOPS WITH MUSTARD AND GREEN PEPPERCORN PAN SAUCE

I really love the balance of flavors in this dish—whole grain mustard and briny green peppercorns come together to cut through the richness of the pork chop. Bone-in chops, which were a real treat at Stonehill, work best here, and make for a stunning plate. I don't recommend cooking pork to a well-done temperature; a steady 140°F is much tastier. Using high-quality meat will yield better results.

· SERVES TWO ·

2 bone-in pork chops

2 tablespoons lard or oil with a high smoke point, such as grapeseed, divided

1 teaspoon ground mustard seed

Salt and pepper

2 medium shallots, halved and thinly sliced

Splash of dry white wine

⅓ cup pork or chicken stock

1 tablespoon whole grain mustard

1 teaspoon brined green peppercorns

Preheat the oven to 400°F.

Place a cast-iron or heavy pan over medium-high heat. Add 1 tablespoon lard or oil and let it heat up. Season the pork chops all over with the mustard seed and generous amounts of salt and pepper. Sear on both sides, 2 minutes per side.

Move the pork to a baking sheet and place in the preheated oven. Roast 5 to 8 minutes, until the internal temperature of the chops reaches 140°. Cooking time will vary based on the chops' thickness, so use a thermometer to be certain. Keep in mind that the chops will continue to cook for a few minutes after removing them from the oven. Let rest for 5 to 7 minutes before serving, so the juices can redistribute.

[CONTINUED]

Meanwhile, make the sauce. If the pan contains any burnt bits, add a splash of water and scrape at the bottom with a wooden spoon, then discard the bits and proceed as normal. If the pan drippings are *not* burnt (that's the goal here), go ahead and add the last tablespoon of fat and the shallots. Sauté over medium heat until softened, about 6 to 7 minutes. Add the wine and scrape at the bottom with a wooden spoon to dislodge any browned bits. Turn the heat to high and add the stock, mustard, and peppercorns. Stir vigorously to mix in completely. Let simmer until the sauce has thickened, about 3 to 4 minutes.

Eat immediately.

WINTER

NOVEMBER

After graduating from culinary school, I begged my family to let me take over the responsibility of cooking for major holidays. My mother is a very good baker, but does not really enjoy time spent over a saucepan and cutting board. She passed the torch, and I had been pulling together the menus for Christmas, Easter, and Thanksgiving ever since—but I liked the job best at Thanksgiving, when I could use my favorite baking spices with wild abandon. This year, my grandparents and great-uncle were coming to dinner, along with one of my father's colleagues who had become a close family friend. "Can I invite Ian?" I asked my mother on the phone one day in early November.

"Of course!" she answered immediately. "Of course. We'd love to have him." And, not missing a beat, "What about turkey?"

"We'll bring it," I replied. Logan's parents had raised a few birds this year and I'd already asked them if we could have one. In the years before Stonehill, my family always just roasted grocery store turkeys, but since joining the farm crew I refused to eat conventionally raised meat, and I knew that Ian preferred to avoid it, too. I felt uneasy about the way feedlot animals were raised and killed and, as a general rule, shied away from hormone- and antibiotic-heavy meat whenever possible. The turkey from Logan's parents was going to be more expensive than the average bird, but it'd be worth it. Plus, I surmised, it would taste a whole lot better.

Ian suggested we brine the turkey—he was still fantasizing about a moist, brined chicken that a friend of his had cooked while I was in Colorado—so the day before Thanksgiving I mixed together raw sugar and salt with a few handfuls of spices and brought it to a boil in a large pot. Once it cooled completely, we submerged the turkey, covered the pot with an ill-fitting lid, and stashed it in the butcher shop cooler. We also planned on bringing a few stalks of Brussels sprouts (despite Ian's worrisome prediction, the drought didn't annihilate our brassicas, although the heads of the Brussels were no bigger than my thumbnail), a couple of acorn squash, eggs, and a few jars of milk. I searched in the milk house fridge for the jars with the thickest creamline and packed them away in Ian's cooler, setting that beside our turkey.

We had offered to take care of farm chores that morning; Lara and Cliff said they'd do them in the evening. Ian and I woke early and decided to split up the work so we could finish faster. I opened the coop and fed the hens, then scooped out grain for the pigs and refilled their water troughs. Ian moved the beef cows and took care of the horses. When we met back in the farmhouse kitchen, he suggested a short ride around the farm on Duke and Bear. "I thought it'd be a nice way to start the holiday," he said, and I nodded enthusiastically as I worked the handle of the burr grinder in a circle to crush some coffee beans.

"Yeah, that's perfect," I said. "Duke just keeps getting better with practice." Ian had been training Duke to allow a rider, but Bear was already comfortable with the extra weight on his back; little seemed to ruffle his feathers. "Let's go right after breakfast," I said, turning the front burner on high as I unwrapped a package of sage-infused breakfast sausage.

Our quick ride turned into a leisurely tour around the entire farm, through the woods and back again. It was chilly outside, but with extra layers on under our jeans and vests, we were able to enjoy the sunshine, which was high and strong by the time we brought the horses back into their stalls. I snuck them a little extra hay when Ian wasn't looking, in honor of Thanksgiving.

WE ARRIVED AT MY PARENTS' HOUSE SHORTLY AFTER NOON, AND I laughed at the nervous look on everyone's faces. "It'll be fine, guys," I said, noting the clock. "We have plenty of time to cook." I was aware that most families had already been sweating away in the kitchen for hours, but, I reasoned, what fun was eating if you didn't have fun cooking? "Besides," I said, "our turkey is small. Dinner'll be ready by six; no problem."

I kept my word. We all sat down shortly after six and filled our glasses with a new bottle of the same Finger Lakes Meritage I had brought to the farm in March, a favorite of both my father and myself. The turkey's skin gleamed golden-brown, and the acorn squash, cut into thick slices, had been roasted until creamy-soft and then sprinkled all over with sage. We had smashed potatoes, a big green salad, and my mother's whole wheat pull-apart rolls, and I even whisked together gravy with the pan drippings from the turkey.

Conversation flowed easily and loudly, and we were all having a great time. Somewhere between a second helping of turkey and dessert, a billboard advertising a jeweler in downtown Syracuse was brought up: it featured a large engagement ring studded with diamonds, and the words, "Ask me!"

"Ugh," I said, setting the tines of my fork down on the rim of my plate. "It's so obnoxious. I would *never* want a big ring like that."

My father's friend chuckled good-naturedly and said, "Well, Ian?" Although Ian kept his head up, he didn't make eye contact with anyone and his neck was quite pink.

"Coffee?" I asked brightly, in an obvious attempt to change the subject. I knew it had been a lighthearted joke, but I was nervous that it had upset Ian. "Who wants coffee?"

Ian and I spent the night in my childhood room. The air in the house seemed hot, even though my parents kept it at sixty degrees from sundown to sunup. I cracked open a window and, out of habit, listened for the animals. All I heard was the distant howl of a coyote as a blast of cold evening air rushed in. I shivered and hopped into bed with Ian and asked if he had been upset by the comment at dinner. He said "no" and I chose to believe him. I burrowed in deeper and kissed his nose and said, "I am thankful for *you*."

"IF THERE'S ONE THING I LOVE," IAN SAID ONE MORNING IN LATE November, digging around in a box under his bed, "it's Christmas."

"Uh, yeah, I realized that," I said. "You started singing carols in June."

"September," he said with a devilish grin, and unearthed a few holiday-themed CDs. "I'll put these in my car. Hey—I forgot to ask." He shuffled the discs in his hands. "How did chores go this afternoon?"

I knew he was referring to the morning's debacle, which involved a frustrating lack of competence, or perhaps just common sense, on my part. The brood cows and steers were still out on pasture—it had snowed once or twice, but not enough to kill the grass and justify digging into the already-too-lean hay supply—and as such, part of the weekend's chores involved moving the cows to a new paddock, then draining, dragging, and refilling their 125-ton tubs of water. I knew how to do this, and how to do it well.

I had successfully turned off the fence's electric charge, opened the gate, and called every last cow through, emptied the tub and dragged it to the next paddock, then yanked the hose up to meet it—everything seemed to be going swimmingly until it came time to reconnect the hose to the tub. The nozzle that protruded from the rubber tank was still filled with frozen water from the cold night, and jamming the hose's connector into it proved utterly impossible. I tried for twenty minutes, sticking my finger into the nozzle in attempt to scrape at the ice, ramming the connector into it, hard, and generally making a fool of myself. The brood cows watched with a bored sort of amusement and I sat back on the ground, defeated.

Ian found me like this, with my knees splayed wide and my elbows resting on my thighs. He had come out—bareback on Duke to surprise me—to help with chores and to show me how much progress the horse had made since his rocky start this summer, when even being led around the barnyard was too much stimulation, too much to ask for.

I tried to explain to him what I thought had gone wrong.

Ian hopped off the horse's back and tied him to a nearby tree. "Well, the thing is that you didn't really do anything wrong." I looked at him incredulously. "You just tried to do it too soon. Once the sun really gets going, at about eleven or twelve, the ice will melt and you'll be able to connect the hose."

I glanced at my watch; it was a quarter to nine. "But I have a cooking class to teach in town at one," I said, bursting into tears.

"Yeah, I know. That's why," he spoke carefully, "it's better not to schedule anything when you're on chores. Usually they go off without a hitch, but if there is a problem, it's so much better to be able to work on it without a deadline."

He was right, but I was frustrated. I tossed my hands up in the air. "You're right, I know, but what do I do about it *today*?"

"Well, that's easy," he said, shifting his weight. "I'll help you today."

"Really?"

"Really. You go get ready for the class, and I'll come back out here in a few hours to connect the hoses."

"Are you sure? It's my responsibility, and I should figure out how to do it."

"Ro, short of bringing out a blowtorch—which you *could* do—the only solution is to wait until the sun melts the ice. And since you don't have time today, I'll help you. It's fine. I promise." I looked skeptical. "I want to."

"Ugh. Why do you put up with me?" I asked, holding the remote up to a line on the fence, turning on the charge. It took, and I tucked the device back into the tool belt, which I slung over my shoulder.

"Honestly, sometimes I don't know," he said with a wink and a grin. He was trying to make me feel better, but it didn't do much good. The morning's frustration, combined with an awareness that I was flaunting my insecurities, made me feel exposed, embarrassed, and worried.

"I know you hate this," I said, tears forming in my eyes. "I'm sorry."

"Hey, come here." He drew me closer and wrapped his arms around my back, squishing my arms and hands up against his chest. "I understand. Chores can be simple, and everything can go fine. But sometimes they don't, and that's frustrating. And it's cute that you're a crying little . . . bunny," he said, pulling back so he could look down at me. I smiled at the reference to my favorite animal, and he used the pad of his thumb to wipe away the streaks on both of my cheekbones. "I've gotten used to it."

"Thank you." I laughed a little and squeezed him tight. We set off in different directions, as I proceeded toward the laying hens and he went to fetch Duke from his post at the tree.

. . .

Back in our bedroom that evening, I wrapped my hands around the mug of tea I'd brought over from the farmhouse. It had acquired a chill on the walk over, and I held it tightly to extract any last bit of warmth. Ian asked again how the afternoon's chores had gone. "Oh, they were fine," I said. "And thank you again."

"Stop thanking me," he said, and then, "You're welcome. And the cooking class?"

"Oh, that was great. I always have so much fun with it." I had taught a lesson in braising beef shanks, then reducing the liquid down into a velvety sauce. I had food on my mind. "Let me make us dinner," I suggested. "I want to."

"You really don't mind?"

"Not . . ." I said, setting my mug down and climbing on top of him on the floor, positioning my knees on either side of his body, " . . . in the least." I kissed his nose, his right cheek and then his left, his forehead and chin, then finally, his mouth. "You're gonna love it."

I popped up and rummaged through the various-size jars we kept on a shelf in the guest room adjacent to ours. I had found the shelving unit, which had five tiers and was painted white, for twenty dollars at an antique shop downtown. We called it the "food shrine" in a nod to the way I fawned over the furnishing and what it contained. A string of small clear Christmas lights that I had woven around the legs cast a soft glow on the adzuki beans, the cornmeal, the petite French lentils. Nothing I saw particularly inspired me that evening, though, and I considered what might be found in the walk-in cooler and house refrigerator. Remembering a thawed package of ground beef I'd set out for lunch on Friday but never got around to cooking, I smiled. I knew just what to do.

"I'll be back," I said, pulling on my brown winter-weather bibs— I had finally purchased a pair—over my tights and legwarmers, yanking one of his winter hats, a knit cap, down over my head. "I love you."

He smiled with an incredible tenderness. "I love you, too, Ro."

I made a right in the barnyard, entering through the milk house where Hazel was cleaning the machine. Cliff had hand-milked when he started the farm, but after a year the herd had grown to six cows and there just wasn't enough time to do it all by hand, so he transitioned to machine milking. Hazel and I stopped and chatted for a while, about the cold snap and my frustration with the frozen hose.

"Oh, god, that's happened to me," Hazel said. "I get so pissed, like I'm out there crying and thinking 'Why won't this just fucking work?'" When she laughed, her nose scrunched up and her cheeks became tiny apples.

"Really?" I brightened a bit, relieved to know it wasn't just me.

I entered the parlor and slid open the once-white, now dirt-flecked door that led to the shop, closing it tightly behind me. Yanking on the string that turned on the bare bulb, I entered the walk-in cooler and rummaged through the plastic tubs and wooden bushels until I found what I was looking for: orange carrots; a few short, fat parsnips; and yellow storage onions, hearty and better-suited for a long winter than the young green variety. I packed them in the canvas bag I had bunched under one arm, and set off for the farmhouse.

The kitchen was empty, save a bread knife on the counter, the remnants of someone's snack on the prep table, and a sinkful of dishes. Typically, I would have pulled a face and immediately let the mess sour my mood, but tonight, I didn't mind. Tonight, I held tight to the fact that Christmas was coming, and that I was lucky to be celebrating it here, with Ian. I wiped the table clean, pulled out the package of beef, then rolled up my sleeves to tidy the space before I began cooking. Upstairs, I could hear strains of Van Morrison on Lara's record player, and I smiled to myself. "Oh, Domino . . ."

Once the dishes were done, I got to work on supper. I scrubbed the carrots and parsnips clean, not bothering to peel them before chopping them into one-inch rounds and then setting them to boil. I turned on the right front burner, hearing it click in quick succession before the flame caught, then spooned a bit of lard into one of the smaller cast-iron pans. As it heated, I chopped the onion and a little garlic for good measure. Into the pan they went, along with clove, allspice, and big pinches of salt and pepper.

I tested the root vegetables with a steak knife; the parsnip piece I speared slid easily back off the knife. I drained the roots and transferred them back to the pot to work them together with a potato masher, adding rivers of cream spooned from the top of a fresh jar of milk, and a few tablespoons of our precious salted butter. I browned the beef with some ginger and added in the last squeeze of a tube of tomato paste, along with beef stock, more salt, more pepper. I added the onions back in, then smoothed the parsnip and carrot mixture—a bright, sunny orange—over the top and I put it all in the oven to broil. I chuckled to myself as I thought about the first time I made shepherd's pie at Stonehill, that very first meal I cooked. Now that I had a better handle on the ingredients, this one looked much more promising.

While I cooked, I thought back to some of the meals we'd prepared and consumed over the past few months. Everyone kept saying that late fall and winter were the absolute worst for eating locally, and while I figured they were right, on some small level the foods I truly loved to eat were the roots in our storage cellar and the hardiest greens getting frosty in the field. It all looked good to me, at least from here. I grinned inwardly as I remembered the previous Sunday: I was pulling dinner together while Ian took a walk around the vegetable field to check on things. "Bring back kale, would you?" I asked. "I'll steam it with garlic and do a miso and sesame oil vinaigrette type thing. If you want." He did want, and promised to bring back enough for the two of us. He arrived in the kitchen forty-five minutes later, the tip of his nose pink and cold, his ears exposed. He held his cap behind his back, and when he deposited it on the table at my hands I saw that it was filled to the brim with Redbor kale leaves and stems. "I didn't want to use a bag," he had said righteously.

As the shepherd's pie came together under the heat, I packed up dishes for the night: two white plates with ridged edges went in the bottom of my grocery bag, and then I rummaged around for proper cutlery. There were a few forks I always avoided, with stubby tines and handles made of black plastic. I chose the two with the longest, most elegant handles and deepest prongs, along with two half-pint jars for the bottle of Finger Lakes Cabernet Franc Ian and I had picked up earlier that week. I also packed a lidded container for leftovers and pulled the skillet from the oven. Transferring the pie from the pan to a separate container seemed like so much work, and the whole thing offered such a striking presentation as it was, so after putting my overalls back on, I just wrapped the pan and its handle with a few more layers of towel and held it in my right hand as I hoisted the grocery bag over my left shoulder.

As I walked along the road from the farmhouse back to our room, I glanced out over the western field. The row of trees looked graceful and sparse in the cold night air, the brood cows and the steers quietly breathing, barely moving. If you didn't know they were still out to pasture, you'd surely miss them as you drove by. My breath escaped my lips in slow, measured puffs; I watched it rise and disperse a few times before heading back to the warmth of Beth's house.

I kicked my boots off on the porch, peeled off the overalls and hung them on a hook by the door, and stepped inside. "Hey, baby," I called as I climbed the stairs.

"Hey, hey, hey!" Ian poked his head around the door frame. "Hey, you've gotta give me a minute. I'm doing something"—he made a goofy face and paused for dramatic effect—"special."

"Ooh," I said, my voice rising upward in tone. "Well then I'll certainly wait." The simple woven chair outside our room was gone, a tumbleweed of dust bunnies in its place. They seemed to have gathered from the middle of the hallway, a sort of no-man's-land that lay between our bedroom and the bathroom. I made a mental note to give it a sweep soon.

From the bedroom, I heard the faint strain of music. "Can I come in?" I asked teasingly. He answered by opening the door a crack and motioning for me. "Oh!" I gasped, my heart swelling and my eyes quickly filling with tears.

"Oh, Ro," Ian said, taking the pan from my hands, leaving them free to fly to my mouth. "I just thought it would be nice to do something like this," he said. "To not eat on the bed." He was being modest, but I could tell he was pleased. I was pleased, too.

He had taken away the piles of paper, books, and binders that typically resided on the writing desk—where he stowed them, I wasn't quite sure, nor did I care—and moved it to the center of the room, in front of one of the big windows that looked out over the machine shop, truck barn, and laying hens' mobile coop. Two chairs sat situated so we could look out at the snow that had just begun falling. The miniature faux evergreen my mother had insisted we take home at Thanksgiving sat in a stand on a chest next to the bed, and though I was initially skeptical about the prospect of a fake tree, I had to admit it looked handsome with tiny white lights poking out from its manicured branches. My laptop lay open on the floor, playing Ella Fitzgerald and Bing Crosby carols, and candles perched precariously on every ledge. A small desk lamp lit the room in a soft glow, its shade wrapped with a reddish-hued scarf Ian sometimes wore tied jauntily around his neck.

"It's beautiful," I said, meaning it completely. A flash of insecurity passed through my mind—*Is this for me, or for Christmas?*—but I waved it away and set the plates on the table, then unpacked the silverware and glasses.

We sat down and clinked jars, the thick glass making a satisfying sound as it connected. An instrumental version of "Christmas Time Is Here" began to play, and I set my elbow on the table, cradling my chin in my hand as I smiled at Ian. "Thank you." If I squinted my eyes, the candles on the windowsill behind him looked just like stars, and the snow was starting to stick on the pane.

"Thank you for cooking," he said as he used a fork to scoop ground beef from the casserole.

"Oh, shoot. I forgot a serving spoon. I'm so sorry."

"Eh, don't need it."

We didn't, really, so I didn't let my mind linger on it for long. I brought a forkful of shepherd's pie to my lips, testing it tentatively. The walk over had cooled it efficiently, so I took a zealous bite. The acidity of the tomatoes and sharpness of the ginger tempered the sweetness of the carrots and parsnips, and it all went very well with the fatty ground beef. "Oh, god," I said, my mouth full. "I don't want to toot my own horn"—I took a moment to raise a flirtatious eyebrow at Ian—"but this is delicious."

Ian chewed thoughtfully. "It is. It's real good, Ro." And I beamed, the wine already turning my neck pink. After dinner, we sat at the table, pouring out another glass, and then another half one, talking about farming and food and hard work and the holiday cheer we were already feeling. We fell asleep that night with my head on his chest, my toes between his legs, the music still playing quietly. The tree stayed lit all night, a beacon of comfort and warmth.

DECEMBER

The freezers in the barn were packed with lard, leaving no room for the actual meat from the pig Jack had just butchered. "The lard has to get rendered this week," he said during a Monday breakfast in December. "Will you have time to do it?"

"Sure," I said eagerly, thrilled to spend a day working on one of my favorite farm projects. I could get at least twenty-five dozen eggs washed, too, and do a little cleaning in the distribution space. "I can, definitely."

After the spring's lard debacle, Jack had walked me through the process in August, checking periodically to make sure I hadn't burned or scorched it as it melted slowly, explaining how to compress the cracklings in an ancient contraption meant to extract as much fat as possible. The project took an entire day, and produced two batches: leaf lard and back fat. Leaf lard, I learned, was rendered from the internal fat around the pig's kidneys, and when treated carefully, came out scentless and milky white, with a mild taste. Back fat was rendered from, well, the external fat from the pig's back, and tasted much more aggressive, more "animal" than the leaf lard. Our members clamored after the leaf, using it largely for piecrusts, but I lusted after the back fat, using it for everything from frying potatoes to rubbing down whole chickens. We stored the lard in quart jars, which were a precious commodity that required a keen eye and patient hunt to find, or else enough savvy to part Cliff from his credit card and make a trip to the town hardware store.

So I knew the drill, and was ready to tackle the job. "I'll do it on Wednesday," I said.

"Great." Jack took a swig of coffee. "I'll take the fat out of the freezers today."

I GOT A LATE START ON THE PROJECT THAT WEDNESDAY, DETAINED BY a loaf of sourdough bread I had decided to bake, and a promise I'd made to Ian that I'd harness Duke and Bear. I had gotten better at the latter, having reduced the time it took me from fifteen minutes per horse to seven. I was nowhere near Ian's two or three, but then, I reasoned, I didn't have the same upper body strength.

Thankfully, Jack had run the fat through the meat grinder before he froze it that fall. Ground lard made for inferior cracklings but liquefied in a hot pot much more quickly. I rooted around in the granary for the fullest tank of propane I could find and carried it to the distribution space, where Jack had laid out the plastic bags of lard on one of the folding tables. I set the tank underneath the burner and got a mild fire burning. Slicing open the bag with a butcher's knife, I dropped the lard in the pot and watched it slide across the bottom, leaving a wet trail of fat in its wake. I repeated the process with three more bags before realizing I should let all of that melt before adding any more, lest the bottom layer burn before I could get to it with the long metal grill spatula that was moonlighting as a stirring spoon. Once I had a nice base of melted lard, I added the rest.

I set up my egg-washing station a few feet away from the lard and breathed in deeply. The air was already funky, and I could feel the smell permeating my hair, flannel scarf, and Carhartt vest. I had five buckets of eggs to wash, a happy sight after the disheartening amount the girls had been laying earlier that month. Despite the light rigged up to a timer and the drawbridge door we closed every night, it was far too chilly for them to lay with any sort of gusto. So Hillary—a volunteer with whom Toby would later fall in love and take back to Colorado—and I carted over huge sheets of plastic, gleaned from old billboards, to the greenhouse. We covered the wooden seeding flats as best we could, in hopes of protecting them from the flurry of dust and hay the hens would no doubt kick up. The first morning Hazel fed them in the greenhouse, she said that it looked like an odd sort of beach, with the hens splayed out luxuriously in the dirt. "I thought they were dead at first, honestly," she said. They were much happier and far warmer and, as thanks, began producing eggs once more.

But it was cold in the barn, and the wet eggs insisted on freezing to the wire-mesh draining table as soon as I deposited them there. I moved the whole thing closer to the lard and hoped that the heat emanating from the pot would encourage drying rather than the formation of ice chips on the clean eggs. Each time I dipped my hands into the bucket of hot water, I sighed with relief, immediately swearing upon removing them and exposing them to the frigid air. They had been permanently red and swollen since November, plus constantly chilled, to Ian's frustration each time I tried to caress his neck with my palm. "Christ, it's like you're the walking dead," he would say, leaping away from me in bed.

I was so focused on my egg project that somehow, despite the increasingly strong scent, I had forgotten about the lard. "Shit!" I said, jumping up and upsetting the table, toppling a few eggs onto the ground. Hank, Toby's dog, who had been lurking close by, came over and lapped up the raw yolks immediately. "Thanks buddy," I said, scratching the crown of his head. "Nice save."

As for my save, I hadn't gotten as lucky. There were bits of pork skin and fat stuck to the bottom of the pot, and it was starting to smell a little roasty. Uh-oh. I scraped at it, hoping to release it from the bottom, and bit at my lip nervously. It'd probably be fine. I hoped it'd be fine. I suddenly felt anxious about the task and thought back to the lard disaster in March. I wasn't being cautious enough and, as usual, was trying to tackle far too many tasks. Affixing a candy thermometer to the side of the pot, I told myself to check it in five minutes, and then set the alarm on my cell phone as a reminder. When it buzzed to alert me, I jumped up again and, in my anxiety, toppled the thermometer into the pot. It hit the bottom with a *clank* and I gulped. At my feet, Hank whimpered. I used the spatula to root around the bottom of the pot, in search of the thermometer that was surely being filled with melted fat. *Clink*— metal hit metal, and I brightened, coaxing the thermometer to the edge of the pot and trying to slide it up the side. I attempted this a half-dozen times before finally getting it to the surface, snatching at it with a grease-soaked hand towel. I rubbed away some of the residue from the face and squinted: 300 degrees. Well, shit. That was way too high. I killed the flame and sat back on my folding chair, irritated with myself and afraid to face Jack.

In the end, he was understanding, and we poured the majority of the batch into a heavy ceramic crock that we set next to the farmhouse stove and used for roasting vegetables and frying eggs. It all turned out all right, but after that, Jack and Hazel handled the lard-making.

In December, Ian and I traveled to Saratoga for "Friendsmas," a tradition he kept with his closest pals. Every year, they'd gather for a collaborative meal between Thanksgiving and Christmas, sharing their favorite foods and plenty of alcohol. By now I knew almost everyone who would be there, and I couldn't wait to make my seasonal cognac-chestnut soup.

We planned on leaving Friday directly after work, so during farmstand I packed our cooler with black radishes, butternut and delicata squash, two chickens, and a few half-gallons of milk, eggs, sausage, and bacon. *Our salary may be small potatoes*, I thought as I struggled to fit everything in the cooler and a wooden box, *but damn if we don't make up for it in goods.* As part of our compensation, we each received a share of the CSA, meaning officially that we could "take what we'd eat for the week," but since we ate most of our meals together, we all loaded our cars with edibles whenever we ventured off the farm. It was a perk that I was especially grateful for.

I had made lunch that day and set aside some extras for dinner in the car: roasted beets tossed in yogurt with balsamic vinegar, oil, and black pepper; plus a salad made with the chewy whole barley from our neighbors' grain farm. "Cover it with water the night before, bring it to a boil, turn it off, and soak it for at least eight hours before cooking it," Tanya explained. "It takes a lot more love than the barley you'd buy at the store. But"—she winked.—"I think it's a lot better." There was a not-insubstantial amount of hulls still in the mix, and while I loved the deeply nutty, roasted flavor, I did find myself picking at my teeth for hours after eating it.

Once Ian and I packed and cleaned up from farmstand, we jumped in the shower together. I hopped from foot to foot as he scrubbed his scalp with the rough pads of his fingers, eschewing, as always, shampoo. "Let me in!" I yelped, attempting to muscle him out from under the modest stream. "I'm cold."

"You're always cold," he said as we toweled off. I turned the wall-mounted heater on full blast. As far as I was concerned, this was the best part of the creaky old farmhouse. We may have seen the occasional mouse, and the windows might have been so thin that they shook with the faintest whisper of wind, but nowhere before had I encountered such a delicious source of aggressive heat.

"Fair," I said, turning around and bending over to let the hot air warm my naked backside. I bent a little too far. "Ouch!" I jumped forward, shocked by a sudden scorch on my ass. "What the fuck!" Ian started laughing, a deep belly guffaw that got even louder when I turned around to inspect the damage and revealed three throbbing red streaks imprinted on the middle of my right cheek.

WHEN WE ARRIVED IN SARATOGA, WE WERE IMMEDIATELY HANDED festive drinks—a vanilla porter for me, maple liqueur in cocoa for Ian. The party was just getting started, but Katelyn and Aaron were already at work in their small and cozy kitchen. They were married, and had recently purchased the house that they lived in with, at various times, Ian and their friends Brian, Jonah, and Marianna. It had been years since they all shacked up together, and when we arrived, Ian marveled at the size of a spruce tree in the front yard. "I remember when it was much, much smaller," he said.

"Yeah, well, we're thinking of cutting it down," Katelyn said, her voice full of apology. "It's hanging over the house, and could be dangerous if it falls . . . plus there's too much shade for anything to grow." Ian just clapped his hand onto the knotty trunk and shook his head. I could tell that he was much more upset than he was letting on.

Over the course of the next few hours, friends and friends of friends trickled in, bringing food to pass and share, bottles of alcohol to open. We had all agreed to make something, and the meal was starting to come together. For dishes composed from so many different brains, we all seemed to be on a similar wavelength. I had made my chestnut soup, scented faintly with cognac and nutmeg, plus a few simple garlic-stuffed roast chickens to carve tableside. We'd also brought flank steak, which Aaron grilled outside. Marianna brought a mélange of root vegetables, their middles soft and edges perfectly crisped, plus barely sweet ginger cookies that almost didn't make it to dessert. Katelyn's dish received the most rave reviews, a clean-tasting salad of pomegranate seeds, bite-size cubes of roasted butternut squash, and raw lacinato kale, massaged with salt and olive oil until tender. She blushed but received the praise happily, and I felt very lucky to be eating such a big meal, such a good meal, with such kind people. Ian sat to my right and Tyler, a friend with a great singing voice and the band to prove it, was to my left. "Here's to Friendsmas," everyone said in unison, raising their various pieces of glassware. "And to being here every year, no matter what." I crossed my fingers tightly under the table and hoped, with every fiber in my body, that I would be, too.

After the dishes were washed and the dining room returned to a slightly cleaner state, we all bundled up and set off for the short walk downtown. We were already a little drunk, and rolled cigarettes for the trip. "I can't do those," Marianna said, referring to Ian's sixty/forty blend of tobacco and herbs. "I have one drag and I'm like—whooo!" She inhaled from hers, noting that it was about twenty percent tobacco.

"I like the head rush," I said, taking the cigarette from Ian's outstretched hand. "It's so pleasant, in a naughty sort of way."

The rest of the night passed in a blur of more drinks, peppered with glasses of seltzer water with lime for me (I could never keep up, and somewhere along the way, had stopped trying), and a whirlwind tour of Saratoga's busiest bars. Everywhere we went, Ian seemed to know someone, and he was always met with loud shouts and enormous hugs as I stood to the side, proud to be with him. I waited through the small talk that ensued for a few minutes before finally extending my own hand and introducing myself. "Hi, I'm Rochelle." I'd glance at Ian, begging him not to make me lay claim on my title.

"Shit, I'm sorry," he'd dive in. "This is Rochelle." He rarely used the word "girlfriend," but did sometimes throw his arm around my shoulder and pull me in tighter to him. In the end, I shrugged off any indignation and figured that most people would probably make the assumption. *And besides,* I scolded myself, *why did I care so much that everyone knew?* I realized suddenly that because we spent so much of our time at Stonehill, where everyone *did* know, it had never really occurred to me to consider how we were supposed to interact off the farm. I admit that I considered a very large part of my identity to be Ian's partner, in farming and everywhere else. Dismissals like this came as a blow to my ego.

As the night wound down, I realized we had detached ourselves from the rest of the group. Although a few were still out, almost everyone had made their way home, and we decided it was time we do the same. As we approached Katelyn and Aaron's house, Ian's gait grew quicker. He seemed to forget that I was trailing behind him, attempting to keep up in my modestly high heels. I scampered after him, my boots making a clicking sound on the pavement. "Babe, babe!" I called. "Are you okay?"

He stopped in front of the big old spruce in our friends' yard, placing one hand on either side of the trunk and situating his cheek to meet it as well. He started to cry, great, deep sobs that frightened me. We had both drunk a lot, and after I caught up with him, I rubbed his back. I wondered if I should run inside for a glass of water.

"Ian," I tried again. "Are you okay?"

"This tree . . . this big, important tree, and it's just going to be cut down, like . . . " He paused to catch his breath and turn around, sliding his back down the trunk as he sank to the ground. "Like it doesn't even fucking matter!" He was crying so hard he was shaking.

I froze. I didn't know how to comfort him, or if that was even possible. I let a few minutes of silence pass between us. "Do you want to sit here, under it, for a while?" I finally offered.

"No." He wiped his nose on the sleeve of his flannel. "No, let's just go inside." He stood and took a few deep breaths, and then it was like nothing had happened. He walked stoically toward the door as I trailed behind him, tip-toeing between drifts of fresh, clean snow.

We didn't mention the interaction the next morning, just both held our throbbing heads and drank glass after glass of water before eagerly accepting the steaming mugs of coffee Katelyn handed us. We all sat on the couch and sipped as we ate leftovers for breakfast. I had a piece of pie and a dollop of plain yogurt, and the boys picked at everything from cold steak to cookies.

We hung around for the morning and the better part of the afternoon, nursing our hangovers with Christmas movies until Ian admitted that we should get moving if we wanted to make it back home by a reasonable time. We hugged Katelyn and Aaron good-bye and packed up the car. As Ian turned onto the highway, I kicked off my boots and drew my feet up under me on the seat. I reached for a blanket on the backseat and wrapped it around my shoulders. "You're pretty sad about that tree, hm?" I said, hinting at last night's scene. I wondered if he even remembered.

"Yeah, it's just shitty," he said. If he did remember, he wasn't going to talk about it.

"Totally shitty," I said, and pulled the blanket tighter.

IT WAS FINALLY TIME TO MOVE THE COWS TO THEIR WINTER PADDOCK. Although the ground wore only a dusting of snow, the forecast called for much more that week, and I wasn't the only one getting frustrated with frozen hose attachments anymore. In preparation for the move, Jack had built fences for two large pens, one for the breeding stock and another for the steers, just as he had in the summer, except that once they got to their new home, they wouldn't move until the ground thawed.

"Why is it called a sacrifice paddock?" I questioned Ian, finally mustering the courage to ask something I'd been wondering for eight months. The crew had referred to the dairy cows' and horses' winter homes as such throughout the summer, and I always nodded, sure of the location but oblivious to the meaning.

Ian looked surprised to be answering this question so late in the game. "They muck up the ground real bad," he said. "It turns into just a total mess of mud and slush. So instead of using it for pasture or hay, you're sacrificing it for a winter space."

"Oh," I said, laughing in spite of myself. "I thought . . ."

"What, you thought we did ritualistic animal sacrifice?"

I shrugged. "Who knows what kind of weird shit you guys were doing before I got here?"

Because the cows had to move across the road to reach their new paddock, Jack and Hazel had constructed an elaborate laneway out of polywire for them to move through. Two reels were hung patiently on fence posts by the gravel parking lot, to be unrolled at the last moment.

I liked moving the cows. Like chicken slaughter or vegetable transplants, it was an all-farm operation, and it was fun to work together with everyone, if only for a few minutes. Nicole, a friend and dairy farmer who was visiting for the week and staying in mine and Ian's guest bedroom, offered to help, too. Jack assigned roles, giving Nicole and I the job of running along the outside of the fence as the cows moved through it—we just had to make certain none slipped out and onto the road as Jack pushed them from behind and Hazel led the brigade from the front.

"Ooh, we have the best job," Nicole said, clapping her hands together both to generate warmth and express excitement. I did the same.

"I know!" I squealed, feeling particularly thankful to be working outside on a chilly but otherwise pleasant—and very bright—day. I danced in place, performing the running man and Nicole followed suit before we both dissolved into giggles on the side of the road.

"Hey," Jack called. "Can you guys pay attention? I'd like to get this done before lunch." I apologized and we nodded, straightening up and waiting for his signal. Toby and Hillary stretched the fence across the road and waved up to Lara, who was at the top of the hill, pausing cars until the animals were all across. The cows snapped to attention quickly, conditioned to associate Jack and forward movement with fresh, new pasture. Nicole and I began jogging alongside, keeping an eye on the smallest steers, as they were the most likely to slip under the polywire. Taur, the bull, had been slaughtered a few weeks prior, having grown too aggressive for Jack's liking. It took four people, a neighbor's tractor, and an entire morning to move his quarters to the hooks in the walk-in cooler. I hadn't been involved in the process, but I did pass by the barnyard shortly after Taur had been killed and transported to the barn, pausing to study a trail of bright red blood that speckled the snow from the milk house all the way around the corner.

The move went off without a hitch. As soon as the cows were in their paddocks, Jack and Hazel set to work reeling up the hundreds of feet of electric fencing that they had set up that morning. "Don't turn the fence back on," Hazel reminded everyone, nodding her head toward the yellow plastic handle at the gate to the laneway. "I'll get it when I'm done here." I shivered. I had only been shocked once, and that was more than enough to remind me to be cautious. It had been late summer, and I was hauling a load of compost out to the steaming pile. Lazily, I assumed the fence was off—as though the extra five seconds it would have taken to check were too much to spare—and grabbed the wire with my fist as I began to lift it over my head and duck under it. That would have been a nasty enough shock, but I happened to also be holding the metal handle of the garden cart with my other hand, and was blasted so badly that I threw down the fence and shoved my fist in my mouth, biting down hard and muttering muffled obscenities.

"Got it," I said to Hazel, and walked off toward the distribution space to grab some meat from the freezer for lunch.

THE COWS WERE HAPPY IN THEIR NEW HOME, BUT THEY WERE ALSO hungry, and let us know it. Every morning they mooed and groaned at everyone who passed their way, demanding that their needs be met in a timely fashion. "Oh, shut *up!*" I snapped more than once when I walked by, perpetually frozen, en route to the horse barn to harness Duke and Bear. "I'd like some fucking arugula, too, but that's not what we signed up for."

All things considered, caring for the cows wasn't a chore I particularly enjoyed. But it was December in the country; it had to be done if we wanted to eat, which we did. *Besides,* I tried to remind myself, picking hayseeds from my blue knit cap, *what else was I going to do with my time?*

The top loft of the barn where Beth kept her horses was filled with decades-old hay, and Cliff told her we'd be happy to clear it out when winter got underway. A taxing chore, it peppered our days for a few weeks. We all wore surgical masks to protect our noses and mouths, but still we breathed in air that quickly agitated into a flurry of moldy hay. We tossed full bales out the window onto a wagon waiting below, and used pitchforks to move loose hay and broken bales. It was a physical job, and although I complained about the dust and the way my eyes itched and watered, it did feel good to peel off layers of clothing and sweat a little. Because when we weren't forking hay, we were tromping through snow to feed the pigs, carting over two dozen bales of hay out to the beef cows, or using a blowtorch to unfreeze the hoses so we could fill the animals' water buckets and troughs. There was little to do in the way of vegetables but dream, so Lara, who was going to take over the position of vegetable manager the next year as Ian transitioned into a greater role with the horses, pored over seed catalogues and called out new varieties of seeds. "Daikon?" she'd ask over breakfast, some of us nodding. "Husk cherry? Radicchio?"

Winter wasn't boring, but it was cold, and the lead up to the holiday season felt a little unsatisfying. I was used to passing the month of December with my nights beside a big fir decked out with heirloom ornaments and a fireplace crackling in the corner. So coming home to the drafty bedroom each night seemed a little lackluster to me. To compensate for the dearth of Christmas cheer we had grasped so fleetingly in November, we listened to carols every night and I gazed longingly at our little tree, staring so hard that the lights blurred into creamy white streaks.

IAN AND I TRAVELED UP NORTH AT THE END OF THE MONTH TO SPEND Christmas with his family. "Are you sure you're okay with this?" he asked. "I know we did Thanksgiving with yours, but . . ." His voice trailed off. "It's not really equal or, you know, fair."

I grinned at him as we took off down the road, my car stuffed with coolers of meat, vegetables, and eggs; bags of clothes and spare pairs of boots in the back. "Honestly, I am very okay with it. I *want* to spend the holiday with your family. I haven't spoken with your mom since we visited this October. And—" I pulled out a pint jar of kraut and unscrewed the top, stuck in a fork, and passed it to him. He wedged it between his legs and kept driving. "I know how important Christmas is to you. I want to be able to give you the gift of being with your family for it." I cracked open a container of brown rice and scooped a spoonful into my mouth. "And we'll be fair about it, I'm sure. Next year, we can do Christmas with mine." He nodded and ate a bite of cabbage.

We drove around the state, visiting friends for a week before heading north. Cliff and Lara planned on spending the majority of the holiday at home, as did Jack and Hazel, so the crew assured us it'd be all right if we took a vacation. We were both excited to spend a stretch of time off the farm. It was always funny, Ian said and I agreed, how quickly you can assimilate into "real life" when you get away from the barnyard.

We stopped in New York City to visit his friends and have brunch at a new restaurant, whose chef I knew from my days as a cook in the city. I had worked with him during a brief stint in corporate catering, and I was heartened to see he had taken his talent to a new level: His restaurant sourced local produce, and everything was homemade. It was just the type of restaurant I would want to open, I thought, if I ever did. Then we took a detour to Massachusetts to see Jonah and Marianna at their home in the woods. They made dinner—braised beef shanks, simmered with root vegetables and pulled from the bone, stirred into a luscious, thick sauce. We ate bowls of it in front of their wood-burning stove with assorted olives that Ian and I purchased in town, and had adzuki bean pudding for dessert. "Oh, this was really nothing," Marianna said as we dipped our spoons into our bowls. "Literally, we barely did a thing to it," but it was rich and sweet and creamy and perfect all the same.

The next morning, Jonah and I pulled together loaves of spelt and wheat bread with flakes of rolled oats on top, then he and Marianna set off for an afternoon of yoga. Ian and I luxuriated in the bath after they left, taking our time getting clean before heading into town to do our Christmas shopping. The hot water grew lukewarm in the claw-footed tub as I rubbed his back with orange-scented soap, watching as it slid down his shoulders in hazy pools. "Citrus always makes me feel more Christmas-y," I said, cupping water in my hands and letting it run down his back. "Clementines in stockings, and orange peel candied with sugar and dipped in dark chocolate . . ."

We took turns shopping in town, one of us holding court at a pleasant little café while the other bustled about and looked for Christmas gifts. While Ian ran around, I wrote letters to family, tucking them into glittery Christmas cards, and drank smoky, acidic Sumatra. When it was my turn to buy things, I marched straight to a kitchenware store and picked up an Italian percolator for coffee. Ian had mentioned a while back that he would like one, but the real allure, I figured, was that anything other than our vat of farm coffee, crunchy with grounds, would be an improvement. "No one else bought this today, right?" I asked. "No tall blond man?" I wanted to be sure.

"Not a one," said the salesclerk, setting it in a bag and handing it across the counter.

I smiled broadly as Ian unwrapped the percolator on Christmas morning, and pulled his youngest niece onto my lap, kissing the top of her head and squeezing her tighter when she squealed. I liked his family, but didn't feel totally comfortable around them yet—like I had to earn their acceptance in the way I worked for Ian's. But his nieces and nephew were easy to please, and I had always loved kids. I tickled Paige's stomach until she squirmed her way out of my arms and dodged behind the chair, peeking out from behind it with laughter in her eyes. We sat on the floor in his parents' living room, with all three of his brothers and their families. I reached for my coffee mug and took a sip, admiring the vintage silver bracelet on my wrist that his sister-in-law had given me. I didn't have a real eye for jewelry, but this was just my style.

I had also gotten Ian an antique milking stool—for when he settled onto his own farm, but also as nice decoration in the interim—and a bottle of good sake with a hand-thrown ceramic decanter and two small cups in a shade of blue that reminded me of tropical water. "It's so much," he said on Christmas morning. "I'm worried that I didn't do enough." He paged through *The Old Man and the Sea*, one of a collection of gently used Hemingway novels I had picked up at a bookstore.

"You did perfectly." I meant it, and leaned over the wrapping and ribbons to kiss him quickly. "The teapot is perfect," I said, patting my new electric kettle. "And you *know* I love this." I flipped open the blade of my very own Leatherman multitool. "Now I won't have to borrow yours!" I was thrilled, and already thinking about the ease with which I'd slice open baling twine; how good it'd look tucked into my pocket. I vowed to keep it sharp.

"That's the whole idea," he said, and I laughed and stuck a bow on his forehead and laughed some more when he left it there.

The rest of the day was quiet. That afternoon, while Ian watched an animated movie with his nieces and nephew, I wrote a letter to Sasha on Christmas stationery. I told her all about how the lake looked in the winter sunlight and what we'd made for breakfast that morning, and for dinner the night before. As I sat, cross-legged on the bed in his mother's guest room, using a hardcover book as a writing surface on the mattress, I realized that I missed my family very much. I called them and they greeted me with so much warmth in their voices that I could almost imagine sitting around the fireplace with them.

"We're having a beautiful day here, too," I said. "Ian and I built a smoker out of old cinder blocks in the backyard, and we're smoking a ham from Stonehill."

"Oh, baby!" my dad said. "I wish you were here. And that ham was, too." We spoke for a few minutes more before saying good-bye. I did wish I was there, or else that Ian was upstairs in the bedroom with me. I felt very lonely, and not Christmas-y at all. And then I remembered something Sasha had told me a few weeks earlier. "Yoga inversions are good for when you're feeling sad," she had said, and while it might have been true, I had never noticed. I unfurled the extra mat I had packed and hoisted myself up into a shoulder stand.

I stayed there for a few minutes, fighting back tears, when Ian came in.

"What are you doing? Is everything okay?" he asked, closing the door behind him.

"Yeah, shoulder stands make you feel less sad," I said matter-of-factly.

"How's that working out for you?" he said, and I rolled onto my side before sitting up.

"Not so great, obviously." I took a deep breath. "I think I just miss my family. You know, home."

Ian shifted his weight before sitting down on the mat next to me. He rubbed my back, but when I rested my head into his chest, he stiffened a little. "I'm sorry you're not really feeling like home here. I know it's tough. And I wish I could be more comforting, but . . . it's hard for me too, right now, to be totally sure and inclusive for you. You know . . ."

"Yeah, I know that. I guess I don't really even want to get into all that tonight. You probably don't, either?" He nodded. "I guess I'm just thinking about all of the traditions my family has this time of year, like how my sister and I still leave out cookies and milk for Santa—we laugh so hard the whole time—and I guess I'm just thinking about how close we all are."

"Do you wish you were there with them, instead?" he asked, and when I didn't answer, "Well, dinner will be ready soon, and that's something you can look forward to."

I thought about the roasted butternut squash and the ham, permeated with wood smoke, and I began to feel a little brighter, if not really festive.

Late that night, Ian and I took a walk together, down the quiet road from his parents' home to the waterfront. We brushed the snow off the rocks that looked out over Lake Placid—a lot had accumulated throughout the day—and sat down, listening to the waves lap up against the dock before heading back toward the warmth of a full house and the promise of leftover butternut squash tart made with coarse pastry flour and ground almond.

As we walked down the road, Ian pushed me away from him by gently pressing on my bicep. "You keep bumping into me!" he said with a good-natured lilt to his voice. "You always have." I looked back behind us and chuckled, pointing at our footprints in the snow. His marched forward in a strict, straight line; mine looped lazily back and forth, making a pattern that looked like water in motion.

"Maybe that's why I have such a hard time driving the horses in a proper line," I said. "I can't even walk in one myself."

"Maybe," he said thoughtfully, really considering it.

"Or maybe," I said, "I just prefer not to."

AFTER CHRISTMAS, WE DECIDED TO TAKE A DETOUR ON OUR WAY BACK home. The farm my father grew up on—it was my uncle's farm, now—wasn't far from Lake Placid, all things considered, and it seemed silly not to visit.

The snow was falling heavily when we pulled in. "This must be the place," Ian said, turning on his turn signal as the covered barns came into view.

"This is the place!" I said, clapping my hands. "It looks so different from when we were younger and would visit. But it's still the Bilow Dairy Farm." The sun hadn't yet set, but it was a grey day and the landscape looked dark. "I like that," I said. "A straightforward name. No whimsy."

"You love whimsy," countered Ian. "You're the biggest whimsy lover of them all!"

"Yeah," I said, crossing my arms across my chest. "But I'm also fond of nostalgia."

My oldest cousin gave us a tour of the farm, taking us everywhere from the milking parlor—it operated twenty-four hours a day—to the office where he tracked their entire herd by computer. "About three thousand," he answered when Ian asked him how large the herd had grown, and nodded stoically when Ian let out a long whistle. They grew their own feed, just like we did, though they went with corn while we fed hay. There were, suffice it to say, a few major differences between our little farm and their large one, but we avoided any large philosophical discussions about it and then walked around a little more once my cousin went back to work.

"Here, look," I said, grabbing Ian's hand and pulling him around the corner of one of the oldest barns. "This was the old hay barn." My cousins and I used to coax the barn cats out for a cuddle, sometimes give concerts for our relatives up in the hay bales. "I have such happy memories of this place," I said, and Ian squeezed my hand twice before we moved on and made our way into the house to help my aunt prepare dinner.

Over pasta with tomato sauce, Italian bread, and lettuce salad, we all relaxed into each other's company. "So you guys really kill all your own animals right on the farm?" my uncle asked, cracking open a beer and passing it to Ian.

"Yeah, Jack'll do it right out in the field while they're grazing," he said, and took a swig of porter.

My uncle started laughing. "That's so *mean!*" he said. "To do it while they're out they're, all happy . . . " He kept chuckling to himself as he let the sentence drift off.

"I think it's actually kind of nice," Ian said. "There's minimal trauma, you know?" I swiped my bread around the plate, letting it become soggy with tomato.

"I don't know, man," my uncle said, but didn't bring it up again, not even when we broke into a jar of moonshine spiked with Maraschino cherries. The next morning, after fueling ourselves with strong black coffee, we drove back to Stonehill, navigating the snowy roads as we wound our way back down to Central New York. We took a day to unpack and visit our own cows in the barn, say hello to Bear and Duke, and reacquaint ourselves with the sensation of hard work and heavy lifting. The next night was New Year's Eve, and although we considered heading to a bar in town, we finally decided to stay put. As we toasted each other at midnight, knocking our half-pint jars together and letting cheap sparkling wine spill over the sides, I settled into the cozy knowledge that there was no place in the world, no other farm at all, where I would rather be.

EARLY JANUARY

One Saturday morning in early January, I woke around seven and luxuriated in bed for a few minutes. Neither Ian nor I had to work, and the promise of a full day stretched ahead of us. Our windows were old, thin, and cracked, letting a lot of cold in, but I jammed my feet into the space between the mattress and his calves and cozied up closer to him. I was warm enough. A tremendous snowstorm had dumped a fresh layer of powder over the entire farm the night before, and fat flakes were still lazily falling. My excitement about being back home had muted quickly, and I soon returned to grumbling about the snow that always seemed to find its way into my socks. "I could stay in bed with you all day," I whispered to Ian, my lips grazing his cheek.

I reached for him under the quilt, but he didn't accept my advance, jumping up instead and heading for the bathroom. By the time he came back, I had pulled on my legwarmers, yanking them up over my thighs, and cozied into a sweater of his that I particularly liked. It was heather grey, made of scratchy wool, with sleeves that hung down over my hands and a few rips in the right elbow. I thought it fit me perfectly, and I loved how the neckline hinted at my collarbone. As he stepped into his underwear I sat on the floor, my back against the bed, looking out at the snow. Something was wrong, and I was waiting.

He sank down next to me and sighed. I turned to him, my face pleading but a bit resigned. "You're still unsure," I offered.

"Ro, I don't understand this. You are such a good partner to me, and I want to be that for you. I hate that we're sitting here, that I'm unsure. I hate that. I want to be excited. I want to play in the fucking snow with you! We should be excited to go do that." His voice rose and grew angry in tone as he waved his hand toward the window.

"So why don't you?" I pulled my knees into my chest and wrapped my arms around my ankles. "Why don't you play in the snow with me? That's what *I* want—I want to play with you and enjoy the weather, and you. You have someone, right here, who loves you and wants to do that with you. Someone who wants to be good to you. I just . . ." My voice trailed off. I suddenly became frightened to assert myself. I shrugged my shoulders, raising my sweater-covered hands in a "fuck-if-I-know" gesture.

He was sitting cross-legged and draped his arms over his legs. "I can't. I don't know why, Ro, but I can't." I was quiet, waiting for him to continue. "I think I need to take some time. This isn't fair to you, and it isn't fair to me, either."

"Are you breaking up with me?" *Finally?* I thought but didn't say.

"I don't know."

I stared stoically out the window, terrified to look at him. It was only a matter of time before tears began forming at the corners of my eyes.

"I don't know what the right thing to do is." He genuinely looked confused.

"Don't leave me," I said, my voice cracking and becoming thick in my throat. I started to cry then, using the baseboard of the bed to steady my head. I was shaking.

"Ro, that isn't fair."

I lifted my eyes and sneered at him through the blurry wetness. "I don't think you are allowed to say that," I said.

"What if we're supposed to be great friends?" I cried harder. "What if, when everything dies down and we move on and stop hurting, what if we continue to be in each other's lives and it's great? I don't want you to miss that—I don't want to miss it either—just because we assumed we'd be something different. Because . . ." His voice got quieter. "Because you assumed we'd be together."

"Well, I can't. I can't just be your friend." My nose was running now, and I swiped at it with my wrist, leaving a streak along the sleeve of his sweater. "I love you, so damn much, and I have always just wanted to be with you." Words were coming quicker now. "Maybe it's easy for you to just be friends, to want that, but I can't. I actually *wanted* to be your partner."

"Don't make it sound like that," he said, his tone tinged with disappointment, defense. "I was a good partner to you; at times

I was really good. But I'm not ready to be real good to you for forever, and you deserve that."

"I was ready to give myself to a life with you, and you just broke my heart. . . ." I trailed off, looking out the window.

"Don't say that," he commanded again, the defensiveness giving way to something more like anger. "That's . . . " He paused, cognizant of the fact that he wasn't, really, in a position to be critical. "That's shitty for me—to hear that this all meant nothing, that I just broke your heart and that's it."

I didn't know what to say. I was angry; it seemed unfair for him to be thinking of his own pride, the integrity of his character at this point, and my petulant stare told him as much. He rubbed his biceps with his hands, his fingers running over the Timothy-hay tattoo that reached up toward his shoulder. I stared sadly at his skin, taut and tan, even in the January chill. I realized how much I would miss him if this was truly the end, considered the fact that I may never again trace my tongue along the grass's roots and up toward its seed head, and I grew very frightened.

"Don't leave me," I said again.

"I need to think about all of this. And I need to be in a space where I can." He stood up. I stayed on the floor. "I'm going to take today to do my own thing. Go into town, write some letters, just think about all of this."

"And we'll talk when you get back?"

"Yeah, but I want you to do your own thing today, too. Think about what you want, what would be good for you. I'll let you know when I'm making my way back." I stayed put as he pulled on pants and a flannel shirt that stretched tight across his chest, as he clipped his wallet onto his belt loop with the silver chain he always wore.

"I love you," I said, perhaps a bit selfishly, as he made his way toward the door.

He paused, looking back at me with his head cocked and his bottom lip stuck out. "I love you too, Ro," he said, and then he disappeared.

I did try to distract myself from my burgeoning fears. Driving would feel good, I decided, and dressed for the cold. I started my Honda, thankful for its hefty seasonal tires as I crunched over the snow, squeaky and clean—I would have gotten stuck if I hadn't been better prepared. I made a mental note to call my father and thank him; he had taught me how to put them on a few weeks before, patiently watching as I situated the jack under my car and wrestled with the lug wrench. I drove around town without any real goal or destination in mind. I drove and listened to "Skinny Love" and cried until I couldn't see the road and then pulled over on a side street in downtown Syracuse and cried some more. Eventually, the car made its way to the Westcott neighborhood, where Ian and I sometimes went for fair-trade coffee and vegan burritos. The vintage clothing shop across the street from the café caught my eye.

I spent the next hour browsing through silk gloves, trying on old hats set at jaunty angles, searching for something beautiful that would make me feel better. My fingers landed on a white lace dress with a deep scoop back and high neckline. The skirt gave way to a slight flare and both it and the bodice were lined with an opaque slip, but the arms, which ended just above my elbows, were just sheer lace. When I tried it on, the thin brown belt fell right at my natural waist. I spun in circles in front of the mirror, admiring the way the skirt flared and twirled. *Wherever will you wear it?* I asked myself out loud, imagining stacking hay bales in the dress with a pair of smart brown leather boots, and giggled in spite of myself. But it made me feel so feminine, such uncomplicated happiness, that I asked the cashier to wrap it up, and to throw in a pair of earrings with a leaf motif for good measure.

On the way home, I stopped by a wine shop and picked up a bottle of Gewürztraminer. The varietal had always been a favorite of mine, at once crisp and refreshing, spicy and warm. It would be just the thing on a cold day that needed a bit of coziness.

I arrived home a few minutes after five and found no sign of Ian. I checked my phone for messages, but had no new ones. The book I'd been devouring before bed each night proved too complicated and taxing to read. I considered calling my sister to talk, but the thought of explaining Ian's uncertainty—of articulating it aloud—seemed even more frustrating than replaying it in my head. I let a stream of the wine tumble into a jar and pulled a coloring book from my nightstand drawer. Sasha had sent it to me as a light-hearted joke, but I suddenly realized that the mindless simplicity of staying within the lines was just what I needed, that creativity within constraints would be more than a sufficient challenge tonight.

As I shaded pictures of unicorns and sipped the Gewürztraminer, I relented to Ian's advice and considered our relationship and what I wanted from it. If I was really honest, it frustrated and angered me that Ian had never returned the amount of dedication, certainty, and love that I offered him. *Surely I want that in kind from my partner,* I thought, choosing a lavender crayon for the unicorn's horn. *Surely I could find that from someone else.*

Somewhere underneath all of that, a small voice that sounded a bit like my own piped up. *Why are you even waiting? Isn't his uncertainty, at the end of it all, actually an answer?* I dropped that thought at the sound of a door downstairs jiggling open. Ian was home. I busied myself with the coloring book and tried to look nonchalant. My heart was racing, but when he opened the door, I counted to five and then looked up slowly, casually. "Hi," I said with a soft smile.

He returned both gestures.

"Did you have a good day? Did it help?" I asked, choosing a steel grey color from the box and continuing to draw in the book.

"It was. I mean, I did. It did. Are you *coloring*?"

I grinned and nodded.

"Oka-ay," he said, drawing out the syllables and raising an eyebrow.

"I bought a dress," I said, apropos of nothing. "Would you like to see it?" He said he would, and I brought it out, smoothing the shoulders over the wooden hanger.

"It is really beautiful," he said, his voice full of resignation. "You'll look real nice in it."

"Do you want to see? Shall I try it on?" I was reaching toward flirtation now.

"Well, sure," he said, and I pulled off my shirt in front of him, crossing my arms and gripping the hem as I yanked upward. "Ro!" His voice was full of mock indignation. I stepped out of my long underwear and into the dress, unhooking my bra and letting that slide off, too.

"See?" I said, lifting my hair and gathering it on the side of my neck. "There's no back."

"I see," he said, and I so badly wanted him to kiss the space between my collarbone and armpit. "Did you eat?" he asked.

"Dinner? No. Do you want me to make something for us?"

"It'll be too late to use the farmhouse," he said, checking his watch. "I don't want to bother Cliff and Lara. What about Ironwood?"

Ironwood was a wood-fired pizza place in a nearby town that, to my indignation, served a Caprese salad in December, but also offered an undeniably delicious pie with salty prosciutto and a mountain of arugula.

"Is that weird? Don't you think that's weird, for us to go out to eat together tonight?" I asked.

"Maybe, but we should embrace the awkward," he said. "I think that some of the best moments in life can be from times like these." I rolled my eyes and grabbed my coat, tying it tight at the waist and slipping on a pair of grey wool fingerless gloves.

"Whatever you say, but you're driving," I said, pouring more of my wine into the jar and screwing on a cap.

WE ARRIVED HOME LATE THAT NIGHT, MY FACE FLUSHED PINK FROM the Gewürztraminer, the Pinot Noir, and the forced heat of the restaurant and car vents. "You really do look pretty in that dress," Ian said as we pulled off our boots and hats.

"Don't leave me," I blurted out, then covered my mouth with my hand. He removed it and placed his lips on mine. "Make love to me," I amended my order. I ascended the staircase, wiggling my fingers behind me. He never took them, but he did follow.

"What does this mean?" I asked him afterward, as we lay in bed. I chewed on the inside of my cheek and added, in my head, *Does this mean you won't go?*

"I'm not ready to end our relationship now," he said, and I shifted uncomfortably.

"Help me understand."

"I mean that I want to try harder to figure it out. I want to . . . keep trying."

And I want to keep loving you, I thought. Instead, I said, "It was the dress, wasn't it?"

"Yes, it was the dress." He grazed his fingers over my bare ribs and I snuggled in closer to him.

I was warm and comfortable under our quilt, thankful to be resting my cheek on his chest, smooth and hot. I felt relieved that the end hadn't come, but as I watched the clock transition from midnight to one to two and then three o'clock, I was also cognizant that this was not sustainable.

LATE JANUARY

As far as I understood it, the Northeast Organic Farming Association's winter conference was an opportunity to socialize and see old friends who were, as you surely were, too busy to make the effort without an excuse. A three-day event that consisted of workshops, panels, guest speakers, and a dance on Saturday night, the NOFA conference was attended by everyone who was anyone in the world of small, local, and sustainable farming.

This year, Cliff and Ian had agreed to give a presentation about farming with draft power, and they had been working on perfecting their speech for weeks. They even brought a bale of hay—to demonstrate to curious farmers looking to ditch their tractors how much they could expect to lift every day, just in feeding their "equipment." The conference was expensive, but as presenters, Cliff and Ian were given free entry. Logan, Toby, and I volunteered to set up and break down the trade show before and after the presentation in exchange for passes.

"It seems silly to me," I said over a breakfast of scrambled eggs and buttery toast one morning. "Requiring farmers to pay so much to attend a conference when we make so little." I pressed my index finger into the bread, and butter oozed out. I stuck my finger in my mouth and shrugged. "Don't you think?"

No one said much; NOFA was the last thing on Stonehill's mind. The dairy cows' production had all but slowed to a crawl and the storage vegetable supply wasn't looking quite as plentiful as it had in November. We had bigger fish to fry and would, everyone said, worry about the conference when we got there. This year's event had the added benefit of being held in Saratoga. There was an element of familiarity about the whole thing for me—visits there were old hat, by now—and Ian was very excited about the excuse to see his childhood friends.

Somehow, the cows continued to produce milk and the vegetables didn't vanish overnight, and we all deemed the situation benign enough to leave for the weekend. Hazel and Jack agreed to stay home and keep things running.

I was drawn to the sessions that promised education on matters of nutrition, sustainability, and the intersection of community and agriculture. The rest of the farm crew attended workshops that, while the subjects may have interested me, seemed over my head. Ian headed off to attend classes with titles such as "Breeding Dairy Stock for Success," and I settled happily into my "Real Foods 101" courses. Saturday was a full day, and by the end of it, my brain felt ready to burst. I was beginning to understand that the majority of farmers who attended the conference already knew most of what was being presented—it was more an opportunity for networking, and to see old pals.

By the time we met up at the end of the afternoon, Ian had convinced a crew of farmer friends to come out dancing in Saratoga. Wearing thick dress pants and tired from a day of note-taking and first introductions, I was in need of a pick-me-up before I rallied. I tugged at his elbow. "You said we could go back to the hotel and freshen up before heading back out for the night," I reminded him. "Can you drive us back now?"

"Ehhh." He rocked back on his heels and scratched his head. "Oh, hey!" He waved to someone across the cafeteria and motioned for him to come our way. "I just don't want to leave now—there's all this momentum and I'm having fun. I really don't want to leave."

"Okay," I said, "but I really do."

"I'll take you," Toby said, pulling on his jacket. "I want to go back and grab a smoke."

"Really?" both Ian and I asked at the same time. "That's so nice of you. Are you sure?" I pressed.

"Yeah, ain't no thing," he said. "I want to go, too."

He drove me back to the hotel where I showered and changed into a slim black tank top and chartreuse cardigan, put on a pair of earrings, applied a little makeup, and felt immensely, immediately better. Toby and I chatted by the car before returning.

"I think it's good," I said, "that I left Ian to freshen up. I don't think it's healthy to be so . . . accommodating, to do whatever he wants to."

"Yeah," Toby replied. "I mean, to be totally honest, guys don't really like that in general. It's better to be with someone who's like 'Oh, I'm gonna go do this thing because I want to, and not worry about what you think or make you entertain me.'"

I furrowed my brow. "Do you think I do that with Ian?"

"You know I love you, Ro," Toby said, grinning through the darkness, but not answering the question in the end. I punched his arm, and we traveled back together to meet up with the rest of the crew.

Our first stop that night was a dive bar that smelled like draft beer and wet wood. I ordered a whiskey and ginger ale and leaned back on the bar to observe the crowd. I watched as Ian introduced his childhood friends to his farming brethren, and I engaged in conversation when brought into it. I wasn't particularly enjoying myself, but I wasn't having a bad time, either. It occurred to me, as I crunched my teeth down on the ice from the bottom of my glass, that I would rather be farming or, surprisingly, writing—that I would rather not be there.

As the mood of the evening transitioned, so did the location. We found ourselves in a busy club with a cover charge, struggling to hear one another over the heavy bass. We took over the dance floor, laughing as women in miniskirts and short dresses handed money to the DJ in exchange for the right to dance on top of the speakers, and we all drank a lot—a lot more than we usually did.

The night ended, eventually, with a brisk walk back to the hotel. It was twenty degrees, and we had a mile to trek, but the air felt good. I talked with Adam, a farmer with an aquaponic greens and tilapia farm in Central New York, about transitioning from being vegan to meat eaters, and he told me what it was like to harvest fish, and how much better whole ones tasted than fillets. Sweaty and hot, smelly and tired, we all tumbled back into our hotel room. Nicole had brought brownies in a crinkled foil package, and everyone snacked on them as we sat on the beds and floor, laughing about the night.

"Every time I smelled cologne," I said, licking fudgy chocolate from my top row of teeth, "I knew I had gotten lost. So I'd go somewhere else on the dance floor and smell B.O. and be like 'Okay, I'm back with my people.'" Everyone laughed, and I beamed. We were a little drunk, and I couldn't help but bring my mind to Elijah, a recently transplanted farmer from the next state over. He was apprenticing with friends, and I had met him the day before at one of the seminars on making and sticking to financial plans for new farms. He was very handsome, and had come out dancing with us. At one point in the evening, everyone else from our group had left the area for drinks, a smoke, or just fresh air.

"It's kind of awkward," I yelled over the music, "when it's just, like, two people on the dance floor."

"Yeah," he said, and I twirled around, throwing my arms up over my head and sinking my hips down into the music. I told that story to our crew, too, but left out how excited I felt to be dancing with him, left out the fact that I wanted to move closer, close the gap between our bodies. But maybe, I reasoned, pressing my lips together, I was just acting out against Ian. It wasn't Elijah's attention, I reminded myself, that I wanted. It was Ian's.

Eventually, we all ambled into the bathroom together, the seven of us brushing our teeth with organic paste. "My tongue is still brown!" I said, sticking it out and inspecting the deposit of chocolate in the middle back.

"Well that means you didn't do a good enough job," Nicole said, shaking the excess water off her brush and setting it back on the sink. I giggled and squeezed a little more toothpaste onto mine. I suddenly recalled a chocolate-themed exchange from the weekend before when, visiting friends in Pittsburgh, Ian and I browsed around a sweets shop for a snack. I was handling bars of ginger- and pistachio-studded dark chocolate, when he quietly whispered in my ear.

"I just want to make sure you remember," he'd said, "that chocolate is one of the most important things to buy fair trade." I felt embarrassed and looked at the package. There was no mention of fair or direct trade. I placed the chocolate back on its stand and instead purchased one that featured a picture of the farmer who'd grown the cacao.

With the lights off, everyone settled down quickly. I listened for the rhythmic breathing that came with deep sleep, the faint whistles and snores. Ian and I shared a bed, and as I burrowed under the sheets and puffy white blanket, I whispered in his ear. "Good night . . ." My words were leading, my lips at his skin. He murmured back and kissed me, his lips soft and quiet on mine.

I ran my hands over his bare chest and stomach, willing his body to relax at the touch. It did, and I let my fingers flutter down to the drawstring of his pants. I circled over the fabric with the pads of my fingers, each revolution seeking an answer: *Is this okay?*

He answered with a slow and deliberate untying of the drawstring at his waistband. I slipped my hand in and down, sliding my tongue along the side of his neck as I did so. His skin was salty, covered in a sheen of sweat from the night's dancing.

He pulled at my flannel pants and I slid them down my legs to the bottom of the bed, moving as deliberately and slowly as I could. Wordlessly, he gripped my palm with his and directed my first two fingers into his mouth, then down to the space between my thighs. He held my jaw as he found my lips with his mouth. I attempted to shift my hand to his body, but he sensed my movement and pushed it back to my own body. *Don't stop. Don't move.* The language translated, and I continued touching myself.

I was aware of every sound; every semi-conscious rustle of comforter and sigh of sheets. I was worried we'd wake our friends, but I also wanted him very much.

He gripped a handful of hair at the crown of my neck and pulled back, hard. It hurt, but I wanted more. He knew this and yanked again, pulled tighter. I made a small noise. He untangled his fingers and hooked both thumbs under my arms, pulling my body up the length of his. We stopped with my lips at the crook of his neck and chest, a perfect diamond-shaped cavern, and I kissed it, brief and wet, before he positioned himself over me.

I wanted to cry out, but he anticipated this and covered my mouth with his hand. We moved together.

"You're going to come," he whispered. His words were hazy and sweet, thick like molasses. I whimpered, and he clapped his hand over my lips again. "I know you are." I nodded, wanting it so desperately and nothing more. I did, my entire body tightening around him as I shuddered and shook and gripped at his biceps. We lay together for a few minutes, laughing silently into each other's mouths before allowing our eyelids to droop down into sleep.

WINTER

CARROT AND PARSNIP SHEPHERD'S PIE

This dish has a special place in my heart. I made a version of it for the first meal I cooked at Stonehill, and have been improving upon it ever since. I'm a sucker for animal fat, so prefer to use ground beef with at least a 20 percent fat content. You may substitute a leaner ratio, but don't expect me to have any sympathy if your pie isn't as unctuous as you had hoped (this isn't to say, of course, that it won't still be lovely!). If you're working with pesticide-free vegetables you feel good about, there's no need to peel them. A hearty rinse and scrub will do the trick just fine. A traditional shepherd's pie is cooked entirely in the oven, but I prefer the stove top method, as it's much more conducive to building deep flavors. Not to mention easier. Do not be deterred by the long ingredient list! They're all common pantry staples.

• SERVES SIX TO EIGHT •

3 cups roughly chopped carrots

2 cups roughly chopped parsnips

6 tablespoons (¾ stick) butter or lard, divided

¼ cup whole milk or heavy cream

2 tablespoons maple syrup

1 teaspoon apple cider vinegar

Salt and pepper

1 cup diced onion

½ teaspoon allspice

¼ teaspoon ground cloves

1 teaspoon ground ginger

2 tablespoons minced garlic

1 pound ground beef

[CONTINUED]

1 tablespoon tomato paste

¼ cup dry red wine

⅓ cup beef stock

Salt and pepper

In a large pot, cover the carrots and parsnips in 2 inches of water. Cover with a lid and bring to a boil. Once at a rolling boil, reduce to a lively simmer and cook until very tender, about 25 minutes.

Drain and transfer the cooked vegetables to a food processor fitted with a chopping blade. Add 4 tablespoons butter, milk, maple syrup, and apple cider vinegar, and process until smooth and creamy. Season with salt and pepper, and set aside. (On other occasions, you can certainly stop here and serve this as a side dish with dinner.)

Meanwhile, in a 9- to 10½-inch cast-iron or ovenproof skillet, melt 1 tablespoon butter over medium heat. Add the onions, allspice, cloves, and ginger and sauté until translucent and soft. Add the garlic and cook for an additional 2 to 3 minutes, then transfer the aromatics to a small bowl.

Add the last tablespoon of butter to the pan and return it to medium-high heat. Add the ground beef and sauté until browned and fully cooked, breaking it apart with a wooden spoon. Add the onions-and-garlic-mixture back to the skillet, along with the tomato paste and wine. Stir, coating the mixture with the paste and wine as it evaporates. Add the stock and stir again, until the liquid is almost entirely evaporated but the mixture is still moist.

Preheat the broiler to high. Spread the puréed carrot and parsnip mixture over the top of the beef, smoothing it with a spoon. Place the skillet on a rimmed baking sheet to catch any drips, and broil until the top is lightly browned, 2 to 4 minutes, depending on the heat of your broiler.

Remove from the oven and let cool slightly. Serve with the rest of the red wine and a bitter green salad, if you're lucky enough to have the goods this time of year.

RAW BRUSSELS SPROUTS AND KALE SALAD

Whenever I talk about Brussels sprouts, I'm always told that I "absolutely must" try them cooked in bacon fat—to which I always reply, "Have we met?" Brussels in bacon fat are good, but I prefer a cleaner preparation, and eat them raw. In the winter, when everything is roasted, broiled, stewed, and simmered into softness, a little give under the teeth is just what I want. This recipe requires a non-local cheat—pomegranate seeds. The vinaigrette takes a bit of time to pull together, but it's worth it. Besides, it's winter—what else are you going to do?

· SERVES SIX TO EIGHT ·

3 medium shallots, skin on

1 tablespoon olive oil

2 cups Brussels sprouts, any brown outer leaves removed

3 cups kale leaves, ribs removed

2 tablespoons apple cider vinegar

1 tablespoon peeled, chopped fresh ginger

¼ cup extra-virgin olive oil

¼ cup plain full-fat yogurt

Salt and pepper

⅓ cup pomegranate seeds

Preheat the oven to 375°F.

Rub the shallots all over with the oil, then place them in a small ovenproof skillet or roasting pan. Roast 45 minutes, until tender and fragrant, shaking the pan periodically. Remove from the heat and let them sit until cool enough to handle.

While the shallots cool, use a sharp chef's knife to finely slice the Brussels sprouts and kale. There's no need to massage or cook the kale if you cut it thinly enough, so be certain you do.

[CONTINUED]

Pop the shallots out of their skin and into a food processor or blender. Add the vinegar, ginger, and olive oil, and purée until completely combined. Move the mixture to a medium mixing bowl and fold in the yogurt. Add a little room temperature water if the mixture seems very thick; it should be thin enough to drizzle. Season well with salt and pepper.

Combine the kale and Brussels sprouts with enough vinaigrette to moisten it all, and mix to coat. Taste and adjust seasoning. Transfer to a serving dish.

To remove the seeds from the pomegranate, slice it into quarters. Hold a quarter, seed-side down, over a large mixing bowl and spank the back of the pomegranate with a wooden spoon, allowing the seeds to fall into the bowl. Repeat with the remaining pomegranate. Sprinkle the seeds over the salad and serve.

CELERIAC PURÉE WITH SAGE AND THYME

I love making this for those who aren't well acquainted with celeriac. It's a brilliant and surprising substitute for mashed potatoes, imbued with the grassy, fresh flavor of celery. I infuse the dairy with thyme and sage so I can enjoy the flavor of the herbs without the tragedy of a mouthful of sage leaf.

· SERVES EIGHT TO TEN ·

4 cups peeled, cubed celeriac, in 1-inch pieces

1 cup whole milk or heavy cream

1 tablespoon dried thyme

1½ tablespoons dried sage

½ cup chicken stock

1 tablespoon buckwheat honey

Salt and pepper

Cover the celeriac with water in a saucepan. Cover with a tight-fitting lid and bring to a boil, then reduce to a lively simmer. Let simmer until the celeriac is very tender, 25 minutes. Remove from the heat and drain.

While the celeriac is cooking, combine the dried herbs and milk or cream in a separate saucepan. Heat gently over low heat, until just barely hinting at a simmer. Remove from the heat and let the infusion steep for as long as it takes the celeriac to cook. Strain out the herbs and discard them.

Combine the celeriac, stock, and infused dairy in the bowl of a food processor. Purée until very smooth. If the mixture looks too loose to stand firm on a plate, put it back in the pot over medium heat to evaporate some of the liquid.

When ready to serve, stir in the honey and season with salt and pepper. Top with extra freshly ground black pepper.

SAVORY LENTIL AND SAUSAGE MASH

If this dish isn't comfort food, I don't know what is. We always had sausage at the ready at Stonehill, thanks to Jack's butchering expertise. I like to use hot Italian links, but any good quality pork sausage will do.

· SERVES FOUR TO SIX ·

2 cups French lentils

4½ cups chicken stock, divided

2 tablespoons lard or butter

1 cup finely chopped leek, white and light green part only
(save the dark green leaves for making stock)

2 tablespoons dried rosemary

4 to 6 large links pork sausage

Salt and pepper

1 cup plain yogurt

Preheat the oven to 375°F.

Pick through the lentils for any small stones or debris, then rinse under water. Place in a saucepan with 4 cups of the stock, then cover and bring to a boil. Once boiling, remove the lid, stir, and reduce the heat to a simmer. Stirring occasionally, cook until tender, 30 minutes, adding extra water if the liquid evaporates before lentils are done. Set aside.

Meanwhile, heat the lard or butter over medium heat in a large cast-iron or heavy ovenproof skillet. Add the leek and rosemary and sauté until tender and translucent, 7 to 8 minutes. Remove from the heat. Add the lentils and remaining ¼ cup stock, then season with salt and pepper. Stir to combine, using a wooden spoon to gently mash the lentils against the bottom and side of the skillet.

Arrange the sausage links over the top of the lentils and place in the preheated oven. Bake for 20 to 25 minutes, turning the sausage over halfway through, until cooked through and browned. Serve family style, with yogurt on the side for dolloping.

SPRING

FEBRUARY

It may have seemed counterintuitive, but with February's harsh winds and brutal temperatures, it felt much colder inside the barn than out of it. If you were working outside, you were most likely doing something physical—carting hay bales back and forth, using a pitchfork to pile up all the loose stuff that had accumulated in the barn, or feeding animals. No matter what chore you were doing, you were walking and moving, and that kept the blood flowing—at least a little bit. I, however, spent a lot of time in the barn.

The barn didn't offer much in the way of shelter, and the jobs had to be completed within its walls tended to be of the stationary variety. Once distribution had been assembled, all you really had to do was be present, greeting CSA members and occasionally running down to the walk-in cooler—which, by contrast, felt positively balmy—to grab a spare bag of parsnips or carrots. Farmstand seemed even harder, chillier, as we lagged through the deep of winter. These customers were not committed to a weekly pickup, so when the temperature dipped down below five degrees, I didn't see too many folks hungry for black radishes and turnips.

To keep myself busy during the farmstand open hours, I washed eggs behind the folding table covered in a red cloth, old metal cash box, and digital scale borrowed from the butcher shop. I always set up the table so that it blocked the four meat freezers—under USDA regulations, we weren't allowed to sell individual cuts of meat to the public (the CSA was exempted, as they already technically owned the animal, or a "share" of the farm), and I didn't want to tempt anyone with packages of Jack's perfectly aged steaks if they weren't available for purchase.

Most customers were regulars, or had at least been there before, and they came in through the milk house with a familiar and confident air, yanking open the refrigerator door before venturing into the second room where the vegetables waited and I shivered. Our staggering milk production had picked back up with the purchase of a shipment of hay from Vermont, but we still couldn't produce enough to meet the demand. We were the only legal raw milk dairy for miles, and people drove for upwards of an hour for a few jars of the stuff.

"No milk today?" they'd call into the barn, hopeful that maybe I had a few jars stashed away somewhere, that they hadn't crossed three counties just for root vegetables.

"No, I'm sorry," I said. "We're milking again in"—I checked my wristwatch—"a half hour, and Toby should be done within an hour after that. You're welcome to wait, or come back around six," I said, knowing that most often, they wouldn't. "We do have plenty of vegetables and," I offered, chipping a few shards of ice from an egg that had hardened onto the drying rack, "fresh eggs." This usually brightened matters a bit, as most everyone liked the prospect of watching their farmer pack the eggs right in front of them. There were plenty in the fridge, but the allure wasn't quite the same. So I'd grab a clean carton from the stack on my left and start setting eggs in, pointy-side down—though sometimes it was hard to tell which was which. Slightly mollified, the customer would drift off toward the bushels of vegetables, browsing around for something delicious.

"Nothing new this week?" they asked, and I felt more sympathetic than annoyed.

"Nope," I'd say, pulling my yellow leather mittens back on and hoisting myself onto a freezer to get a little closer to the tiny heat lamp affixed to the barn's ceiling beams. "Still the same stuff. The same delicious stuff, if it helps." What we harvested that fall was what we had to offer, and because there was no heated greenhouse, there were no new vegetables to get excited about. I felt doubly guilty about this at farmstand, knowing that we were stashing away some of the best roots in the cooler, reserving them for distribution. We had so few celeriac and kohlrabi, that I wasn't sure they would even last through the winter for our CSA members. "Have you ever made chocolate cake with beets?" I'd ask the customer, and they would wearily eye the crate of fat red roots.

Filling their reusable bags—or our supply of used plastic grocery bags, if they forgot their own—with potatoes, onions, carrots, and eggs, they'd hand me a few bills, I'd give them a few back, and then I'd watch them leave, listening for the slam of the storm door behind them. "Alone again," I'd sigh, watching Ian cruise by with the horses attached to the wagon, or Jack trek past with a hammer and a tool belt, or Cliff sporting a goofy grin and with a spring in his step. In the height of summer, farmstand lasted from 2:00 until 6:30, but I had convinced Cliff to close at 5:30 come winter. In the last hour, the only light in the barn came from the bare light bulbs and string of lights purchased for Cliff's anniversary party, causing me to grow sleepy and lose momentum around four.

One particularly bitter afternoon shortly after two, I heard the familiar clank and clatter of empty half-gallon jars being returned in the milk house bushel. "Come on in!" I called, shaking off a burlap sack that had covered the carrots.

"Hello," Tracy said, smiling sweetly.

"Oh, hi!" I said. "I was wondering where you were at pickup yesterday."

"Doctor's appointment," she said, her eyes lighting up when she saw the winter leeks. I loved how excited food made her, and her enthusiasm and gratitude about the same old storage crops was admittedly infectious. "Here; it's my latest batch." She handed over a pint jar of purple sauerkraut. "It's kind of weird, I think. I'm not sure if I actually like it."

"Well, I'm sure I will," I said with a smile, remembering her promise to supply me with kraut. "I love anything fermented."

"Me too. I feel like we have a lot in common," she said.

"Yeah, I feel that way, too." I didn't have a lot of girlfriends, and I was nervous to make them, but something about Tracy made me feel at ease, like we had known each other forever.

"You kind of remind me of my sister, actually," she said. "Something about your mouth, or jawline, I think."

I touched my chin with my mitten. "Oh, I have secret stuff for you. Hold on." I ran down to the walk-in to grab the bags of celeriac and root vegetables. "Plus, there's meat in the freezers." I pushed aside my folding table blockade. "Have at it. Lamb sausage this week."

Although Jack had slaughtered the last of the lambs before the cold weather arrived, he had frozen much of it, thawing portions periodically for ground meat and sausage. It was always a huge treat, especially when it went into links of spicy-sweet merguez.

Tracy and I chatted for the better part of a half hour before I noticed her teeth chattering. "You should get out of here," I said. "They pay me to sit in this."

"I do have a few more errands to run," she said, then placed a delicate pause between us. "Hey, some friends of mine are going to a show in town this Saturday night. *The Full Monty*. It's kind of silly, but all in good fun. Would you"—she took a breath—"want to come?"

"I would love that." I said, emphasizing the verb. "Thank you. Thank you for asking, seriously." I was already anticipating an evening off the farm, and really looking forward to getting to know Tracy a little better. We made plans to meet, parted ways, and I unscrewed the top of my mason jar of coffee, excited to take a sip until I realized it had gone stone-cold.

THE NEXT NIGHT, I RAN A STRAIGHTENING IRON THROUGH MY HAIR in the bathroom as Ian showered. "I'm happy you're getting out there, Ro," he said through the steam. "It'll be good for you to make a friend."

"Yeah, I'm really stoked about it. I like her—a lot. It kind of feels like we're already close."

He drew open the shower curtain and I handed him his towel. "You have attachment issues," he said, half serious and half not. He shook water droplets from his hair. "As in, you fall in love with people really quickly."

"Well, yeah, I guess." My hair was still damp and sizzled under the hot plates of the iron. "I mean, I don't connect to a lot of people. So when I do, I just—know. It's like I can sense who they are immediately."

He nodded, considering this. "Well, it's not my way, but hey." I nodded back and ran my fingernails down his abdomen. He flexed his muscles. I kissed his shoulder.

Tracy and I had planned to meet in a public parking lot where I would leave my car so we could drive over to the theatre together. "You know the McDonald's in the shopping plaza?" she said. "It's about midway between us, and it's well lit. It's not the ideal location, but it's safe."

She was already there when I pulled in, so I turned off my ignition and scurried over to meet her. "Ugh," she said, breathing in. "My car already smells like freaking fast food." I inhaled. She was right, and we both laughed.

"Such an illicit meeting spot!" I said, and we both giggled nervously. As we made our way to the theatre, she asked me what it was like to work on the farm and live there, too. We talked about our opinions about what food should be, and how it was unfortunate that most people had it so backward. "Just take real ingredients and don't fuck them up," I said, and she nodded vigorously, her hands tight around the steering wheel.

"Hell, yes!"

As we waited in line with our tickets, talk turned tentatively to stickier matters, like happiness and security, love and lack thereof. I slowly turned the conversation from general farm-life stress to my frustrations and fears about Ian. "He's just not sure," I said. "And he doesn't know if he'll ever be." She listened patiently. "We go through these bouts of everything being great—being wonderful. It's always when he's not up in his head about it—but then he expresses doubt or uncertainty. Says he doesn't feel fully committed to me. And he doesn't know why. But that he wants to be. But that he doesn't. But that maybe the problem is him. That maybe it's me. I don't know. I feel like it must be me," I said, looking down at my hands.

"I am so sorry," Tracy said, and I knew that she meant it, but before we could discuss it further, her girlfriends arrived, and talk turned light, to an analysis of whether there'd actually be full-frontal nudity in the evening's performance (there was, but only for the briefest of seconds, and we all roared with deep laughter).

On the ride home, Tracy and I continued to open up to one another. She talked about feelings of self-worth and confidence, and

I admitted that, for the last year or so, I didn't have much of it. It wasn't until I began working on the farm, I told her, that I started to gain some self-esteem. "I can remember when I realized that I was someone worth knowing—even if I was a work in progress. I was actually picking Duke's feet," I said. Tracy listened. "I couldn't get him to pick up his back hoof, and I was getting so mad at myself, like I was this terrible person for not being able to make a horse do what I wanted. And then I realized that even if I was having a bad day, the fact remained that I was still doing something completely outside my comfort zone—and that I was opening myself up to learning." I paused for a moment. "I don't know. It made me feel proud of myself."

We arrived back at the McDonald's parking lot and sat in the car, talking and gripping each other's hands, for another hour before finally saying good-bye. When I arrived home, I received a text message from her: *Thank you for coming. I guess we really went for the full monty tonight, in how much we shared. I love you!* My heart felt swollen. I loved her too, and read the message out loud to Ian, who rolled his eyes and laughed. "You do love everyone." I colored red, but couldn't help but feel that, for the first time in months, I was truly supported, accepted, wanted, and at that moment, I realized I wanted more of it.

MARCH

March felt hostile, cold, bleak. Everyone was short with one another, snapping about personal space and jobs poorly performed. The coldest days felt unbearably bitter, and each fresh snowfall reminded the crew that we were not out of the woods quite yet.

I was supposed to teach a cooking class on baking with local flour on the third Sunday of the month, but beyond setting aside a few cups of coarse hard winter wheat from the jars in the distribution space, I hadn't given it much thought. When it came down to it, I assumed I would just bake bread the way I always did for farm meals, impossibly dense loaves that would win no prizes for beauty but got the job done.

I'd cobbled together a recipe of sorts from a mixture of Jim Lahey's no-knead method, Jonah's patient teaching from our visit to him and Marianna in Massachusetts, and my typical a-bit-of-this, bit-of-that kitchen wisdom. I started with three cups of flour and often added a pinch of nutmeg, ground cardamom, or black pepper, plus a healthy shower of salt. I used a heavy wooden spoon to mix in enough water to moisten the flour without making it a soppy mess, always wondering if I should follow the no-knead instructions of a cautiously conservative stir or Jonah's method of fifty strokes done with a loose and relaxed palm periodically dipped in water. I usually landed somewhere in the middle.

Every baking recipe I'd ever encountered called for a sheen of oil in the proofing bowl, but with our olive oil in such high demand (vinaigrettes, you know) and lard being positively unacceptable for salad dressing, I opted to use it where I could. So the proofing bowls got coated in pork fat.

I would cover the bowl with the cleanest tea towel I could find and slip it into the germination chamber, which held steady at a toasty temperature. I pulled all of this together after washing up the breakfast dishes, around 8:30 am, then wandered outside to complete a few tasks on my morning chore list. At 10:30, I found my way back inside to discover a whole new set of dishes waiting for me on the counter.

I passed by the plates and grabbed the dough out of the germ chamber. By this point, it had blossomed into a ball twice its size. I turned the dough out onto a cutting board, kneaded it, and put the entire thing, cutting board and all, back in the chamber, pretending I hadn't noticed the spiders lurking in the back and exploring the flats.

Back in the kitchen, I cranked the oven and set a cast-iron Dutch oven in the bottom half of it. Forty-five more minutes stacking hay, feeding cattle, or sorting carrots and I'd come back in, ready to cook lunch. I gingerly set the pot on the prep table and threw another handful of flour in its general direction, dusting the bottom and sides, then transferred the dough to the pot and returned it to the oven. Once the top became a dark brown crust and a tap from my knuckle sounded hollow, I removed the pot from the oven and set the bread on a wire cooling rack on the middle of the table.

And so with all of this in mind, I figured that I could teach a class without too much of a plan. When I woke that Sunday, sleepy and chilly, I admitted I had better stop procrastinating and get to work. The bed was cold—Ian had already gone off to do chores—so I yanked on leggings and his old sweater, piled my hair into a messy bun, and pulled a fleece headband down over my ears. It was 7:30, an hour before we were technically allowed to enter the farmhouse on weekends, but I figured an exception could be made, just this once.

I stopped in the barn to pick up my flour, and as I rounded the corner to the farmhouse, I encountered Lara leaning back in one of the wooden folding chairs, feet propped up on a garden cart, reading a book in front of a large pot of sap boiling away over a kerosene flame.

"Hey," I said, not waiting for her to respond. "Do you mind if I grab some baking time in the kitchen?" Fate seemed to be smiling on me; with Cliff milking and Lara tending the sap, I wouldn't wake either of them as I pulled together the dough.

"No, that's fine," she said, never taking her eyes from the book in her hands. I ducked inside and shivered. Cliff requested we keep the temperature at sixty-four degrees, but I wondered if it wasn't much colder than that in the drafty old house. I spent the next hour pulling together two doughs—one to bake before the cooking class, and another with which to demonstrate proper folding and shaping technique—and simmering some rolled oats in a can of coconut milk for breakfast. I was pouring hot water over a pot of gunpowder green tea leaves when Lara came into the house and up the stairs, her feet heavy and stomping. She seemed irritated, but I couldn't place why. As I waited for the doughs to proof, I idly flipped through the local newspaper and pulled Ian's sweater tightly around my midsection. It really was quite cold.

My dishes washed and breads puffing along, I slipped my feet back into my winter boots and waved good-bye to Lara, who had since taken back her post by the pot. "Um, hey," she said, setting her book down. My stomach flopped. "I don't know if you forgot, but we asked that no one come in the house before 8:30 on weekends. That's still a rule." Somewhere along the way this morning, we had experienced a communication breakdown. I couldn't blame her: The farmhouse was a communal space, but she lived there. I would find it maddening.

My face burned crimson, my neck felt hot. "Sure. I know that, but . . ." I felt my voice catch in my throat and swallowed hard. We had obviously misunderstood each other, and it seemed silly to rehash how I had seen things. "But I figured that it'd be okay because Cliff was milking and you were awake, out here. I'm sorry. I didn't mean to disrespect you."

She mumbled something under her breath and I felt nervous. We both turned away from one another at the same time and I stalked off toward Beth's house. As I rinsed off under a stream of hot water, I thought about the encounter and felt a flash of irritation, bitter and angry on my tongue. Lara and I used to get along, but ever since the winter holidays it seemed that we couldn't stand each other. I felt anxious and insecure, like her voice dripped with disdain whenever addressing me. But then, everyone seemed on edge.

I was lying on the bed on my back, still wrapped in Ian's big red towel, when he walked in from the morning's chores. "How'd it go?" I asked as he stripped down to his boxer shorts.

"Fine," he said, rubbing his hands together vigorously before unwrapping my towel and placing a palm on either side of my waist. I kissed his mouth and then rolled over onto my side.

"Lara and I had a drama this morning," I said, propping my chin on my knuckle. Ian looked weary as I recalled the exchange. He was quiet when I finished. "What do you think I should do? What would you do?" I asked the questions in rapid succession.

"Well I don't think you should talk about it with her until you feel strong enough to do so confidently," he said, running a hand through his hair. "You know I understand when you start to cry, but I think she does poorly with that. It'll make things worse if you're emotional."

I burrowed under the blanket and quilt, hiding my face with my hands. "Ugh."

"But I would talk to her. When you feel like you can. I mean, that's what I would do."

On the last Friday of the month, I was finishing up things at the farmstand and packing away the last few dozen eggs that sat drying. It had been a slow day, made a little brighter by a lengthy visit from one of my favorite customers, a young mother who always bought a pint jar of frozen chicken livers. "I purée them and put them in hamburger," she said, her eyes twinkling. "At the end of this year— but definitely not before—I'm going to tell my husband."

Inside the butcher shop, Jack was wiping down the band saw and wrapping the last of the steaks from Thursday's pickup. There were a few extras—our members hadn't nabbed them all—and I was excited to cook a few for lunch sometime soon. It was almost 5:30, and I was pretty sure we'd seen our last customer of the day. I was tired, I was cold, and I just wanted to be done.

"Um." Jack suddenly stood in the doorway. I looked up, watching a puff of breath become visible as it escaped my lips. "I want to make sure you know that you can't use the butcher shop scrubbies for egg washing." There was a warning tone in his voice, and I looked down at my overturned bucket and stack of cartons. I had my own coarse scrubbing pad for the eggs. And of course I knew not to wipe shit away from them with the same one that was used for cleaning boning knives and the meat grinder.

"Of course I know that," I snapped.

"Okay," he said, his expression giving away skepticism. "Because the one from the butcher shop is missing and I don't know who else would use it."

"I don't know either," I said, my voice shaking. "But it wasn't me."

"Right." He turned his back and walked away.

At 5:35, Ian came dutifully to help me pack up the vegetables and carry them back down to the walk-in cooler. We worked quietly and efficiently, both eager to be done for the day and eat dinner. Cliff, Lara, Jack, and Hazel were all planning on weekend getaways, so the rest of us were on our own for the meal. As we walked along the shoulder of the road toward the farmhouse, I recounted the conversation I'd had with Jack.

"It was just so disrespectful—his tone was so fucking condescending," I spat. Ian was quiet, kept his gaze forward. "Like, 'Did *you* use the scrubbie?' when he knows damn well I would never do that!" I paused. "I mean, I hope he knows."

We turned into the driveway and my heart stopped. Jack was standing at his truck, a mildly amused smile playing at his lips. Surely, he had heard.

"Um, hi," I said, then hurried into the house, my face on fire.

Toby, Hillary, Ian, and I ate on the couch, leftover beef shank stew and mashed rutabaga with rosemary. I could barely choke down the root mash as I whined about getting caught. Jack intimidated me at times, and the last thing I wanted was to be on his bad side. "He had to have heard me—he had to. But there's that really awkward issue of *maybe he didn't,* so I definitely shouldn't bring it up because I don't want to make a thing out of it if I don't have to."

Toby mopped up broth with a chunk of brown bread. "Yeah, Ro, that's tough. I wouldn't want to be in your position right now."

"Really, you can just ignore it and if he does approach you when he comes back," Hillary said logically, "just explain that you were annoyed and needed to vent. We all do it. No one can fault you for blowing off steam to your boyfriend. I'm sure he does it with Hazel all the time. He'll understand."

I looked to Ian for reassurance, but he just shrugged. I was confused about his silence—something seemed off—but I also knew that my social anxiety and the seemingly increasing rift between the farm crew and myself was a sore spot for him. Maybe he was thinking I just wasn't cut out for farmwork. After dinner, we walked back to Beth's and took turns in the shower. I was drying my hair when Ian emerged, toweling off his head as well.

"Do you want to have a glass of wine?" he asked and I nodded. I pulled the cork from a bottle of Côtes du Rhone that we had started a few days prior, and poured it into two jars.

"Cheers," I said, clinking my glass to his and smiling up at him. I took a sip and sighed: earthy, funky, deep. It was exactly what I wanted. I relished in a long breath and reminded myself to be thankful for everything I had, despite the day's frustrations.

Ian sat down at the writing desk, perched uncomfortably on the edge of his chair. "Ro . . ." he began. My breath caught in my throat. "I don't feel good."

"What do you mean?" My voice was plump with anxiety.

"You know what I mean." His was pleading. I knew what he meant.

"Are you *fucking* kidding me?" I hissed. "Are you fucking seriously going to do this to me right now?" I sank onto the bed and gripped my jar until my knuckles turned white.

He set down the wine and cradled his forehead in his hands. When he finally spoke, his voice was quiet. "Why does it matter when I do it?"

"I cannot—I cannot believe you're going to do this to me *now*," I said, impossibly, jarringly aware that it was the end.

"Well, I couldn't do it last weekend because you were on chores and I didn't want you to have to deal with it then." He looked like he was in a great deal of pain. "And next weekend is Easter."

"Oh, that's so kind of you," I said, taking an enormous slug of my wine. It burned going down my throat and I realized I wanted to get very drunk. "That is so enormously kind."

"Ro, I tried. I tried so hard, and I just don't know what's wrong.

I don't know if we're not the right match, or if some flaw in me is making it hard to fully commit to you. But I can't." I glared at him through my sadness. "And I can't figure it out while trying to be in a relationship with you. It's confusing me to be together and wrap my head around it. I have lain awake in bed so many nights, thinking I need to end it, but then I see you in the morning and I get confused all over again. So"—he sipped, held the wine in his mouth for a moment and swallowed—"I need to be by myself, to not date anyone at all. At least until the end of the year. At least until December."

I clenched my jaw and willed tears to come. None did, but I felt a searing headache beginning directly between my eyes. "I want to have a cigarette. Please roll one for me."

He silently took the case of tobacco from his nightstand and began wrapping a pinch of it into a paper. "It's not very good," he said when he finished, inspecting the bulges and tufts of tobacco and herbs poking out either end. "I've never been good at this."

"I don't care." I took the cigarette from him and struck a match. He opened the window with a sigh.

"I cannot believe you put me through all of this for nothing," I said, picking threads of tobacco from my teeth. He winced, and I remembered our conversation months earlier. He motioned for the cigarette. I handed it over.

"It wasn't for nothing." His voice became defensive. "I did love you, I do, and I'm trying to figure this out. Don't you think it's wrong to say this wasn't worthwhile just because it didn't meet your expectations? Don't you think that's short-sighted?"

I snatched the cigarette back from him. "No," I said instead. "I wanted to be with you and I would have given you everything."

"I know," he said quietly. "But that's the problem. You gave too much of yourself before I was ready." I snorted. He repeated what sounded to me like a tired line: "We could end up being incredible friends, both happy with someone else, or maybe alone. I don't know. But you do know how I feel about expectations. I think that you're blind to other outcomes that could be just as good or better because you've convinced yourself you only want this one thing."

I nodded, too angry, too sad to say anything. I refilled my jar with the rest of the wine and handed it to him. He took a sip, and I took the glass back. Neither of us said anything for a while. Finally, anger grew soft around the edges, became something closer to fear. "Can we sleep in bed together tonight—one last time?" I whispered.

He drew me into his arms, with the correct amount of reservation, and kissed the top of my head. "We can do that."

EARLY APRIL

I moved into the guest room adjacent to the bedroom we had shared. An equally nice space, if a bit darker, it held the food shrine, our dressers, my closet, and our yoga mats. There was a twin bed with a hard mattress that we'd pushed against the wall and piled with pillows. I had originally intended it as a reading space for myself in the evenings, a place for us to "do our own things," but the cozy glow of our bedroom always seemed so much more inviting, and I always found a reason not to do my own thing.

But now the room was mine, and I wasn't entirely sure how to fill the emptiness. A film of dust covered just about everything, and I spent that Sunday cleaning it. After shoving all of the furniture into the middle of the room, I ran a rag under the faucet, then wrung it out and let it partially air-dry for a few minutes, the way my mother had taught me when I was younger. I ran the rag along the baseboards, the walls, the frame of the bed and the door, and, in lieu of a vacuum cleaner, crawled around the floor with a small red Dustbuster, stopping every thirty seconds to empty clots of dirt, hay, and hair into a trash bag I hung over the door handle. There was no screen on the window, but I opened it anyway, figuring a little fresh air was worth any bees or flies that happened to find their way inside.

Ian came home from somewhere—a coffee shop, I presumed, noting his shoulder bag and the rimmed glasses that sat on his nose— in the afternoon and surveyed the space. "Nice work," he said. "It looks great in here, Ro."

"Thanks," I said, not sure what else I should offer.

He inclined his head to his dresser and shelf full of sweaters. "Do you . . ." He stopped himself mid-sentence and dropped his bag on our bed. On his bed. "Do you want me to take this out of here?"

"I don't know," I said, folding my legs at the knees and resting my bottom on my feet. "Do *you* want to take it out of here? What if . . ." I couldn't bring myself to continue.

"What if you move back in?" he offered gently.

I nodded, my eyes filling with tears. "What if I move back in, and then we have to do it all over again?"

He laughed, running a hand through his hair and shaking it out at the ends. "Well, then we'll schlep it back in here," he said. "I'm not worried about that."

My heart leapt—*maybe*—but I just nodded again. I didn't have the courage, or the heart to tell him that it was really the feeling of finality, of distinct closure, that worried me. Removing his dresser meant removing him, and I wasn't ready to do that. "What are you doing this afternoon?" I asked in spite of myself.

"Oh, think I'll do a little work with Duke," he said. "He's been so much better lately—calmer."

"That's great," I said, with insistence. "I'm so happy for him. It's because of you; I hope you know that. I hope you realize it."

"Well, I don't know. I still lose my temper more often than I should with him," he said, giving away disappointment and frustration.

I ran my fingers along my arm. The open window coaxed in a chill, but the late-afternoon sun felt cozy, nice on my skin. The catalpa tree caught the light in the prettiest way, holding it in its branches briefly before throwing it on the floor between us. "But you always give him another chance," I responded quietly, looking up at him with a sad smile.

"Ro . . ." There was both a warning tone and nostalgic tinge to my name.

"Don't you? Don't you think he deserves that?" I asked.

"Are we talking about our relationship or my horse?"

I tried to look casual. "Maybe both?"

"I don't know." He sounded tired. "I don't know if I want to. I just need time to figure this out." I picked up my rag again and began running it between the posts of the headboard. My moment had passed; he wasn't interested in engaging. He would be again. I let it go.

"Enjoy the horses," I said.

"Ro . . ."

"Go, go!" There was forced cheer in my voice, and I was happy to know that the falsity was apparent. "You're not a part of this," I said, sweeping my hand over my newly acquired domain. "Let me do my thing here."

He backed out of my room and into his, hesitating slightly before pulling the door shut.

THAT NIGHT, I UNROLLED MY YOGA MAT AND TURNED ON A MIX OF chants. I began moving through sun salutations, pausing extra long in downward dog to enjoy the sensation of release in my lower back. I could hear Ian in the room next door. The slightest movements, which I guessed to be pen on journal, made what seemed like very loud noises, and I began to blush when I considered the fact that Logan, who lived across the hall, used to tease that he could hear us in the evenings. Apparently sound traveled well in the creaky old farmhouse.

I lay in *shavasana* for quite some time, thinking about sleeping in his bed and willing tears to come, but none did. Giving up, I blew out the candles I'd lit, left my mat unfurled on the floor in defiance of Ian, who once told me that he preferred re-rolling the foam mats and storing them away properly. Crawling into bed and pulling the red jersey sheet—a gift from friends who'd stayed and expressed shock that we didn't, actually, have any sheets for the small mattress—up around my neck, I sighed deeply. The bed was cold and I was lonely.

I tiptoed across the floor and opened the door separating us with a tentative hand. Ian was lying in the middle of his mattress, his back resting against propped pillows, a book cracked at the spine and open on his chest. *Alice in Wonderland.* I stood in front of him and bit at my lip. I made the smallest of coughs. He stirred, observing me through bleary eyes. His hair looked wild, the brown-blond strands covering the floral-patterned pillow. "What's up, Ro?"

"Can I come in?"

"Well, you're in now," he said sleepily.

"You know what I mean," I responded, one of my knees already on his bed. He nodded and lifted his left arm, opening a space for me to crawl into. I pressed my nose into his armpit, kissed his skin, and breathed in his scent. The light in the room shone soft and quiet, emanating from just one lamp on his nightstand. He turned over, his back to me. It didn't feel so much like a rejection as it did a request, so I curled my body around his, bending my waist to accommodate his backside into my lap. I kissed his bare shoulders, ran my fingernails in light traces over his biceps. He made small murmurs of pleasure, one third asleep, another third enjoying the touch, and the last third too confused to stop it.

After a few minutes, I moved my hand to myself, began touching my body through the fabric of my underwear. My knuckles knocked into his backbone; I made sure of this, made sure he knew what I was doing. I began to mimic the sounds he had made earlier—soft and quiet—as I moved my fingers into and under my waistband. I closed my eyes and pictured his hands on me instead of my own, and when I peered through my lashes, it was equally satisfying and sad to see his neck and back inches from my nose. I kept moving until he turned, urgent and quick, grabbing at my shoulders with his hands. He pressed his mouth on mine firmly.

"I need this; you know I do," I pleaded, and I didn't have to say any more. His hands were on me, in me, and I was once more transported to that elusive place between satisfaction and desire.

LATE APRIL, EARLY MAY

In April, shortly after Ian delivered the first note of finality, I had called a meeting with Cliff in the common room of Beth's house. The kitchen table at the farmhouse was too busy to have a proper meeting, always bustling with activity—a farmer wandering in for a cup of tea, a volunteer looking for the bathroom, Cliff and Lara's two cats stretching their bodies out lazily on top of a laptop or paperwork.

As Cliff settled into a winged armchair and opened his three-ring binder, I sat in the low-slung couch across from him, considering the room. In the fall, the whole crew had crammed around a laptop set up on the side table to watch the Presidential debates together, sipping Logan's homemade ginger beer and eating Alfalfa cheese with fancy crackers. A month later, we had watched movies and drank ginger beer mixed with whiskey.

Shae had given yoga classes for us in that room, too, every Tuesday during the few months she lived on the farm, before she moved to Africa. She tailored the lessons to the needs of farmers' bodies and minds, encouraging us gently during *shavasana* to close our eyes and quiet our minds, to know that there, for those last five minutes, no animals needed to be fed, no weeds pulled, no food made. She walked to each one of us and pressed her palms into our shoulders. When she got to me, I always tried to release the tension in my body, to imagine myself melting into the ground. Sometimes, the whole crew came, but most often it was just Cliff, Lara, Ian, and me.

As Cliff scribbled the date in the binder, I smiled sadly at the faded brocade fabric lining the chairs, the small plush horse propped up in a corner, the books on riding and farming, and the paintings and photographs of a life outside, a life made of hard work. I was going to miss this room, and I was going to miss this farm.

"So, obviously, we need to talk and check in," I said. Cliff knew about the breakup. Everyone knew. The morning after it happened, I stood simmering oats in the kitchen, holding it together all right, but when Lara and Cliff came in from chores and asked how my morning was going, I burst into tears. They took me to Ironwood that night, and we all drank wine and ate a lot of pizza, with gelato for dessert. The next day, after a walk, I came home to a letter from Lara on my pillow, a letter about new opportunities, and strength, and true love and what it looks like, and the fact that it does not hurt, not like this.

"You've told the whole damn farm," Ian said a week later, before taking a deep breath and assuring me that, if it would help, if it was what I desired, then it was my choice and I was free to do so. I thought about this now and sighed deeply.

"*Obviously* we need to check in," I repeated. "I've given this a lot of thought, and I just don't think . . ." I stopped, swallowing hard. I really didn't want to cry. "I just don't think this is healthy for me, to be working here. It's not good for me. I want to give you time to find someone new, or figure out how you'll move forward without me," I said, "and I also want to stay until this year's CSA is over. I feel like I owe it to our members." Cliff listened, his pen resting on the paper, his hands folded. "But I think that after May, I need to leave."

"I appreciate the time, and the notice," he said as a formality, and then: "But you know, I hope you know, if you do want to stay, we can find a way to make this work. We can find a way to make it better— another place to live, something. I just don't want you to feel like you have to leave, if it isn't what you really want."

There was no point trying to plug up the tears that were falling freely now, running in streaks through the dirt on my cheeks. Cliff waited until I was ready. "I don't know what I want," I said, finally, wiping my nose on my wrist. "But I think this is what I should do."

THE WEEKS SEEMED TO PASS SLOWLY THROUGH A HAZY CLOUD OF sadness, but by the time my last weekend on chore duty rolled around, I felt surprised. I wasn't totally sure I was ready to leave. Still, there was a lightness around the knowledge, one everyone laughed about at meals. "Last weekend for feeding pigs," Hazel said. "Last time closing the chicken coop late at night!" Toby high-fived me. "Last time watering the greenhouse," Lara nodded in the direction of the hoop house. "Last time," I said with a heavy sigh and an already nostalgic smile over the rim of my coffee cup.

I had been spending more and more time in the kitchen, baking breads and pulling together stews that required plenty of mindless chopping, slicing, and simmering. I often listened to the news as I worked in the kitchen and sometimes turned on music, but lately the sad songs that came on were too much and made me feel a heavy amount of grief. I'd slam my computer shut and run up the stairs halfway to Cliff and Lara's quarters, just to get away from the rest of the crew, curling my legs into my chest and crying into my kneecaps. If Ian was in the house—and he sometimes was, doing paperwork or writing emails—he would always walk quietly up the steps to meet me, would always rub my back and whisper that he was sorry that things were so very hard. "I know that if I chose to have a committed partner, forever, I would have that in you," he'd tell me. "I'm just trying to figure out if that's what I *should* choose, what I want."

I let him comfort me, but it never felt very satisfying. We continued to go to bed separately, but more often than not, one of us would knock softly at the other's wall, and we'd wind up tangled in each other. Once, after our breathing slowed to normal, I kissed his chest and walked back to my room—but I grew so lonely that after that I gave up the pretense and just snuggled in closer to him as we both drifted off into sleep.

That was at night. During the workday, everything was business as usual. We had welcomed two new batches of broiler chicks on the farm—the first ones were just about done being cute, growing quickly into their ugly, alien-like stage, and were living in the mobile coops over fresh pasture. I knew from experience—from lessons with Ian the May before—that I just wasn't strong enough to move all that wood and wire mesh on my own. Jack promised he would build a second dolly for the back of the coops, to make moving them easier. I wished he didn't have to, but I also knew I wasn't the only one on the farm who needed them. That comforted me a little, because I was grappling with some regret over the fact that I was leaving weaker, less capable than I had planned and hoped.

But that week brought more than its fair share of surprises for Jack, most of them of the unpleasant sort. One of the sows got out of her paddock and it took four of us and the majority of the afternoon to herd her back in. There was a steer to slaughter, pasture plans to create. Friday came, and the dollies were still on the to-do list. I wondered how I was going to move the coops.

I finished my day's work, packing up from farmstand and collecting the eggs as a favor for Hazel. I had plans that night to meet my friend Enid, the cheesemaker from Alfalfa, for a drink at a bar in downtown Syracuse. I stood under the shower for longer than was necessary, letting the stream of water hit the crown of my head and run down my body in rivers, swirling at my feet in the perpetually clogged tub. As I rubbed hemp-scented lotion into my knees after the shower, my phone rang. It was Jack. I picked up reluctantly. "Hey!" My voice sounded cheery.

"Hey, do you have a minute to go over weekend chores?" he asked. I looked at the clock. I did; I wasn't supposed to meet Enid for another hour. But I didn't want to. I was clean, officially de-farmed. I didn't smell, and there was not a speck of hay to be found on my person. "I do," I said, and tossed off my towel, then threw on a racer-back cotton tank top and my torn cargo pants. I grabbed a pair of Ian's socks and yanked them on my feet before shoving them in my barn boots. On my way out the door, I ran into Ian.

"Where you going?" he wanted to know, or at least he asked.

"To meet Jack," I said. "Weekend chore education—you know."

"Oh, I know," he said.

He had spent the previous weekend downstate with friends, and before he left, I told him that something needed to change. "This isn't healthy," I had said. "I need to know if you want to be with me . . . or if you don't." I paused for effect. "Because this is killing me." In the darkest corner of my heart, I knew that he didn't want to, but I suppose I had hoped that the ultimatum would make him admit it to the both of us.

I thought about that in the doorway and said, "I'm going to meet Enid tonight for a drink."

His face brightened. I knew he had been worried, concerned over the gripping sadness that enveloped me and cast a dark cloud over our living space. When we weren't sleeping together, I was sniffling in the next room, or shuffling down the hallway, barely lifting my feet or my chin. "Hey, that's great!" he said, his voice full of positivity and cheer.

"Yeah," I said with a sigh, thinking of the half-open bottle of wine I had on my dresser, and wondered if it would be appropriate to have a nip before heading out.

"Well, be safe," he said,

"What time are you leaving?" He and his friend Brian were going to visit some of their childhood crew in Philadelphia, to see the house they had just purchased and moved into. I was supremely jealous and felt dejected.

"As soon as I get clean," he said. "Brian's hanging out with Toby right now."

I smiled—for real, this time—when I thought of Brian. Earlier that afternoon, the two of us had taken a walk. It was the first time I'd seen him since things ended. He was Ian's friend first, but I loved him very much, and was hopeful that he'd stay in my life. The two of us had taken a walk out to the broilers and the mobile greenhouse. We spoke about normal things and not-sad things for the first few minutes, but by the time we reached the tiny young spinach, I couldn't hold back any longer. With tears pricking at the corners of my eyes, I asked Brian what he thought about the whole affair. "I mean," I started, jamming my hands in my pockets, my thumbs sticking out of the fabric, "has he talked to you about it?"

"I mean, you know," he said, scratching at the back of his head uncomfortably. "He's confused. I know he told you that. I think he just needs to figure out some shit."

"But . . ." I tried to press further.

"I love you both," he said, and my tears started to really flow. "I want you both to be happy." The faintest breeze ruffled my hair and disturbed the grass, which was reaching up well past our ankles.

"I just don't understand," I said, through hiccups and sobs, "why he doesn't want to be with me. I would give—I've given—him everything."

I couldn't breathe, so I placed my right index finger on my right nostril and blew hard. Snot flew out of my nose and onto the ground. "You know?" I said, still sniffling.

"Well, um," he said, on the verge of a joke. "Have you considered it might be because of reasons like . . . that?" He motioned to the ground where my mucus had landed, and I started laughing so hard, I doubled over at the waist and had to steady myself with my elbows on my knees, my head in my palms.

I wanted to tell Ian about it now, to recall the story, but as I opened my mouth to do so, I realized that the only reason to do so would be to grasp at reconciliation, in hopes that that my outdoorsy aptitude and spunky nature would land me back in his favor. So instead I pressed my lips together and brought my first two fingers to my forehead in a salute. "Tell Andrew and Eloise I said hi." I paused, unable to contain myself. Unable to do what people kept telling me I should, to stop doing what I knew I shouldn't. "I wish I could go with you."

"I know you do." His words stung and I brushed past him, latching the storm door behind me with a firm click. I ran down the driveway, past the barn that housed Beth's riding horses, past the broiler coop where the youngest chicks lived. The grass made scratching sounds against my boots and pant legs. The sun was getting lower in the sky, though not yet threatening evening, and the whole field seemed to glow with a golden sheen.

I saw Jack standing in the middle of the pasture, reeling up a fence line. He looked tired, but happy. I waved and made a turn, cutting across the grass to meet him. "Hey," I said, "thanks for meeting me. I do appreciate it." And I did; without Jack's reminders and detailed instructions, chores always seemed to be a bit stickier.

"No problem," he said. "So these are the paddocks for the steers," he said, motioning to the one they were in and the subsequent two, built exactly the same shape and size, measured out by paces. "You won't have to move their water tomorrow morning," he said, "but you will on Sunday." He and Hazel always positioned their tubs in between two paddocks, giving the beef cattle access on either side to make the arduous chore of emptying and refilling water a bit easier.

The brood cows were farther out in the field, and their water wouldn't have to be moved at all, just refilled every day as it got drunk down. "Really?" I said pumping my fist in the air. "Thank you so freaking much." He laughed, and that made me feel good. For the brood cows, I just had to drop the line and reel it up, finishing the weekend with one very large paddock. "This makes me so supremely happy; you have no idea."

He smiled patiently. "Want to go over broiler chores?" I nodded, and listened as he reminded me how to open the tops of the mobile coops, to top off their feeders with grain and to detach and rinse out their water bowls from the stream of hose, to reattach them and make sure the water was flowing. Either he or Cliff would handle the mobile coops in the morning, thanks to the lack of an extra dolly and my inability to move them without it. I thanked him again and he waved it off. "Well, I mean, it just makes sense for us to do it all." He reminded me to bed down the stationary coop twice a day, paying extra-close attention to the areas where the birds tended to congregate, along the wall, under the heat lamps, and around the feeders. He reminded me to clean their water bowls, to top off their feeder, and to herd them back in the coop at night, to test the charge on the electric polywire fence that surrounded the whole thing.

We chatted briefly about the pigs—there were plenty to attend to, between the feeders and the boar and sows, plus their piglets, some born as recently as last week. "If any of the broilers are dead," Jack said solemnly, "and some probably will be, bring them over to the feeders and toss 'em in." There had been a rash of chicken deaths, owing, Jack presumed, to heart attack in thanks to their rapid weight gain and enormous size. "Some of them were definitely six-pounders," he had said a few days earlier with a wistful tone.

"Got it," I said to Jack.

"And that's about it," he wrapped up. "You know the deal with the layers—open the coop in the morning, feed, collect afternoon eggs, and close it back up once they roost—and I presume you know what to do with horses?" His voice dropped a shade with the last few words. Horses were Ian's domain, and Jack wanted to tread carefully. I had, at that point, spoken about my heartbreak and aches over Ian with everyone on the farm except Jack. He just didn't seem like someone to confide in, in large part, I thought, because he seemed so in control of his own emotion that I doubted he'd want to entertain mine. Plus, I was still stinging over the scrubbie incident.

"Yeah. I know what to do."

"Cool. I'll be around all weekend, so if you have any questions you can call me," he said. I gave him a high five and ran off back in the direction of Beth's house.

I WOKE EARLY THE NEXT MORNING, AIDED BY THE ALARM CLOCK, MY head pounding ever so slightly. I had drunk a bit too much with Enid, but it wasn't anything a big glass of water and some cold, fresh air couldn't fix. I arched my back and curled up under the familiar sheets, which felt warm and soft against my skin. I had slept in Ian's and my old bed. I had been considering it, for familiarity's sake and comfort, but when he told me I was welcome to, that I might find it nicer than the hard, small mattress in my darker room, I knew for certain that I would. His pillows smelled like hay, soap, and the *nag champa* incense he burned, and I rolled over onto my stomach, cramming my face into one. I lay like that for a few minutes before getting out of bed to start the day.

Pants on, socks on, boots on, jogging bra and tank top over head, sweatshirt zipped, hair gathered in a functional braid, and I was out the door. "What to do first?" I said out loud, glancing at the fields on either side of the road. My knife was tucked into my pocket and I had the familiar leather of the toolbelt slung over my arm; I was ready for anything. Opening the layers' coop seemed like a logical first step, but I so dreaded the task of moving beef cattle—largely due to my lack of fencing experience and subsequent anxiety over it—that I marched off in that direction, eager to get it out of the way and off my to-do list.

"Caaaahhhm aaahhnn," I called again and again, the emphasis most prominent on the vowels, willing the most stubborn brood cows to move forward into fresh pasture as I wound up the polywire. "Come on." I had always felt a little self-conscious calling cattle, like my voice was somehow less authentic and authoritative than Jack's, Ian's, Hazel's, Cliff's, Lara's. But as the littlest calf—born that week, spotty black and white, with big ears—trotted to keep up with the crew and almost tripped over his mother's hooves, I felt calmer, quieter. Who cared about the timbre of my voice? Certainly not the cows. Certainly not anyone who mattered. I suddenly realized that this truly was the last weekend I'd have to complete chores; at least here, on this farm, in this way. On this land. With these animals. I straightened my back and lifted my chin a little higher. *How foolish you would be not to enjoy this*, I reminded myself and took a few minutes to memorize the way the moos sounded more like groans, the surprisingly loud sound of grass being torn and chewed.

As I approached the pigs, a small army of piglets squealed and shuddered, running away from me and into their hut as quickly as their tiny legs could carry them. I removed the lid to their tub of grain, working as quietly as I could, mindful of Toby and Hillary asleep in the cabin a few yards away. I fed everyone and sat back on my haunches to watch the sows and Mr. Peanut, the boar, shove their noses in the grain, jockeying for the prime positions at the feeder.

Pig and cow chores completed, I crossed the road and entered the barnyard. Most of the hens were already up and out of their coop, having made efficient use of the small back door. They would be moved out to pasture soon, but for the time being, their coop was still parked in the compost. We had experienced a fair bit of precipitation, leaving the ground a mess. I waded through the mud, my boots sticking a bit, and pulled on my work gloves, then unwrapped the rope from around the latch and lowered the drawbridge door. I tried to bring it down gently, but the rope slipped through my hands and the top of the door hit the ground with a thud. Oops. I walked around the structure, letting down the bars that kept the hens from laying in their nest boxes overnight, and scooped out three buckets of grain for the feeders. They flocked frantically to each one, leaving their posts and following me as I walked, and I shook my head. I would miss the way they moved in one large group that seemed to simultaneously comfort and irritate itself. I would miss the gurgling, belly-deep cooing sound they made as they poked around in the grass. I would miss them.

I tried to order myself to appreciate it, to enjoy the labor and the early morning air, but I just couldn't seem to bring myself into the present. When I tapped into my emotion, all I felt was sadness, pain, fear. All I felt was Ian.

I THOUGHT BACK TO MY BIRTHDAY THE WEEKEND EARLIER, AND HOW absent it had felt without him. He left on Friday, the day before my birthday, to visit friends downstate. Since March he had always seemed to be visiting friends, and it made me nervous that he was pulling away indefinitely. As he packed I sat on his bed, rubbing at my eyes and begging him not to leave. Not to leave the farm for the weekend. Not to leave me.

"I know this is shitty for you," he said. "I feel bad that I'm not going to be with you on your birthday, but it's not right for us. Not right now. If we do end up together, I promise I will make this up to you." I started to protest, but he interrupted. "I promise," he said. "If we end up together."

The next morning, I woke up early and said "Happy birthday, Ro," out loud to myself before I got out of bed and drove to a coffee shop where I ordered a frothy cappuccino and a piece of biscotti. I ate slowly, savoring the flavors, then walked to the lake where I tightened the scarf around my neck—it was still a bit chilly—and parked myself on a bench and read for hours. I paused periodically, setting the book down to answer calls from my parents and sister wishing me well. "You're officially over the quarter-of-a-century hump," Sasha said when I picked up my phone, and I told her that I felt about triple that. "You'll see. Spring will be here soon," and I hoped she was right.

That night, Hillary and Toby planned a dinner with the rest of the farm crew. Hillary's mother had lent her house for the occasion, and by the time I arrived, not only was everyone there, they had all brought a dish to share. We enjoyed wine and beer, plus Stonehill chicken—marinated in fresh green herbs and then grilled—a quinoa salad with chopped bell pepper, leafy greens and berries, a hearty round loaf of bread dotted with pecans and raisins, plus cheeses from Alfalfa and almonds and olives for snacking. There was a toast to my birthday, but until dessert, talk centered around farm chores and jokes, and I was thankful not to be at the center of attention. I just wasn't feeling up to it. As Toby washed the dishes, Hillary lit a few candles that she stuck in a pear *clafoutis*—a barely sweet tart that borders on pudding. "I knew it was your favorite," she said, and I hugged her, wrapping my arms around her back and squeezing tightly.

Ian arrived back home Sunday night; I was asleep already, or else pretending to be, and we didn't have a chance to speak until the next evening. When we did, he took a deep breath and looked at his hands, then looked at me. "I have spent a lot of time thinking about this," he said. "I don't want to tell you no, but I can't tell you yes. So I *have* to say no." I stared dully into the flickering flame of a candle, comatose and unresponsive. "I am sorry, but I have to say this—I need to be honest—I want to have the experience of meeting someone new. I'm not done with that, with the excitement and anticipation of potential. Or I don't want to be." I turned my gaze to him, slowly, and my face was a mess of pain. "And that does confuse me—it *does*, Ro, don't look at me like that—because I think that ultimately what I want is a committed partner who loves me entirely and . . . you are that. So there. It's confusing."

"Well, please don't see anyone until I leave." I wasn't crying, but my voice was on the verge. "Please don't fuck anyone until I go." I was acting irrational and we both knew it, but I couldn't help myself. *There has to be a better reason than that*, I thought.

He was irritated. "Okay—well." He took a deep breath. "I obviously don't want to hurt you, but why does it matter? I mean, if I do it one day before you leave or one after? What's the real difference? Why does it matter?"

"Because it just does!" I exploded, spreading my fingers in the air and clenching them like talons. At a tremendous impasse, neither of us spoke.

"Okay," I said and backed out of his bedroom, into my own, slamming the door and collapsing on my mattress. I didn't sleep at all that night, sobbing and letting guttural cries escape from deep in my belly long past midnight. Around eleven, I felt a rage bubble up inside me, and I threw my fist against the wall, shouted *"FUCK! GOD!"* through clenched teeth. Ian threw open the door and flew into the room, crouched down next to my bed.

"I get that you are sad," he said, his voice angry and fast. "I understand that, and I'm *sorry* for it. I know you're hurting, and I don't want to tell you not to feel what you feel. But"—he took a breath—"you are being so *selfish* right now. Other people live in this house, Rochelle." The use of my name in full, a step away from familiarity, felt as devastating as his scolding and I just wailed louder, tried to muffle myself with my pillow.

I considered all of this as I opened my pocketknife with my thumb and sliced through the twine holding the hay bales together, letting the flakes tumble into the horses' metal feeder. Was I being selfish? Probably, I admitted. I shoved Pat away with my elbow. "Not yet," I said. "You wait." I opened another bale. "Okay. You can go now." She buried her face in the hay, chewing noisily. I knew that Ian didn't want to hurt me, and I knew that the fact I was in pain hurt him all the more. He was not malicious, he was not unkind, and he was not a *bad person*. But I couldn't help but think that if he was, this would all be a bit easier.

MID-MAY

Spring was still maddeningly cold, and the crew was getting sick of wearing insulated overalls every day. Every time a fresh quilt of snow was dumped down over the fields and barnyard, I exclaimed, pulling out a sheet pan of roasted squash or potatoes and calling everyone in to breakfast, that it would surely be the last. But the final snowfall didn't come until an afternoon in mid-May. I was working in the trailer typically used for transporting the livestock to and from their winter and summer paddocks and for bringing chickens to slaughter in the barnyard. It was loaded now with old planks of wood, salvaged from the newly renovated machine shop. Because Cliff was thrifty, and also because he had a soft spot for nostalgia, he wanted to save all of the wood, as well as the thick, heavy nails that dotted each plank. The task of using both a hammer and a crowbar to remove the hardware was an ongoing one assigned to anyone willing, but it looked like I might finish the job that day if I worked hard. The trailer offered a little shelter, but outside, the wind howled and bossed around the snow that fell in sheets, picking it up and swirling it in cyclones before it touched the ground. The sky was a menacing grey.

"Fuck. This. Shit," I yelled to Hazel as she trudged by, wrapped in a scarf that reached up over her mouth and a hat with the hood of her Carhartt jacket pulled up over it. She threw her mitten-covered hands up in the air and shook her head in disbelief before walking on to collect the eggs.

THE SNOW DID MELT, EVENTUALLY, AND WE ALL BEGAN TO TAKE NOTICE of the farm's rough and weathered beauty again. The property included a forest with a riding trail that cut through the heart of it, a lively little river and plenty of trees. "You've should really go see the trillium," Beth said one Thursday morning as I hauled burlap sacks of storage onions and shallots from her basement. In want of a proper dry storage cellar, Beth's basement was the next best thing, if a little warm and wet to be considered optimal. Most of the onions were going squishy and soft, and I remembered the amount we tossed in the compost the previous year.

"Is it in bloom?" I asked, hoisting a bag up by its neck, supporting its bottom with my other hand.

"All over! The entire ground is covered." I smiled at the thought, and promised her I'd take a walk that weekend. "Well don't wait too long," she said, taking off toward the mailbox, her dog galloping ahead. "It won't be there forever."

So that Saturday, I took a walk in the woods. Coming from Beth's, I followed the path around the vegetable field—past where the dill grew, past the corn—and through the pigs' paddocks. I waved to the piglets, who still squealed and scampered, as I cut across the stream, stepping daintily on rocks that stood taller than the water. I hiked up the incline, and considered how different it felt to be on foot than on the back of a horse. When I reached the clearing at the top of the hill, my breath caught in my throat. The ground was a blanket of trillium, entirely white. If you squinted, it looked as though it had snowed the night before, but if you opened your eyes fully, you would take notice of the green leaves under the trilliums' petals, the tight buds on the tree branches. I picked five or six flowers and gripped them in my palm before emerging from the forest at the top of the hill. The sun felt warm and welcome on my shoulders, and beyond all of the fields, miles in the distance, I could see the lake sparkling.

I swung by the barnyard on my way back to the house, grabbing a pint jar and filling it with water in the milk house. I dropped the flowers in, then pulled them back out, snapping off their bottoms so they fell more gracefully around the jar's rim. "Trillium!" I said, running into Lara on the concrete pad. She was hauling the hose reel out to the greenhouse to water the spinach she'd planted earlier. It was small still, but would be ready for harvest soon.

"Isn't that a protected species?" She asked, then, seeing the crestfallen look on my face, assured me that it was probably fine.

"There's just so much of it . . . " I said in feeble defense. Lara laughed and agreed that it was beautiful, that she looked forward to its springtime blooms, too, and I didn't feel so guilty.

I set the jar on my dresser, but the room was dark, its one window not quite coaxing in the sunlight. I stood, my hands on my hips, and considered it. I was almost ready to leave the farm. My things were half-packed, knick-knacks in boxes, two open suitcases full of clothes—one for farmwear, another for "real person" clothes. The flowers looked confused in the room, too beautiful to be lost in the chaos.

I knocked on the door that separated Ian's and my bedrooms, rapping quietly on the wood with my knuckle. "Ian?" I called, and waited for an answer. None came, so I turned the handle slowly and called his name again. "Ian?"

He was gone, somewhere, and his room was quiet. I stood still, breathed in deeply, looked around. His bed was made, the green quilt pulled up to meet the pillows. The edges of his flannel sheets hung out sloppily along the side of the bed, and I tucked them into the frame. The old wallpaper caught the light that streamed in from the windows, making the faded yellow of the paper all the more obvious, though in a pleasant sort of way. The wooden boxes, borrowed from the barnyard, were still crammed with books, though some were mine and I made a mental note to retrieve them before I left. His yoga mat was curled up and resting in the corner, the ceramic mug I brought back from Colorado empty but dirty on his nightstand. Two braided rugs sat on the sides of the room, and the wooden floor was peppered with tufts of dust in various sizes. The air smelled sweet.

I walked back into my bedroom and retrieved the vase of trillium, its many petals gently bobbing in the air, then brought it back to Ian's room. I set it on a heavy coaster in the middle of the writing desk, and then I turned and left the room.

As I drove away from Stonehill Farm for the last time, my tires spinning in the mud, I kept my gaze on the fields and the barns in the rearview mirror. I watched as they grew smaller and smaller, until they slipped completely from my view.

RECIPES FOR

SPRING

CHEESY SCRAMBLED EGGS WITH CHARD

This is a dish we didn't make often on the farm after learning that Toby absolutely, positively hated the taste of cooked chard. I happen to love it, and think it adds an earthy sweetness to an otherwise ho-hum breakfast staple. The stems of springtime chard are tender enough to toss in the pan with the leaves, but if you find yourself with particularly woody stems, you may do well to remove and chop them, then sauté them for a few extra minutes to take the edge off.

· SERVES SIX TO EIGHT ·

2 tablespoons butter

1 leek, white and light green part, finely chopped (save the dark green part for making stock)

4 cups chopped chard leaves and stems

1 teaspoon ground coriander

Salt and pepper

12 eggs

⅓ cup whole milk

⅓ cup fresh goat or sheep cheese

1 whole scallion, finely chopped

Heat a large skillet over medium heat and add the butter. Once melted, add the leek, chard stems if tough, coriander, salt, and pepper, and sauté until tender and soft, about five to six minutes. Add the chard and sauté until wilted—it will cook down considerably.

[CONTINUED]

Meanwhile, crack the eggs into a mixing bowl. Use a fork or whisk to break them apart and beat in the milk. Season with salt and pepper. Turn the heat to medium-low, add the eggs to the pan with the cooked leek and chard, and stir constantly until the eggs have begun to set. Patience is key here; don't rush things with a high heat, or you'll end up with dry eggs.

Once the eggs have just begun to set, remove them from the heat and stir in the fresh cheese. Top with the scallions and serve immediately.

WHOLE WHEAT PANCAKES WITH RHUBARB SAUCE

Pancakes were always a hit on the farm—unless we were out of maple syrup. I was in the middle of making a batch of pancakes in the early spring when I realized we had none in the house, and hadn't yet tapped the trees. Luckily, there was tangy-sweet rhubarb close at hand, and a bit of raw sugar. I like this version of pancakes just as much as the original. We used whole wheat pastry flour on the farm because that's all we had, but if it's too heavy for you, feel free to cut the recipe with 1 cup white flour. One last note: I don't sweeten pancake batter, for virtue of dolloping sweet topping over it all. One must find restraint somewhere.

• SERVES SIX TO EIGHT •

FOR THE PANCAKES:

2 cups whole wheat pastry flour

2 teaspoons baking powder

1 teaspoon baking soda

1 teaspoon cinnamon

Pinch of salt

4 tablespoons (½ stick) butter, plus 4 to 6 tablespoons for cooking

2 eggs

2 cups milk

FOR THE RHUBARB SAUCE:

½ cup sugar

⅓ cup water

3 cups chopped rhubarb

¼ teaspoon grated nutmeg

[CONTINUED]

Set the oven to its lowest temperature.

In a large mixing bowl, combine the flour, baking soda and powder, cinnamon, and salt. Whisk to combine. In a separate bowl, whisk together the melted butter, eggs, and milk. Add the wet ingredients to the dry and stir to combine, getting rid of any lumps.

Preheat a griddle or large cast-iron skillet over medium heat. Melt 1 tablespoon butter over the surface, then ladle in ¼ cup batter. Repeat if you can fit multiple pancakes in your pan or griddle. Cook until the top begins to bubble, 2 to 3 minutes. Flip the pancakes over and cook for an additional 1 to 2 minutes. Remove the pancakes from the heat and place on a baking sheet in the warm oven. Repeat with the remaining batter.

To make the rhubarb sauce, combine the sugar and water in a saucepan big enough to hold all of the rhubarb. Bring to a boil, then add the rhubarb and nutmeg and reduce the heat to a lively simmer. Let simmer for 10 to 15 minutes, stirring frequently, until the rhubarb breaks down and becomes soft. The sauce will be chunky. Serve warm over pancakes, or let cool and store in the refrigerator to use over ice cream.

CHARD PESTO

You can make pesto with just about any green, and while basil tends to get the most attention, I think raw chard adds a welcome heartiness. It isn't the most vibrant green color once it's mixed up (in fact, it's quite brown), but give it a chance anyway. I like to eat this pesto slathered on bread.

· MAKES 2 CUPS ·

1 cup walnuts

2 fat garlic cloves

4 cups coarsely chopped chard leaves, stems removed
(save the stems for another use)

⅓ cup extra virgin olive oil

1 tablespoon pumpkinseed oil

⅓ cup whole ricotta cheese

Kosher salt and pepper

Preheat the oven to 350°F. Spread the walnuts in a single layer on a baking sheet, and place in the oven. Roast for 8 to 10 minutes, until the nuts smell fragrant. Remove from the oven and let cool completely before proceeding.

Smash and peel the garlic cloves, then drop them in the bowl of a food processor. Run the machine until they're finely puréed, scraping down the sides of the bowl once or twice. Add the walnuts, then pulse 4 to 5 times, until the nuts are broken up but still chunky. Add the chard. With the processor running, add the oils in a stream, then transfer the pesto to a medium mixing bowl. Use a wooden spoon to stir in the cheese, then season to taste.

MINT AND SAGE ICED TEA

When it comes to herbs, why should soups and roasts get all the fun? I love a big glass of herbal tea—and when it's homemade, all the better. Here, I combine bright, energizing mint with cozy sage. The herbs taste pretty sweet already, so you really don't need to add much sugar. You can always make a double batch of this tea and keep it in your fridge; it definitely won't go to waste.

· SERVES FOUR ·

2 tablespoons raw sugar

4 cups plus 2 teaspoons water, divided

⅔ cup fresh mint leaves, picked from the stem, plus extra for garnishing

½ cup fresh sage leaves, picked from the stem

Place the sugar in a small saucepot with two teaspoons water. Bring it to a boil, stirring constantly, until the sugar dissolves, then remove from the heat—this won't take more than a minute or two.

Meanwhile, place the herbs on a cutting board and use the handle of a knife to bruise the leaves by pressing down on them and working the handle back and forth; this helps release their aromas and flavors.

Place the leaves in a teapot. Boil four cups of water, remove it from the heat, and pour it over the leaves. Let it steep for 8 minutes, then remove the herbs and discard. Stir in the sugar syrup.

Fill four glasses with ice cubes and a few mint leaves. Pour the tea over the ice and serve immediately. Alternately, you may transfer to a jug and cool in the fridge.

ACKNOWLEDGMENTS

Writing a book is exhilarating—I highly recommend it. It is, however, also exhausting, and I do not recommend doing so without an extraordinarily talented, patient, and forgiving support system.

I cannot put into words—which is embarrassing, as I am a writer—how grateful I am to Sasha Tropp and Cara Bedick for their impeccable edits; for their tireless attention to detail, their ability to see the forest when I was stuck in the trees, and for their gracious tuning of my voice when I went off-key. Thank you, also, to Matthew Lore, for making it all happen; to Rachel Stout, for believing in the project from the very beginning and being my best advocate; and to Dan Roche, for planting the seed before I knew it could germinate.

Thank you, also, to the crew at the farm—Beth, Cliff, Lara, Jack, Hazel, Toby, Hillary, Logan, Dylan, and, yes, Ian—for accepting me as a volunteer and for letting me stay. Thank you for all you have taught me, for your friendship and insight, and for being exemplary examples of the driving force behind responsible, sustainable agriculture.

To my parents and sister: Your love, support, and belief in me honestly may be a little biased, but I love you so much for it. I am proud to be a part of our family.

To Jared, for your patience, for your strength. For waiting.

ABOUT THE AUTHOR

ROCHELLE BILOW has worked as a farmer, food writer, line cook, and cooking instructor (among other things that are not relevant here). She lives in Brooklyn, cooks with lard regularly, and finally landed her dream gig as a staff writer at *Bon Appétit*. This is her first book.